*Family, gender, and
 population in the Middle*

DATE

Family, Gender, and Population in the Middle East

Family, Gender, and Population in the Middle East

Policies in Context

Edited by

Carla Makhlouf Obermeyer

The American University in Cairo Press

Chapter 1, *Reproductive Rights in the West and in the Middle East: A Cross-Cultural Perspective* by Carla Makhlouf Obermeyer, was first published in 1995 in *Human Rights Quarterly* vol. 17, no.2, and is reprinted by permission of *Human Rights Quarterly*.

Chapter 11, *Rethinking Family Planning Policy in Light of Reproductive Health Research* by Huda Zurayk, Nabil Younis, and Hind Khattab, is copyright © 1994 by The Population Council and is reprinted by permission of The Population Council.

Dar el Kutub No. 8749/94 (cloth)
              4877/95 (paper)
ISBN 977 424 357 9 (cloth)
     977 424 368 4 (paper)

Library of Congress Cataloging-in-Publication Data:

                                                           95-960433
Obermeyer, Carla Makhlouf.
     Family, gender, and population in the Middle East : policies in context / edited by Carla Makhlouf Obermeyer.— [Cairo] : American University in Cairo Press, 1995.
     p.

Printed in Egypt at the Printshop of the American University in Cairo

Contents

List of Tables   vii

List of Figures   ix

Foreword *by Carolyn Makinson*   xi

Acknowledgments   xv

Introduction: A Region of Diversity and Change
    Carla Makhlouf Obermeyer   1

OVERVIEW: INTERNATIONAL AND REGIONAL PERSPECTIVES ON
REPRODUCTIVE CHOICE

  1.   Reproductive Rights in the West and in the Middle East:
      A Cross-Cultural Perspective
      Carla Makhlouf Obermeyer   16

THE FAMILY, THE STATE, AND THE LAW: POLITICS AND POPULATION

  2.   The Fertility Transition in Turkey:
      Reforms, Policies, and Family Structure
      Cem Behar   36

  3.   State, Women, and Civil Society:
      An Evaluation of Egypt's Population Policy
      Saad Eddin Ibrahim   57

  4.   Fertility Transition in the Mashriq and the Maghrib:
      Education, Emigration, and the Diffusion of Ideas
      Youssef Courbage   80

  5.   Population Policy and Gender Equity in
      Post-Revolutionary Iran
      Homa Hoodfar   105

WOMEN IN FAMILIES: CULTURAL CONSTRAINTS AND OPPORTUNITIES

  6.   Women, Uncertainty, and Reproduction in Morocco
      Rahma Bourqia   136

7. Women's Autonomy and Gender Roles in
Egyptian Families
Laila Nawar, Cynthia B. Lloyd, Barbara Ibrahim   147

8. Changing Hierarchies of Gender and Generation in
the Arab World
Philippe Fargues   179

HEALTH AND FAMILY PLANNING SERVICES: FOCUSING ON WOMEN
9. Target-Setting in Family Planning Programs:
Controversies and Challenges
Karima Khalil, Cynthia Myntti   199

10. Broadening Contraceptive Choice: Lessons from Egypt
Ezzeldin O. Hassan, Mahmoud F. Fathalla   216

11. Rethinking Family Planning Policy in Light of
Reproductive Health Research
Huda Zurayk, Nabil Younis, Hind Khattab   232

Notes on Contributors   259

Tables

Introduction
1. Demographic and socioeconomic indicators in
   countries of the Middle East   4

Chapter 2
1. The demographic transition in Turkey   39
2. Percentage of married women using contraceptives   40
3. Future fertility and mortality projections   40
4. Total fertility rate in Turkey   41
5. Family planning methods used by married women   45
6. Use of family planning by characteristics of women   46
7. Literacy rates in Turkey   49
8. Percentage of men and women in each educational level   49

Chapter 3
1. The population issue and Egypt's relevant actors   64
2. Comparison of community leaders on population issues   71
3. Knowledge, views, and practices of reproductive women   74

Chapter 4
1. Trends in fertility by education level, Syria   92

Chapter 5
1. Contraceptive use among women in Markazi province   116
2. Information source on family planning   117
3. Annual rate of population growth in Iran   119

Chapter 7
1. Household type by selected characteristics   150
2. Marriage arrangements of Egyptian women   155
3. Attitudes to personal autonomy among married women   157
4. Various aspects of autonomous behavior   159
5. Women engaged in income-generating activities   161
6. Gender roles in decision-making   163
7. Gender roles in decision-making   164

8. Gender roles and family decision-making 165
9. Mean autonomy level by background variables 167
10. Allocation of women's earnings 170
11. Reproductive intentions and behavior 172
12. Desired and completed fertility by autonomy level 173
13. Aspirations for daughters 174

Chapter 9
1. Total fertility rate objectives: Egypt and Tunisia 201
2. Contraceptive prevalence rate objectives 201

Chapter 10
1. Percentage of couples using contraceptives 219
2. Knowledge and use of methods 221
3. Perception of pill safety among women 222

Chapter 11
1. Measurement of gynecological and related morbidity 235
2. Use of contraception by marital status 238
3. Use of contraception by age group 239
4. Gynecological and related morbidity conditions 239
5. Prevalence of one or more morbidity conditions 240
6. Gynecological and related morbidity conditions 241
7. Conditions among women using contraceptives 243
8. IUD users with multiple conditions 243
9. IUD users with reproductive tract infections 244
10. Individual pill users with hypertension 244
11. IUD users and pill users by source of contraceptives 246
12. Prevalence of symptoms as reported in the interview 247
13. Consultation of physician by women with symptoms 247
14. Consultation, treatment, and outcome 248

Figures

Chapter 4
1. Total fertility rate in Egypt and Morocco   95
2. Female mean age at marriage in Egypt and Morocco   95
3. Infant mortality in Egypt and Morocco   96
4. Population in the largest cities in Egypt and Morocco   96
5. GDP per capita at constant price in Egypt and Morocco   97
6. Female illiteracy in Egypt and Morocco   97
7. School enrollment rate in Egypt and Morocco   98
8. Females in labor force in Egypt and Morocco   98
9. Share of taxes in Egypt and Morocco   99

Chapter 8
1. Fertility and wealth in the Arab world   180
2. Birth rate and education of women in the Gaza Strip   184
3. Average gap in education between men and women   187
4. Educational inequality between generations of men   189
5. Family structure and political violence in Egypt   192
6. Level of education and political violence in Egypt   193

Chapter 10
1. Current use of contraception in Egypt by method   220
2. Trends in contraceptive prevalence in Egypt   220

Foreword

The papers in this book go to press in a climate very different from the one prevailing when they were solicited and presented. Now, the International Conference on Population and Development (ICPD) is behind us. Its Programme of Action—which calls for population policies to address social development beyond family planning, and for family planning to be placed in a broader reproductive health framework—met with approval from widely differing constituencies in the population and development fields, and was adopted by the official delegations of 179 states. Even the Holy See joined the general consensus for the first time at a population conference, while noting its reservations regarding certain sections of the document.

Two years ago, such a consensus seemed improbable to many of us. At informal meetings and public debates, women's health advocates and members of the mainstream family planning community often found themselves at loggerheads. Yet it was evident that many representatives of both sides genuinely felt that they had women's best interests at heart. Some of us found ourselves agreeing with much on both sides. But in trying to find common ground, there was both an absence of empirical data on important questions, and an absence of theoretical frameworks which could facilitate the reconciliation of competing values.

In the summer of 1992, Barbara Ibrahim, The Population Council's Senior Representative in Cairo, posed the question: was there a way that the work of scholars in the Middle East—both empirical research and theoretical analysis—could inform the debate? The papers in this volume provide the answer . . . in the affirmative.

The papers offer a rich and varied menu. Some consider controversial topics closely related to family planning services, such as target setting (Khalil and Myntti), and Egyptian successes and failures with regard to the introduction of new and experimental contraceptive methods (Hassan and Fathalla). One paper in particular, by Zurayk,

Younis, and Khattab, documents research that provides solid support for those who insist that family planning must be provided in the context of reproductive health services. The authors present data showing very high prevalence rates of reproductive tract infections and other gynecological morbidities in a rural area of Egypt, and alarmingly high proportions of women using contraceptive methods for which they have clear contraindications.

Those who prefer sweeping hypotheses on broad social phenomena should read the papers by Courbage and Fargues. Courbage attributes the difference between Morocco and Egypt in the historical pace of fertility decline to the different destinations of international migrants from these two countries: Moroccans have tended to migrate to low-fertility European countries, while Egyptians have migrated to the pro-natalist countries of the Gulf. Fargues has the courage to advance an ingenious explanation for the current political violence in Egypt. Reversing the usual tendency to study demographic change as the dependent variable, he looks at the effect on the social order of strains brought about at the family level by demographic changes which have influenced intergenerational relations.

Reading the papers in this volume, it is hard to understand why demographers from other regions—in particular the United States—have for so long neglected research on the fascinating countries of the Middle East. And it is hard not to be critical of some of the few studies that do exist for their rather superficial and stereotypical treatment of the diverse countries of the region, and the diverse manifestations of its dominant religion, Islam.

Happily, several of the present papers, prepared by Middle Eastern scholars, will begin to set the record straight. In addition, they chart new ground on issues relevant to women around the world, not just in the Middle East. One of these is the need to better define and measure widely used but little understood concepts such as women's status and autonomy. Another is the need for open and constructive debate as to how the rights and freedom of the individual may be reconciled with other values, which emphasize the individual's responsibilities to others and to the social order. The case study on Iran provides an intriguing and counterintuitive example of the attempts of women in one country to redefine their roles and gain new rights within an Islamic framework (Hoodfar). And other papers in the volume illustrate attempts to reconcile new ideas on women's rights with traditional values, which define men's and women's identities in relation to their roles in the family and the community (Nawar, Lloyd, and Ibrahim; Obermeyer).

With ICPD behind us, several challenges remain. We need to ensure that changes are made in the real world as well as on paper, and to document how well programs and policies live up to the new standards. Moreover, we need to maintain the momentum of intellectual inquiry, which was initially occasioned by the conference: the willingness to question long-held assumptions, and the search for new ethical and philosophical approaches. If the present papers are anything to go by, the scholars represented here are likely to be major contributors to these endeavors.

Carolyn Makinson
December 1994

Acknowledgments

This book is the result of a program of research sponsored by The Population Council, and conducted as a joint activity of its Research Division and the Office for West Asia and North Africa in Cairo. Financial support for the studies and the symposium held in Cairo February 7–9, 1994, was generously provided by the United Nations Fund for Population Activities (UNFPA), the Andrew Mellon Foundation, the Rockefeller Foundation, and the Middle East and North Africa regional office of the Ford Foundation.

I am grateful to the Cairo office of The Population Council, and in particular to Barbara Ibrahim, for the invitation to work on a topic in which I have had a longstanding interest, and for helping make my stay in Cairo a most productive time; and to the Department of Population and International Health at Harvard University for its flexibility in granting me several leaves in the course of the project. The Research Division of The Population Council in New York played a key role in organizing the international symposium at which the papers gathered here were presented, and I would like to thank Cynthia Lloyd and Kristin Morrell. Elizabeth Ransom assisted with the editing and preparation of the manuscript, sometimes under considerable pressure, and her help is greatly appreciated.

Introduction

A Region of Diversity and Change

Carla Makhlouf Obermeyer

BACKGROUND: FAMILY, GENDER, AND POPULATION POLICY

Although international debates about the role of population policy have gradually come to acknowledge the multiplicity of the forces shaping the demography of nations, until recently a rather simplistic view prevailed with respect to the situation in the Middle East and North Africa. Even comparatively well-informed observers believed that the region was lagging behind the rest of the developing world, and they attributed the apparent persistence of high fertility and mortality to the influence of Islam and the low status of women. In the last few years, however, the acceleration of mortality decline and the continuing drop in fertility have considerably changed the demographic profile of the region, and underscored the diversity in the paths taken by different countries. At the same time, a growing body of research has begun to clarify the multiple dimensions of the demographic transition, and has uncovered unexpected patterns which call into question easy generalizations about the region.

The attention that the International Conference on Population and Development (held in Cairo in September 1994) was to focus on the Middle East provided the impetus, in the course of the preceding year, for bringing together a group of scholars who would review population policies in the region, in light of international debates and recent demographic and socioeconomic data. The project was also designed to bridge the gap between what appeared to be opposing sides of the population debate: those advocating fertility limitation to foster national development and preserve global environmental resources, and those concerned about the protection of the rights of women and the well-being of individuals. By providing a regional focus for these debates, the project would contribute to reducing the polarization of views on the international scene concerning the definition, scope, and implementation of population policies.

In the spring of 1993, at the invitation of The Population Council, a small group of researchers representing different backgrounds and disciplines met in Cairo to discuss the ways in which the issues being debated on the global scene related to the current situation in the region. Building on research which suggests that the formulation and impact of population policies is, to a great extent, a function of the forces that shape gender relations and the functioning of families, the aim was to offer new insights about the ways in which these forces operate in the Middle East. Following the first meeting, the group of researchers was expanded to provide a broader coverage of the issues, papers were commissioned, and another workshop was held in Cairo in the fall of 1993. These efforts culminated in an international symposium entitled "Family, Gender, and Population Policy: International Debates and Middle Eastern Realities," convened in Cairo from February 7 to 9, 1994.

The chapters that follow are revised versions of the presentations made at the symposium.[1] The first part of the book analyzes the political conditions under which population policies are formulated and implemented, in particular the legal, religious, and symbolic aspects of the relation between the state and the individual. The second part of the book focuses on the constraints that household/family structures represent for individual behavior, and more specifically the ways in which the distribution of resources and responsibilities within the family affects reproductive choices. The third part considers the extent to which health and family planning services are effective in improving the well-being of the populations they serve, while responding to the needs of individual women. These chapters provide new, sometimes provocative, perspectives on the transformations that have been taking place in the region.

THE MIDDLE EAST AND NORTH AFRICA: SIMILARITIES AND
CONTRASTS

The Middle East as referred to in this book encompasses the countries
of the Arab world, in addition to Iran and Turkey. Similar but not
identical groupings of these countries are sometimes classified (for
example by the United Nations) under the headings of the Middle East
and North Africa, or West Asia and North Africa. Neither the
strategies for categorizing the countries, nor the criteria of inclusion/
exclusion are without fault, reflecting as they often do changing
political or administrative realities. The one regional classification
that has the merit of reflecting a large degree of linguistic and political
homogeneity is that which would group all countries that use Arabic
as the official language and are members of the League of Arab
States.[2] While such a strategy would have the advantage of simplicity,
it would lead to the exclusion of two large countries that share a
number of common cultural traits with the Arab world, and have been
closely linked to it historically. Indeed Turkey and Iran, each with over
60 million inhabitants, present fascinating illustrations of the divergent policies that have been followed in the region, the former based
on secularism, the other on a theocracy. The decision was therefore
made to use a broader definition of the Middle East, which includes
the Maghrib, the Nile Valley, Western Asia, the Arabian Peninsula,
Iran, and Turkey.

The region as a whole is predominantly Muslim, and the majority
of the people share a common language, Arabic. History has also at
different times connected the countries of the region, and shaped
common social institutions. Until the middle of this century, a
pretransitional demographic regime prevailed, large families were the
norm, and mortality was high throughout the region. Although the
forces that were to transform the demographic profile of the region had
long been at work, as recently as the mid-1980s some scholars had
argued that the demographic transition was lagging as a result of
Islamic doctrine, and in particular because of the way in which it
defines a subordinate status for women. Such statements could be
made only on the basis of figures that were compiled just before
substantial declines in fertility and mortality became apparent
throughout the region.

Today, the diversity in indicators is striking (see Table 1). The
large gaps in per capita income and in the degree of urbanization are

Carla Makhlouf Obermeyer

Table 1: Demographic and socioeconomic indicators in countries of the Middle East, most recent data[a]

Country	1 Population (millions, '95)	2 GNP per capita (US$, '92)	3 Percent urban ('90–95)	4 Total fertility rate ('90–95)	5 Infant mortality rate ('90–95)	6 Life expectancy at birth ('90–95)			7 Adult literacy (%, '90)	8 Female enrollment ratio in primary school (%, '92)[b]
						Total	Male	Female		
Algeria	28.0	1,840	53	3.9	42	67	68	67	61	88
Bahrain	0.5	7,130	83	4.2	16	72	70	74	79	102
Djibouti	0.4	–	81	6.5	115	48	47	50	–	–
Egypt	60.0	640	44	3.9c	62	64	62	65	50	93
Iran	60.0	2,200	58	5.0	36	68	67	68	56	105
Iraq	20.0	2,340d	73	5.3	44	66	65	68	62	102
Jordan	4.2	1,120	69	5.6	34	68	66	70	82	98
Kuwait	1.5	13,400e	93	5.9	11	75	73	78	74	–
Lebanon	3.0	2,150d	86	2.5	11	69	67	71	81	110
Libya	5.4	5,420e	84	6.7	68	63	62	65	66	–
Mauritania	2.3	530	49	6.5	117	52	50	53	35	43
Morocco	27.0	1,030	47	3.8	57	63	62	65	52	53
Oman	2.1	6,480	12	7.8	26	70	68	72	–	95
Palestine[f]	2.2	–	51	7.8	28	69	–	–	76	108
Qatar	0.5	16,750	90	4.5	23	71	69	74	–	100
Saudi Arabia	17.8	7,510	78	6.5	52	70	68	71	64	72
Somalia	9.2	170e	25	6.6	122	53	52	54	27	–

Table 1 contd.

Country	1 Population (millions, '95)	2 GNP per capita (US$, '92)	3 Percent urban ('90–95)	4 Total fertility rate ('90–95)	5 Infant mortality rate ('90–95)	6 Life expectancy at birth ('90–95)			7 Adult literacy (%, '90)	8 Female enrollment ratio in primary school (%, '92)[b]
						Total	Male	Female		
Sudan	28.1	480[c]	23	6.3	65	52	51	53	28	43
Syria	14.6	1,160[c]	51	4.2	35	67	65	69	67	103
Tunisia	8.9	1,720	57	3.2	36	68	67	69	68	109
Turkey	60.8	1,980	64	2.7	53	67	65	69	82	111
UAE	1.9	22,020	82	5.9	24	74	73	75	–[g]	114
Yemen	14.5	528	31	7.9	83	50	50	50	41	44

Sources: Columns 1, 6: United Nations, 1994 Revision. Population figures for Egypt and Iran are based on Courbage and Fargues, 1992, and Ladier and Hourcade, 1995, respectively. The figure for Jordan excludes the West Bank. Column 2: World Bank, 1994. Column 3: United Nations, 1992 Revision. Columns 4, 5: Latest survey available: Demographic and Health Surveys (DHS) for Egypt, Morocco, Tunisia, Jordan, Yemen; Pan Arab Project for Child Development (PAPCHILD) surveys for Algeria, Mauritania, Syria; Gulf Child Survey (GCS) for Saudi Arabia and the countries of the Gulf; other countries, estimates from Courbage and Fargues, 1992; Courbage and Khlat, 1993; and ESCWA, 1992. Columns 7, 8: UNDP, 1994

– Not available

[a] Different sources of data on the region present very different estimates for several of the indicators. For example, United Nations sources (1994) give higher population figures for Egypt (63 million), Iran (67 million), and Jordan (5.4 million). The difficulty of providing correct estimates is especially acute in the case of Gulf countries, which all have substantial non-national populations, and where different figures are obtained when all residents are included. Moreover, in several countries (Iraq, Kuwait, Lebanon, Sudan), war conditions have both affected demographic indicators and made it more difficult to monitor their trends. In others (Jordan, Palestine), a fluid political situation makes the exact enumeration of national populations subject to debate.

[b] Enrollment ratios are expressed as a percentage of the total population of primary-school age; for countries with universal primary education, the gross enrollment ratio may exceed 100 percent because some pupils are above or below the official primary-school age

[c] Courbage (this volume) argues that the latest DHS underestimates Egypt's fertility because of its sampling frame, and that the TFR is closer to 4.4

[d] 1987   [e] 1988   [f] Palestine figures refer to the West Bank, Gaza Strip, and East Jerusalem, and are calculated from CBS, 1993

[g] Data not available, but illiteracy is estimated at less than 5 percent (World Bank, 1994)

The editor is grateful to Youssef Courbage for his help in checking and updating the figures in this table a reflection of the dissimilar economic bases of the different countries, from the 'coupon clippers'[3] whose economy is based mainly on oil revenues (Bahrain, Kuwait, Libya, Oman, Qatar, and the United Arab Emirates) and the 'oil industrializers' (Algeria, Iraq, and Saudi Arabia) to the 'watchmakers' who concentrate on skill-intensive manufactures (Jordan, Lebanon, Tunisia, and Syria) and the 'agro-poor' (Sudan, Mauritania, Somalia, and Yemen), with other countries relying on a combination of agriculture and industry (Iran and Turkey, in a substantially higher income bracket than Egypt and Morocco).

While growth rates remain above 2 percent annually across most of the region (and above 3 percent in five countries), reflecting the momentum of earlier decades, fertility rates have begun to drop substantially in several countries. Indeed, although women still bear more than five children in over half the countries of the region, total fertility rates are down from an average of almost 7 for all countries during the period 1950–55, and are at or under 4 in eight of the countries. Infant mortality rates have dropped substantially across the region; while almost all countries started above 175 deaths per thousand live births during the period 1950–55, rates are now down below 70 per thousand in all but the four 'agro-poor' countries. Throughout the region, women's life expectancies are higher than men's by an average of three years, suggesting that the high maternal mortality and the differential treatment of female children that may have characterized parts of the region in the past[4] have been greatly attenuated. Moreover, in thirteen out of eighteen countries for which school statistics are available, female enrollment ratios are close to 100 percent, indicating that the gender gaps in education are rapidly closing, and suggesting that further reductions in fertility are likely.

A consideration of the patterns and trends evidenced by demographic indicators shows, not surprisingly, a poor fit with economic factors. It is true that the poorest countries tend to have higher fertility, but high total fertility rates are also found in some of the wealthiest countries, and the most rapid fertility declines have taken place in some of the poorer countries (Egypt, Tunisia, Turkey, and Morocco).

Perhaps more interestingly, the correlation with explicit government policy on population is also far from uniform. Several countries have a policy aimed at encouraging high fertility (Saudi Arabia, Kuwait, and Iraq), but they by no means have the highest fertility— Kuwait in fact has one of the lowest fertility rates, despite the government's support for large families as a way to decrease reliance on foreign labor. Most countries of the region do not have an explicit position on population, but their governments support the provision of family planning services. In some countries, such as Egypt, Tunisia, and Turkey, fertility-reduction policies have been in place for several decades, and have, in the latter two cases, been associated with fairly rapid fertility decline. Other countries have only recently adopted such principles, like Algeria, which in 1985 reversed a tradition of advocating development as the best contraceptive in favor of a more direct strategy, and Yemen, which in 1991 formulated a comprehensive population and development policy. But the most dramatic reversals are those which occurred in post-revolutionary Iran. The Islamic leadership at first rejected the policy put in place by the shah in favor of a vehemently pro-natalist stand. The government subsequently reversed that position after its ability to provide for its citizens was called into question by the results of a national survey showing rapid growth. Iran has now embarked on a vigorous family planning program.

ISLAM AND POPULATION: "FLEXIBLE LIKE A ROPE"?[5]

The policies formulated over time by various governments have been divergent in both their explicit and their implicit goals, even though they must ultimately be justified with reference to shari'a (Islamic law).[6] To what extent this apparent flexibility of Islamic doctrine can extend to notions of reproductive choice as they have evolved in the West is a question that is addressed in chapter 1. Much of what is written about notions of gender in Islam emphasizes the non-egalitarian aspects of the doctrine with respect to marriage and family relationships, and consequently its incompatibility with the notions of equality that are at the heart of reproductive rights formulations. And yet beyond these apparently fundamental differences, the chapter argues, women-centered views on both sides of the debate provide elements for a possible convergence of ideas. Critiques of Western liberal thought by feminists have suggested new approaches to the notions of equality and autonomy; and at the same time, Muslim feminists and human rights advocates have questioned the dominance of jurisprudence and called for a return to what they see as the true message of the religion, one that is egalitarian and universalistic. The chapter brings to light these elements of convergence, and explores how they can be used to broaden the bases of policies aimed at improving human welfare.

While the potential for equality is present in the religious doctrine, across the region the policies that deal with reproductive behavior have generally taken a more traditional approach to gender relations. Even where sweeping reforms of the laws regulating women's status were undertaken, they were the outcome of nationalist goals rather than state feminism, as Cem Behar argues in his review of the population policy of Turkey (chapter 2). The precociousness of the transition in Turkey, according to Behar, was the result of a multiplicity of forces, among which the reforms of women's legal status were very important. But as in Tunisia (the only other Muslim country that reformed its Code of Personal Status to prohibit polygyny and unilateral repudiation, and put in place an egalitarian marriage and divorce legislation), although the reforms were pervasive and redefined gender roles,[7] they were undertaken as part of a modernizing program, and their feminist outcomes were somewhat unintended. Nevertheless, by radically altering family relationships and strengthening the conjugal bond, these reforms were a key element behind the early onset of the fertility transition.

Another important feature of the demographic transition in Turkey is that, as in historical Europe, its onset preceded the development of modern contraceptives. Behar's research reveals that historically, men in Turkey took a great deal of initiative in family planning.[8] While it may be surprising to find such a pattern in a nineteenth-century Turkey ruled by Sultans, this is yet another indication that male responsibility—associated everywhere with the limitation of births— was to be found in the region at a relatively early time.

The case of Iran illustrates the flexibility of Islamic ideology in adapting to changing circumstances, and questions the assumption that it is incompatible with feminism. As Homa Hoodfar shows in chapter 5, after it reversed its pro-natalist policy of the early years, the Islamic Republic adopted a strategy of consensus building around the necessity of family planning. The government has been successful in increasing popular commitment to family planning by combining Islamic discourse with modern ideas about population issues, and propagating its ideas through the Friday sermon and other media. In this, it relied on an interpretation of the scriptures that stresses quality of offspring rather than quantity, and justifies birth control as a means to strengthen the community of believers and reduce their dependence on outside powers. The regime has also advocated women's participation in the implementation of the goals of the Republic, even though such a strategy is in conflict with the idea of female domesticity that has been central to its notion of the ideal Muslim society. These contradictions have provided an opportunity for women activists to question traditional notions of gender roles, and to use the ambivalent ideological positions of the government to launch their women-centered interpretation of Islam.

STATE POLICY OR SOCIETAL FORCES?

The diversity in governments' objectives and the changing context in which population policies are implemented are themes that echo through several chapters in this book. Egypt provides an example of a policy that received increasing commitment over time on the part of the leadership, but fell short of many of its goals. In his analysis, Saad Eddin Ibrahim (chapter 3) attributes the policy's limited impact to the varying degree of allegiance of different echelons in the social structure, in particular to the lukewarm support it receives from some mid-level government officials and physicians. Even though the findings of this survey may not be representative of the country as a whole, they do raise the question of whether a pervasive conviction about the relevance of population issues and a commitment to the ideology of fertility reduction (which in Iran's case were found to be important) are necessary conditions for the success of family planning programs.

The experience of Morocco would seem to answer this question in the negative. Indeed, Morocco does not even have a population policy as such, although the government has, since the mid-1970s, been supporting family planning programs. Youssef Courbage (chapter 4) presents Morocco as one of the unexpected success stories of fertility decline. Despite its disadvantageous position with respect to many of the factors that are usually associated with fertility decline (including its economic mode of production, standards of living, infant mortality, patterns of urbanization, and levels of education), the pace of fertility decline has been relatively rapid, especially by comparison with a country such as Egypt, where these indicators were more favorable.

Courbage attributes this to the interplay of several socioeconomic forces, principal among which are the increase in female employment, government fiscal policies, and the patterns of migration of Moroccans to the West. These changes have contributed to raising women's autonomy, increasing the cost of children, and undermining traditional world views. Thus a combination of ideational and economic factors brings changes to the structure of the family and women's roles within it, and in turn translates into reproductive decisions that are conducive to fertility decline.

FAMILIES IN TRANSITION

The extent to which the demographic transitions under way in the region have been accompanied by transformations of the family and a redefinition of gender roles is another major theme that recurs through several chapters of the book. The notion of individualist choice in reproductive matters that is advocated as indispensable, not only to the exercise of human rights but also as a more appropriate strategy for fertility limitation, is potentially in conflict with the cultural ethos of the region, in which family and community play a considerable role. Indeed, the tension between family values and individual rights which has marked many of the international debates is especially striking in the Middle East because of the particular way in which prevalent definitions of women's roles are inextricably linked to notions of the family. It is therefore important to understand to what extent the concepts of autonomy and choice, as they have developed in the Western tradition, are relevant in a different cultural context.

In chapter 7, Laila Nawar, Cynthia Lloyd, and Barbara Ibrahim address just such a question, through a careful analysis of data from a survey of Egyptian households. While the study confirms the relatively low levels of autonomy among Egyptian women and the importance of education and employment for the exercise of independence, it also reveals several unexpected findings. Women had a stronger voice in decisions most relevant to them, such as family planning, and believed that such decisions should be jointly made by husbands and wives. In addition, women with little autonomy expressed the desire and the conviction that their daughters would have much greater leeway than they themselves had: four-fifths approved of their daughters working, and over half thought they should have no more than two children. Such aspirations suggest a great potential for changing gender roles in a not too distant future.

The limitations on women's reproductive decisions are also illustrated by Rahma Bourqia's discussion (chapter 6) of women's strategies in rural Morocco. The insecurity that characterizes the lives of many village women is rooted both in the subsistence conditions of the rural economy and in the uncertainties inherent in the unequal system of marriage. Fears of divorce and polygyny lead women to have more children as a way of "clipping the husband's wings" and as an insurance policy for their old age. At the same time, however, women's discourse about children shows that they are keenly aware that childbearing is only one of the possible strategies against insecurity. That education is, in their opinion, a more desirable asset, suggests that they would favor changes in their life conditions.

Starting from very different types of data, and using comparative trends across several countries, Philippe Fargues (chapter 8) discusses the direction of change that can be discerned from an examination of current gender and generational gaps. The gender gap in schooling, which is today at its highest level, appears to be strengthening the traditional social order. At the same time, the lag between the decline of mortality and that of fertility has resulted in a gap between generations, manifested in the disparity between the monopoly of power of the over-fifty generation and the quasi-monopoly on formal knowledge of the younger generations. This results in a situation that has great potential for cleavages leading to protest against the social order. But if we project both of these imbalances into the future, it becomes clear that they are but a temporary phenomenon. Indeed, the balanced sex ratios in primary school suggest that the sharp sex and age differentials in education that are currently so pervasive will, in a couple of decades, have all but disappeared, and with them the confrontations that have characterized previous generations in the Middle East.

It is comforting to think that the forces that today create situations of strife and define constraints on the exercise of freedom and reproductive choice may be somewhat ephemeral, and that considerably different social arrangements can emerge from contemporary conflicts. The research findings presented here document the complex links between demographic forces and their cultural context, both at the micro-level of the household and at the macro-level of regional trends. They draw our attention to the particular ways in which demographic transitions and social transformations interact in the region, at times reinforcing tradition, at other times undermining it.

BROADENING CHOICE AND PRESERVING HEALTH

The expansion of the scope of population policies worldwide has been accompanied by a greater awareness of the need to consider the effect family planning programs have on individuals, not merely the impact they have at the aggregate level of fertility. The increased emphasis on quality of care has thus shifted attention to the ways in which family planning programs can expand the reproductive options for individuals, while preserving their health and well-being. The last three chapters in the book reflect on these issues in the context of Middle Eastern countries.

One of the major obstacles to the improved quality of care in family planning programs has been the use of incentives to reach numerical targets in the distribution of contraceptives. In chapter 9, Karima Khalil and Cynthia Myntti summarize the drawbacks of the preoccupation with numbers—of acceptors and of contraceptives distributed—that have marked the use of targets worldwide. While targeting has been limited in the Middle East as a whole, there have been some concerns over the use of incentives and quotas in Egypt. These are fortunately starting to be addressed, and there are signs of a change in the way programs are evaluated and of a shift towards client-based perspectives.

Similar concerns and lessons emerge from the review by Ezzeldin Hassan and Mahmoud Fathalla (chapter 10) of Egypt's experience with the introduction of different contraceptive methods. Oral contraceptives were initially made available to women without providing sufficient information on their use, or counseling about alternative methods. As a result of improper use, estimated at about 60 percent of women, the failure of the pill was much higher in Egypt than in other parts of the world. Similar problems emerged when injectable contraceptives were first introduced, leading to widespread dissatisfaction and distrust. The lessons learned from these two experiences were put to use in the introduction of plans for contraceptive implants, and efforts are under way to provide adequate training and make the system more responsive to women's requests.

Patterns of contraceptive use are thus the outcome of both the choice of available contraceptives and the extent to which providers are attentive to women's needs. One of the dimensions that had until recently been neglected is the interaction between the use of contraception and the health of the woman who relies on it. Indeed, for three decades the distribution of contraceptive methods seemed to be built on the assumption that women are healthy, and that only the side-effects specifically associated with a given method needed to be addressed. The Giza morbidity study has now provided clear evidence that this is an untenable assumption, both scientifically and ethically. Chapter 11, by Hoda Zurayk, Nabil Younis, and Hind Khattab, reports on the high prevalence of reproductive tract infections, prolapse, and related morbidities among women in two Egyptian villages, and underscores the heavy burden of illness that many women come to take as a natural part of womanhood. The associations that the authors found between the use of contraceptives and morbidity conditions also raise serious questions about the neglect of the health dimension in family planning. Because it is backed by careful analyses, their call for a rethinking of family planning is having a considerable impact on both the research community and advocates for women's health.

In sum, these reviews of reproductive health in the Middle East underscore the need for a reassessment of family planning programs in the region, and support a new approach that would both provide means to help individuals reach their reproductive intentions and ensure their health and well-being. How the combination of health and family planning can be achieved, in other words how reproductive health programs are to be defined, administered, and funded are questions that will require a mobilization of resources and good will in the decade to come.

INDIVIDUAL CHOICES AND SOCIAL CONSTRAINTS

The transitions now under way in societies of the Middle East have, in many respects, been unanticipated. Fertility is declining in countries with apparently unfavorable socioeconomic conditions, and lagging in others with high levels of income and education. In some countries with a tradition of openness to the West, governments are under pressure from religious conservative groups to revoke the reforms that were earlier enacted to mitigate gender inequality, while in others, activists working within the framework of traditional Islamic laws have achieved a number of feminist goals. The forces that are transforming the region have resulted in sometimes opposing trends. Increasing levels of education hold the promise of expanding options for individuals, improving societal indicators, and fostering gender equality, while worsening economic conditions threaten these advances and create a climate of despondency. The greater openness to dialogue that marked the International Conference on Population and Development has also been accompanied by a hardening of previously more tolerant positions, such as has been the case with abortion. The resurgence of veiling in the region is symbolic of many of the ambiguities that surround changes in reproductive choices, since it can be both an overt sign of the constraints on women and a means to express one's adherence to norms of proper personal conduct. The chapters of this volume provide insights into how some of these contradictions are defined, and raise questions for further investigation about notions of rights and expressions of women's autonomy, men's responsibilities in the family, the role of state policies, and the scope of family planning programs. Based on a solid grasp of the dynamics of one region of the world, their findings contribute to a better understanding of the articulation of individual motivations, collective norms, and real options that constitute the background of reproductive decisions everywhere.

REFERENCES

CBS. 1993. *Statistical abstracts.* Jerusalem: Central Bureau of Statistics.
Courbage, Y. and P. Fargues. 1992. *L'avenir démographique de la rive sud de la Méditerranée.* Paris: Institut National d'Etudes Démographiques.
Courbage, Y. and M. Khlat. 1993. Population structure and growth in the Arab world: Recent trends. Paper presented at the Arab Population Conference, Amman, April 1993.
Economic and Social Commission for Western Asia (ESCWA). 1992. *Population situation in the ESCWA region 1990.* Baghdad: ESCWA.
Ladier, M. and B. Hourcade. 1995. *Les paradoxes de l'évolution démographique en Iran.* Paris: Institut National d'Etudes Démographiques.
Obermeyer, C. Makhlouf. 1992. Women, Islam and politics: The demography of Arab countries. *Population and Development* 18/1:33–60.

Richards, A. and J. Waterbury. 1990. *A political economy of the Middle East.*
    Boulder: Westview Press.
United Nations. 1993. *World population prospects: The 1992 revision.* New
    York: United Nations Population Division.
United Nations. 1994. *World population prospects: The 1994 revision.* New
    York: United Nations Population Division.
United Nations Development Programme (UNDP). 1994. *Human develop-
    ment report.* New York: Oxford University Press.
World Bank. 1994. *World development report, 1994.* New York: Oxford
    University Press.

NOTES

1   A summary of the major ideas discussed at the symposium has been
    published in *Family, Gender and Population Policy: Views from the
    Middle East,* Cairo: The Population Council, 1994.
2   Indeed, in a previous work (Obermeyer, 1992), I limited my analyses to
    countries of the Arab world for precisely this reason.
3   This taxonomy is adapted from Richards and Waterbury (1990).
4   Analyses of data on infant mortality suggest that in some countries a small
    excess in female child mortality was found in past decades, which has
    been attributed to son preference and possible discrimination against
    female children.
5   The expression is cited by Homa Hoodfar, quoting one of her informants.
6   The major exception is Turkey, which adopted a secular code of law
    under Atatürk, and to a lesser extent Lebanon, which is not constituted as
    a Muslim state because of the presence of a substantial Christian popu-
    lation (although the government has traditionally been structured around
    a confessional distribution of power).
7   It is important to note, however, that while Atatürk clearly broke with the
    Ottoman past and advocated complete state secularism, Bourguiba justi-
    fied the reforms of Tunisian law with reference to Islamic doctrine.
8   This is still the case today, with over half of contracepting couples using
    withdrawal as their method of family planning. In other countries of the
    region, withdrawal accounts for a much lower proportion of contracep-
    tive use.

1

Reproductive Rights in the West and in the Middle East: A Cross-Cultural Perspective

Carla Makhlouf Obermeyer

In recent months, a number of international conferences focusing on human rights and population have added a certain urgency to the search for definitions of reproductive rights that would be acceptable cross-culturally. In the last three decades, discussions of reproductive rights at each of the international conferences on population have been marked by subtle but important changes in emphasis (Freedman and Isaacs, 1993). These have come in response to evolving ideas about the rationale for reproductive rights and its implications for population policy, as well as to changes in power relations on the global scene. One key issue on the international agenda is the extent to which definitions of human rights can be transposed to non-Western cultures in ways that avoid both "homogenizing universalism" and "paralyzing relativism" (Cook, 1993a).

The purpose of this chapter is to explore the commonalities that can be found between notions of reproductive rights as they developed in the Western tradition and the principles that define gender rights in Islam. This is a daunting task, which requires some knowledge about several disciplinary domains and involves a comparative analysis of two philosophical and legal traditions that have often been at odds historically. In addition, the issue of women's rights in Islam is one that has brought about a polarization of viewpoints—and recent regional and international developments have done little to defuse the tension between them. Clearly, this is hazardous intellectual territory, where only the overly optimistic would willingly tread. I am convinced, however, that careful research will uncover more common ground than appears at first. It is this belief that motivates my pursuit.

One has to recognize at the outset that the discourse about women and their rights in the Middle East has often been dominated by the more uncompromising positions on both sides, and moreover that the exchange of these extreme views has usually excluded women, who are the group most vulnerable to abuses of reproductive rights. By contrast, woman-centered perspectives coming from both sides can provide new elements for a dialogue. More specifically, Western feminists who have questioned traditional liberal notions of autonomy and individualism in light of the reality of women's reproductive experience have opened the door for a redefinition of rights that is more conducive to dialogue than earlier formulations. At the same time, there are elements in Islam that can be interpreted to justify a more egalitarian approach to reproductive rights, one that is more responsive to women's needs and is espoused by a large number of Muslims. This chapter aims to bring to light these two tendencies and show that their shared concern for the welfare of women and men can contribute to bridging the apparent gap between them.

UNIVERSALISM AND RELATIVISM: ANTHROPOLOGICAL PERSPEC-
TIVES

The process of translating legal and ethical concepts of rights between two different cultures is an extremely arduous task, and it is useful here to pause for a moment and draw on the anthropological literature, which provides many illustrations of the dilemmas that arise from encounters between different normative systems (Herskovits, 1947; Lévi-Strauss, 1963; Hatch, 1983). Unable to find equivalents to his/her concepts of rights and wrongs, and confronted with behaviors that seem morally unacceptable, the anthropologist can adopt one of two equally undesirable stances: the first is that individuals in cultures that do not possess the same notions of rights will need to be 'educated' and 'enlightened' in the ways of liberal thinking—an undertaking with all the dangers of cultural imperialism; and the second is the detached relativist view[1] that since any ethical principle is only applicable in a given context, the anthropologist will have to acquiesce even to practices that appear to violate human dignity.[2]

This dilemma has received a great deal of attention from anthropologists who have at various times had to confront value systems that were antithetical to their beliefs.[3] Recently, there have been attempts to break out of the impasse of universalism versus relativism, and develop a new approach to human rights. Several researchers have examined the bases for the universality of human rights (Panikkar, 1982; Donnelly, 1989). Some have questioned the strict presumption of universality upon which human rights are based, in part because it is founded on the erroneous belief that all people think in a similar fashion; they have argued against developing a "single catalogue" of rights because this ignores the variability in value systems and is not based on sufficient knowledge of how people in other cultures conceive of rights. At the same time, however, the anthropological literature suggests that there is a considerable degree of flexibility in formulating notions of human dignity: morals systems based on either rights or duties can accommodate human rights, and there is no inherent contradiction between individual and group formulations of rights (Renteln, 1988a). It is increasingly recognized that while absolute universals cannot be found, it is possible, indeed desirable, to seek common denominators across cultures, which in turn can be used to develop contextually relevant notions of reproductive rights.

DEFINING REPRODUCTIVE RIGHTS

Since the Universal Declaration of Human Rights of 1948, all formulations of human rights are premised on the principle of the equality of all human beings and their inherent dignity. Human rights as defined in various international documents comprise the right to life, to freedom from all forms of discrimination, to liberty, and to security; the right to marry and found a family; the right to privacy and to education—all these are usually referred to as "first generation rights"; "second generation rights" include social, economic, and cultural rights, as well as access to health care (Cook, 1993b).[4] In the West, reproductive rights have roots in a long tradition that emphasizes the bodily integrity of individuals, and their right to protection against coercion by others (Petchesky, 1990), and they have also been formulated as elaborations of the right to found a family. They have been the focus of much public attention because of the important part they play in the defense by the women's movement of the right of all women to control their bodies, including their right to safe abortion. In official documents drafted at each of the international conferences on population, reproductive rights are defined as the right of individuals to decide "freely and responsibly" about the number and spacing of their children (earlier formulations had emphasized couples while later ones stressed individuals). Decisions about procreation require that individuals have access to information concerning reproductive matters, and have the power and resources needed to carry out their decisions—in other words, reproductive rights are dependent on individuals' ability to exercise their basic rights as human beings. Therefore an examination of reproductive rights entails a consideration of the status of women in society.

It is not the purpose here, however, to undertake a general review of women's status in Islam and in the West. The social reality of women's status is complex, and does not lend itself to some simplistic scoring system that would allow international comparisons—indeed, such comparisons often fail to do justice to the ambiguities that surround women's status in all cultures. One must, however, note three important points. Firstly, that the notion of complete equality between the sexes is central to international human rights documents. Secondly, it has to be recognized that complete gender equality is nowhere a reality, and that even those societies that hold such equality as an ideal have by no means achieved it—hence the importance of pledges to eliminate gender-based injustice, such as the Convention for the Elimination of all Forms of Discrimination Against Women (CEDAW). The third point is that not all cultures subscribe to the idea of complete equality as it is spelled out in human rights documents, and the ambivalence of some countries is clearly expressed by their refusal to ratify the CEDAW convention, or by their addition of preambles and reservations to the international documents. Several countries of the Middle East have expressed such reservations, despite the fact that other Muslim countries participated in drafting the Universal Declaration of 1948, and the fact that the 1972 Charter of the Islamic Conference (the organization of Islamic countries) expressly endorses international law and fundamental human rights as compatible with Islamic values (Mayer, 1991). Such ambivalence raises a key issue that underlies the rest of this discussion, namely whether equality as defined in international documents is indispensable to improving the welfare of women and protecting their reproductive rights.

THE MIDDLE EAST AND THE WEST: APPARENT CONTRADICTIONS

The researcher embarking on a quest for common ground is at first taken by the polarization of opinions on the subject of women's position in societies of the Middle East, and in particular the prevalent view that there is a basic incompatibility between on the one hand the notions of universality and equality that are at the core of reproductive rights as human rights, and on the other the Islamic emphasis on complementarity rather than equality in gender roles.[5] It seems that, at whatever level we situate ourselves, the ethical, the legal, or the social, differences are at first more striking than commonalities, and we must face the old predicament of anthropologists: how to deal with the fact that the values that seem central to one culture, in this case the group of cultures referred to as Western, are in contradiction with those of another group of societies, those referred to as Muslim.

Before going any further in our comparisons, it is important to mention that both these constructs—Western and Muslim—are overly general in that they ignore the diversity that exists within each broadly defined culture from the point of view of both ideology and practice.[6] In the case of Islam, several scholars have argued that one has to distinguish between what is Muslim—that is, practiced by people who are considered Muslim—and what is Islamic—that is, reflecting the essential values of the religion (Arkoun, 1984). This distinction is most useful because it separates the ideal of the religion from its implementation by various sects, and acknowledges diversity while protecting the central core of the religion against totalitarian claims. This is especially important at a time when militant groups are engaged in intense competition to assert their monopoly over the truth. Moreover, there is a good deal of evidence from many regions of the world suggesting that societal definitions of women's roles and reproductive rights are affected more by local and international politics than by religious doctrine as such.[7] Therefore, the prevalent polarization as discussed in this paper is not inherent in the two value systems but is a product of power relations between groups.

Such subtleties are usually ignored by those who render the fateful diagnosis of incompatibility between 'Islam' and 'the West.' All too often, scholars from both sides have emphasized the more extreme interpretations of the situation. Thus for instance, in explaining Iran's refusal to ratify the CEDAW convention, Sultanhussein Tabandeh argues that human rights as developed in the West are incompatible with Islam, and implicitly endorses a relativist stance—that is, 'your' values are not relevant to 'our' tradition (1970). Western scholars examining the legal codes in countries of the region find a number of instances where they conflict with the universalist human rights statements endorsed by governments, and some draw the conclusion that the religion lacks "any willingness to recognize women as full equal human beings who deserve the same rights and freedoms as men. Instead, discrimination against women is treated as something entirely natural" (Mayer, 1991:136). Analyses by Middle Easterners often stress the striking differences in status between men and women, and characterize Middle Eastern societies as fundamentally unjust. Typical of these views are statements such as those made by Hisham Sharabi, who argues that Arab society is "neopatriarchal," and embodies much that is dysfunctional and pathological. "The dominant ideology of neopatriarchal society [is] a conservative relentless male oriented ideology, which tended to assign privilege and power to the male at the expense of the female, keeping the latter under crippling legal and social constraints" (Sharabi, 1988: 33).

What this all means is that this whole area of research and action is burdened by a heavy baggage of conventional models and preconceived notions. There are a number of factors that account for the power of such stereotypes and the polarization of views. Some of them have to do with the distrust that often characterizes relations between more developed nations and those that they have dominated politically and economically—in other words, with a fundamental 'north–south' tension, one that is vehemently expressed at the many international conferences dealing with development, population, or human rights. The emergence of groups in the Middle East claiming that they hold the key to a regeneration of society through the application of literal interpretations of the sacred texts, and the threat that they have come to constitute against established governments, are additional elements that further hinder candid communication about these issues.

Another key factor is that Islam, like the other two monotheistic religions of the Middle East, emerged in a specific temporal context that can be characterized as patriarchal, a context that is to a certain extent reflected in the sacred texts (Ahmed, 1992). Although the emergence of Islam in Arabia is widely believed to have resulted in an improvement in women's status, and although reformists and feminists have repeatedly argued that the doctrine lends itself to an egalitarian interpretation, the historically dominant tradition in Islam, as in other traditional creeds, stresses the fundamental differences between the sexes and defines different social roles and legal statuses for men and women.[8] The dominance of this interpretation is further reinforced by research that is inattentive to the discrepancy in societies of the region between the ideology of male dominance and the reality of women's autonomy. It is in fact no coincidence that until a couple of decades ago, all analyses of Middle Eastern societies were carried out by men, who had limited access to the domestic sphere of the family, and thus ignored a significant domain of social life, one that often contradicted the monolithic message communicated in the male-dominated public sphere.

There is another set of factors that account for the prevalence of the polarization of views. It is a function of the powerful dichotomies that are often seen to embody the essence of the Western and Islamic traditions. Philosophical comparisons and theoretical elaborations (which have also been dominated by the thinking of the establishment on both sides) have often emphasized the fundamentally different premises from which each tradition starts. Thus, it is argued, whereas Western thinking about human ethical issues is seen as based on pure reason, in Islam reason *('aql)* is considered insufficient, and incapable of evaluating the divine law.[9] The reason–revelation dichotomy is strengthened by the notion that Islam stresses not the rights of human beings but, rather, their duties to obey God, and that therefore human rights cannot be defined without recourse to revealed religion. A further opposition is seen to exist between the Western idea that the individual is inherently valuable and the Islamic emphasis on the *umma* (community of believers) as the locus of moral valuations.[10] Comparative analyses of political structures in Western and non-Western societies tend to focus on the relationship between the state and traditional kinship structures as the basis of order. For instance, Max Weber's classic study (1953) defines the modern state in terms of the development of rational–legal authority, bureaucracy, liberal-ism, and capitalism, and contrasts it with societies based on traditional familial structures or charismatic authority. Western political philoso-phers of the liberal tradition see the state as both a guarantor of rights and an institution against which the individual needs protection, while states in other parts of the world are seen to have a different moral status in relation to society.[11] Such differences are seen to extend to formulations of the roles of men and women. Western liberal formu-lations assume the existence of the conventional nuclear family with its emphasis on the conjugal bond and its role as a retreat from the competitive world (McKinnon, 1989; Naffine, 1990), whereas the more pervasive kinship structures of Middle Eastern societies empha-size intergenerational links (Goode, 1970). The legal implication of such differences is a further contrast between the civil and criminal codes of Western countries and what has been described as a "consti-tutional chasm" in the Middle East: in all countries, with the exception of Turkey, and (to a lesser degree) Tunisia, laws derived from shari'a regulate personal and family status, while laws inspired by the civil codes of Western countries regulate economic transactions.

All these dichotomies can be helpful in constructing 'ideal types' that are a good starting point for cross-cultural comparisons, and they may or may not stand up to empirical testing. The point is, however, that regardless of their scientific value as tools of analysis, these dichotomies have a certain appeal because they clearly categorize the world into two sides—black and white, 'us' and 'them'—and thus spare us the need to get down to the reality of the many shades of gray that make up real cultures. Moreover, by linking perceived cultural differences to powerful philosophical foundations, they suggest that differences are fundamental, and hence immutable. In fact, if we critically examine these so-called fundamental differences, two major points become clear. Firstly, the Western tradition is by no means uniformly representative of Westerners' opinions or behaviors—indeed, much of what is seen as typical of this tradition is increasingly questioned as a product of the evolution of a society that is also unequal and dominated by men, as well as by the ideology of the marketplace. In particular, critiques by Western feminists are provid-ing new elements that mitigate this dominance, and help find points of convergence with other cultures. Secondly, and similarly, the domi-nant interpretations of Islam with their emphasis on jurisprudence are by no means a necessary development of the religion. Today as well as in the past, Muslim feminists and mystics provide us with alternative visions that are more attentive to the needs of individuals and more open to dialogue about women's situation. In other words, while a cursory comparison of Islam and standard Western liberalism would suggest substantial incompatibilities between the two traditions, woman-centered perspectives on both sides help define a new approach to these issues, one that is situated somewhere between the two traditions. In order to move toward this middle ground, we need to consider both the elements provided by Western feminists' critiques and those that exist within Islam.

COMMONALITIES AND POINTS OF CONVERGENCE: WOMEN'S PERSPECTIVES

Western feminist approaches to the law "start with the conviction of women's unjust subordination, and they evaluate the law in terms of how it contributes to the dismantling of such injustice" (Cook, 1993a). There are two key elements here: firstly, the challenge to the neutrality of the law: "In a gendered world where sexes are not equal, the application to women of seemingly neutral laws . . . does not have a gender neutral result" (Naffine, 1990). In other words, although in the traditional liberal view the state appears to be gender-blind and impartial, some feminists argue that it is in fact far from neutral (McKinnon, 1989). The prototype human being that is abstracted as the subject of the law is in fact an "able-bodied, autonomous, rational, educated, married, competitive and essentially self-interested" male entrepreneur (Naffine, 1990:52). Therefore, standard formulations of human rights do not really apply to human beings in a universal manner, and equal treatment that does not acknowledge both the inherent bias of the law and women's specificity is bound to perpetuate injustice.

A second important element in Western feminist critiques is the reluctance to wholeheartedly adopt male-derived notions of autonomy because they are in contradiction with the reality of women's reproductive experience and their patterns of caretaking. Although in principle a positive value, autonomy fails in practice (Cook, 1993c). As Nedelsky puts it, "the values we cherish [freedom, self-determination] have come to us embedded in a theory that denies the reality we know: the centrality of relationships in constituting the self." It thus becomes necessary to reconceive autonomy in a way that would combine "the claim of the constitutiveness of social relations with the value of self-determination" (1989:9–10), and better reflect women's involvement in relationships of nurturance and care. By modifying the two key notions of equality and autonomy, feminist theory does in fact temper the abstract universalism of human rights, and provides an approach that is more relevant to the reality of women's lives. In so doing, it takes a step toward other cultural elaborations of gender that emphasize differences rather than ignoring them. While cautioning about the tendency of male-dominated groups to use the argument of cultural diversity to oppose human rights, formulations of reproductive rights are increasingly respectful of the diversity of contexts in which these rights are defined and implemented (Correa and Petchesky, 1994).

At the same time, it is also possible to find within Islam certain elements that mitigate the inequalities stemming from the legal tradition. While the legal doctrine deals with women only as wives and mothers—there are no discussions of either men or women except insofar as they belong in familial roles—the scriptures also address men and women as believers who are all to be judged according to merit.[12] A number of Qur'anic verses address men and women as believers and stress their equality. This clear recognition of individual believers as equal in the sight of God is key to the universalist ethos of Islam. Some researchers have argued that, in fact, the development of all the 'schools' of Islamic jurisprudence is the result of a one-sided reading of the scriptures, and that it has now become necessary to take a fresh look at the texts and restore the centrality of the more universalistic verses (An-Na'im, 1990)[13]. Moreover, the legalistic emphasis of the various 'schools' has developed at the expense of other aspects of the religion. Indeed, as the Japanese Islamic scholar Murata has argued in her book *The Tao of Islam* (1992), there is a vibrant Sufi (mystical) tradition in Islam that is unencumbered by the legalistic burden of the dominant tradition and is based on a much more egalitarian ethos when it comes to gender.[14]

Similarly, although the non-egalitarian aspects of marriage, inheritance, and court testimony in Islam are well known—a man inherits twice as much, his legal testimony is worth that of two women, he has a unilateral right to divorce his wife, and he can marry more than one woman—interpretations of the bases of men's position have varied greatly. The Qur'anic statements that God has "preferred men" who are "in charge of women" (IV:34) and are "a degree higher" than women (II:228) are somewhat ambiguous, and there has been a good deal of argument about their exact definition and implications.[15] This implies some leeway in interpreting them in a more egalitarian fashion. In addition, Islam recognizes women's right to own property and manage their own affairs.[16] This aspect of Islamic doctrine is one that could be used to reinforce the potential for women's autonomy and equality, but it has received a great deal less attention than the unequal aspects of the doctrine.[17] Muslim feminists believe that those statements in the scriptures that stress the equality of believers before God are the authentic message of Islam, while those suggesting discrimination against women are merely reflections of the temporal conditions in which the religion developed, and a distortion of its inherent egalitarianism (Ahmed, 1986, 1992; Mernissi, 1985, 1992).

Another important element that is often overlooked is the emphasis in the scriptures on mutual consent rather than coercion as a basis for relations between men and women.[18] The Qur'an gives clear instructions about mutual consent between spouses in decisions related to child care, namely breast-feeding and weaning. "A mother should not be made to suffer because of her child, nor should he to whom the child is born (be made to suffer) because of his child. . . . If they desire to wean the child by mutual consent and (after) consultation, it is no sin for them" (Qur'an, II:233). There are also statements in the Hadith (compilations of the sayings of the Prophet Muhammad) concerning the use of contraceptive methods, which emphasize the need to obtain the wife's consent before practicing 'azl (withdrawal), because it may interfere with her enjoyment of sex or her desire for children. Several scholars have in fact noted that Islam is quite open in recognizing the importance of sexual enjoyment for both partners within marriage (Bouhdiba, 1975; Musallam, 1983).[19] Although little research has been carried out on this subject, there are indications that women have a sense of entitlement to sexual satisfaction in marriage (Khattab, 1992). Islamic doctrine is also quite flexible when it comes to the use of contraceptive methods (Bowen, 1991; Omran, 1992). Concerning abortion, the general Islamic position is to allow it until ensoulment, which is believed to take place after the first trimester, and except for the Maliki school of law, this results in a rather liberal policy.[20] Thus, several important components of a reproductive rights approach are encouraged in Islam.

There also exists the potential for an approach toward marriage that would be based on agreement rather than dominance and submission. This tendency, however, has been muted in comparison with the clear asymmetry in gender roles that is apparent in marriage practices in Muslim societies, as well as in the writings about these practices by both Muslim scholars and Western analysts. The standard view is that men have the obligation to financially provide for the family, and the right to expect obedience from their wives, while women's duties are confined to companionship and the care of children, and their rights limited to financial support and equal treatment in the case of polygyny (Abu Zahra, 1955; Rahman, 1980). This asymmetry is built around three key concepts: the first is *wilaya* (guardianship), which means that a woman needs a guardian to act on her behalf, and that a father is the legal guardian of his children; the second is *nafaqa*, which refers to the financial support that a man owes to his wife and children; and the third is *hadana,* which summarizes the right and duty of women to care for their young children, along with the fact that these are limited by the father's legal guardianship. Analyses of shari'a as it has been codified in the laws of Personal Status in different Muslim countries (Chamari, 1991; Nouredine, 1991; Rchid, 1991) demonstrate the unequivocal way in which man's role as the head of the household is spelled out, and the resulting difficulties of defending women's rights under such a legal system. These include the potential for the coercion of girls into early marriage; a divorce legislation that is clearly disadvantageous to women; limitations that a husband can put on his wife's right to work and freedom of movement; the fact that marriage to a non-Muslim is allowed for men but not women; and the fact that the ability to grant children legal status and citizenship are the prerogative of men and are only granted to women under exceptional circumstances.

All these obstacles, however, are not necessarily insurmountable within the framework of Islamic jurisprudence. One major reason has to do with the fact that the texts on which marriage legislation is based, like all religious texts, contain some ambiguities and lend themselves to widely different interpretations. This makes it possible to promulgate reforms without breaking with the tradition, a strategy that was adopted in Tunisia to abolish *talaq* (repudiation at the husband's request) and replace it with an egalitarian set of divorce procedures; to outlaw polygyny as contrary to the true intent of the scriptures; and also to decrease the claim of male relatives to inheritance, thus weakening links to the extended family and strengthening the conjugal bond.

Along somewhat different lines, but with similar results, women in different parts of the Muslim world have been trying to use shari'a to their advantage. Thus, for instance, feminists in post-revolutionary Iran have capitalized on the idea, shared among all the interpretations of Islam, that a husband has no legal right to his wife's labor or property, since her only duties are to provide him with companionship and to ensure proper care of the children. They have argued that in case of divorce the man must compensate his wife for the labor she contributed to the management of his household. Such legislation has contributed to raising the costs of divorce for men, and defining the conditions for a better legal settlement for women than they had before. It has also called into question the asymmetry in the husband–wife relationship by recognizing the importance of the woman's contribution and giving it concrete value. Another indication of the adaptability of the cultural context is that in many countries there are legal codes that have been superimposed on the Personal Status Code and clearly contradict it. Thus, for instance, most countries of the region have laws stating that all citizens are equal, labor codes emphasizing the right to work, and health laws insuring universal coverage. Although the aims behind such laws were often nationalist rather than feminist, the result has been to open the door to conflicting interpretations, and consequently to change, as these egalitarian laws can theoretically be used to support women's rights.

A further reason for the flexibility that exists concerning gender relations is that marriage in Islam is an explicit contract, which can include a number of provisions. "Marriage is not a sacrament . . . still less is it a bondage. It is a civil contract between one free servant of Allah and another free servant of Allah" (Pickthall, 1966:161). The contractual nature of marriage makes it possible to insert provisions that protect the woman against arbitrary divorce or polygyny, and guarantee her right to work or her freedom of movement. This method has been regularly used throughout history, but it has unfortunately been the privilege of those who have both the necessary knowledge of the law and the means to influence its application. Currently there are efforts by Muslim feminists and legal scholars in several countries, including Egypt and Iran, to develop a more egalitarian 'model marriage contract' that would be the standard for all contracts, and gradually allow for a more egalitarian definition of gender relations.

In sum, the existence of egalitarian elements in the scriptures, the ambiguity of some of the texts, the contradictions between different normative structures, and the efforts of reformists all contribute to defining a remarkably dynamic situation. Whether this potential will be directed toward dialogue that aims at improving the welfare of women, men, and families or be stifled by intolerant indictments on both sides will depend in large part on politics at the local and international levels. We have to hope that enlightened scholarly exchange, along with prudent policy formulation, will exert some beneficial influence on these political circumstances.

CONCLUSION

The most general inference that can be drawn from this review is that while superficial comparisons would lead us to believe that we are dealing with two incompatible systems of norms relating to gender and reproductive rights, further probing reveals a much greater potential for convergence. One implication of this is that further comparative studies of the ethical and legal bases of reproductive rights in each of these traditions are likely to uncover even greater possibilities for common themes to emerge. To do this, it is necessary to go beyond the general legal and normative level that has been the focus of this chapter, and attempt to understand reproductive rights in their particular contexts. How men and women perceive reproductive rights and to what extent their decisions and behavior reflect a concern over such rights are questions that require multidisciplinary research, and they are now starting to be addressed. Only when we can comprehend local notions of rights can we begin the two-way process of translation, and develop culturally relevant definitions and policies. At the same time, since legal reforms and ideas about rights can only provide a receptive context for changes in behavior, and do not by themselves produce these changes, it is important also to devote our attention to the practical realities that would support or hinder these reforms. These range from the economic and health infrastructure, to patterns of family formation and dissolution, and the diffusion of ideas through education and exchange—in other words to all those conditions that are a prerequisite to the exercise of human rights.

ACKNOWLEDGMENTS

This chapter has benefited from the valuable comments of Rebecca Cook, Barbara Ibrahim, Gerald Obermeyer, Michael Reich, and Huda Zurayk. Their help is gratefully acknowledged.

REFERENCES

AbdulRauf, M. 1977. *The Islamic view of women.* Cited in Bowen, 1992.
Abu Zahra, M. 1955. Family law. In M. Khadduri and H. J. Liebesney (eds.) *Law in the Middle East.* Washington, D.C.: Middle East Institute.
Ahmed, L. 1986. Women and the advent of Islam. *Signs: Journal of Women in Culture and Society.* 11/4:665–91.
———. 1992. *Women and gender in Islam: Historical roots of a modern debate.* New Haven and London: Yale University Press.
Arkoun, M. 1984. *Pour une critique de la raison Islamique.* Paris: Masonneuve.
Berthoud, G. 1989. Droits de l'homme et savoirs anthropologiques. *Identität: Evolution oder Differenz. Festgabe für Professor Hugo Huber.* Freiburg: Universitätsverlag (Studia Ethnographica Friburgensia, 15). Pp. 137–66.
Bouhdiba, A. 1975. *La sexualité en Islam.* Paris: Presses Universitaires de France.
Bowen, D. L. 1991. Islam and family planning. Unpublished paper, Europe, Middle East and North Africa Region Technical Department, World Bank. Washington, D.C.: World Bank.
———. 1992. Islam and the position of women. Unpublished paper, Europe, Middle East and North Africa Region Technical Department, World Bank. Washington, D.C.: World Bank.
Chamari, A. 1991. *La femme et la loi en Tunisie.* Casablanca: Editions Le Fennec.
Cook, R. 1993a. Women's international human rights law. *Human Rights Quarterly.* 15/2:230–61.
———. 1993b. International human rights and women's reproductive health. *Studies in Family Planning.* 24/2:73–86.
———. 1993c. Feminism and the four principles. In R. Gillon (ed.), *Principles of health care ethics.* New York: John Wiley and Sons.
Correa, S. and R. Petchesky. 1994. Reproductive and sexual rights: Feminist perspectives. In G. Sen, A. Germain, and L. Chen, *Population reconsidered.* Cambridge: Harvard University Press.
Donnelly, J. 1989. *Universal human rights in theory and practice.* Ithaca: Cornell University Press.

Downing, T. and G. Kushner. 1988. *Human rights and anthropology.* Cultural Survival Report 24. Cambridge, Mass.: Cultural Survival.

Finkielkraut, A. 1987. *La défaite de la pensée.* Paris: Gallimard.

Freedman, L. P. and S. L. Isaacs. 1993. Human rights and reproductive choice. *Studies in Family Planning.* 24/1:18–30.

Goode, W. J. 1970. *World revolution and family patterns.* New York: Free Press.

Hashmi, S. 1992. Is there an ethics of humanitarian intervention? Harvard Center for Population and Development Studies. Working Paper no. 2 (February 1992).

Hatch, E. 1983. *Culture and morality: The relativity of values in anthropology.* New York: Columbia University Press.

Herskovits, M. 1947. Statement on human rights. *American Anthropologist.* 49/4:539–43.

Kandiyoti, D. (ed.). 1991. *Women, Islam, and the state.* London: Macmillan.

Khattab, H. 1992. *Silent endurance.* Cairo: UNICEF and The Population Council.

Laroui, A. 1978. *La crise des intellectuels Arabes: Traditionalism ou historicisme.* Paris: Maspero.

Lévi-Strauss, C. 1963. *Structural anthropology.* New York: Basic Books.

McKinnon, K. A. 1989. *Toward a feminist theory of the state.* Cambridge: Harvard University Press.

Mayer, A. E. 1991. *Islam and human rights: Tradition and politics.* Boulder and San Francisco: Westview Press.

Mernissi, F. 1985. *Beyond the veil: Male–female dynamics in a modern Muslim society.* Cambridge, Mass.: Schenkman, 1975; London: Al Saqi Books, 1985.

———. 1987. Femininity as subversion: Reflection on the Muslim concept of nushuz. In D. Eck and D. Jain (eds.), *Speaking of faith: Global perspectives on women, religion, and social change.* Philadelphia: New Society.

———. 1992. *Islam and democracy.* Reading, Mass.: Addison-Wesley.

Murata, S. 1992. *The Tao of Islam: A sourcebook on gender relationships in Islamic thought.* New York: State University of New York Press.

Musallam, B. 1983. *Sex and society in Islam.* Cambridge: Cambridge University Press.

Naffine, N. 1990. *Law and the sexes: Explorations in feminist jurisprudence.* Sydney: Allen and Unwin.

An-Na'im, A. A. 1987. The rights of women and international law in the Muslim context. *Whittier Law Review.* 9:491–516.

———. 1990. *Toward an Islamic reformation: Civil liberties, human rights, and international law.* Syracuse: Syracuse University Press.

Nedelsky, J. 1989. Reconceiving autonomy: Sources, thoughts and possibilities. *Yale Journal of Law and Feminism.* 1:7–36.

Nouredine, S. 1991. *Femme et loi en Algérie.* Casablanca: Editions Le Fennec.

Obermeyer, C. Makhlouf. 1992. Islam, women, and politics. *Population and Development Review.* 18/1:33–57.

———. 1994. Reproductive choice in Islam: Gender and state in Iran and Tunisia. *Studies in Family Planning.* 25/1:41–51.

Omran, A. R. 1992. *Family planning in the legacy of Islam.* London and New York: Routledge.

Ong, A. 1990. State versus Islam: Malay families, women's bodies, and the body politic in Malaysia. *American Ethnologist.* 17/2:258–76.

Panikkar, R. 1982. Is the notion of human rights a Western concept? *Diogenes.* 120:75–102.

Petchesky, R. 1990. *Abortion and woman's choice: The state, sexuality, and reproductive freedom.* Boston: Northeastern University.

Petchesky, R. and J. Weiner. 1990. Feminist perspectives on human rights since 1985. Unpublished paper, Reproductive Rights Education Project, Hunter College, New York.

Pickthall, M. 1966. *The cultural side of Islam.* Lahore: Ashraf Press.

Qur'an. 1930. *The meaning of the glorious Koran: An explanatory translation.* Trans. M. Pickthall. London: Alfred A. Knopf.

Qutb, M. 1964. *Islam: The misunderstood religion.* Kuwait: Darul Bayan.

Rahman, Fazlur. 1980. A survey of modernization of Muslim family law. *International Journal of Middle East Studies.* 11:451–65.

Rawls, J. 1971. *A theory of justice.* Cambridge: Harvard University Press.

Rchid, A. M. 1991. *La femme et la loi au Maroc.* Casablanca: Editions Le Fennec.

Renteln, A. D. 1988a. The concept of human rights. *Anthropos.* 83:343–64.

———. 1988b. Relativism and the search for human rights. *American Anthropologist.* 90:56–72.

———. 1988c. A cross-cultural approach to validating human rights: The case of retribution tied to proportionality. In Cingranelli, D. (ed.), *Human rights: Theory and measurement.* New York: St. Martin's Press. Pp. 7–41

Sha'rawi, M. M. 1982. *Issues concerning the Muslim woman.* Cairo: Dar al-Muslim. Cited in Stowasser, 1987b.

Sharabi, H. 1988. *Neopatriarchy: A theory of distorted change in Arab society.* New York and Oxford: Oxford University Press.

Schirmer, J. 1988. The dilemma of cultural diversity and equivalency in universal human rights standards. In T. Downing and G. Kushner (eds.), *Human rights and anthropology.* Cultural Survival Report 24. Cambridge, Mass.: Cultural Survival.

Stowasser, B. F. 1987a. Liberated equal or protected dependent? Contemporary religious paradigms on women's status in Islam. *Arab Studies Quarterly.* 9/3: 260–83

————. 1987b. *The Islamic impulse*. London and Sydney: Croom Helm.

Tabandeh, S. 1970. *A Muslim commentary on the universal declaration of human rights*. Iran: Goulding and Co., Ltd.

Weber, M. 1953. *From Max Weber: Essays in sociology*. New York: Oxford University Press.

NOTES

1   Of course, as has repeatedly been pointed out, the relativists do in the end subscribe to certain values, namely tolerance and respect for cultural integrity, and it is paradoxically in the name of these values that they defend cultural relativism.

2   "Le relativisme débouche sur l'éloge de la servitude" (Finkielkraut 1987:131).

3   The first formal statement on relativism as a tenet of the anthropological credo was made by Herskovits in the aftermath of World War II, as the General Assembly of the United Nations was working on the Universal Declaration of Human Rights. It reflects the difficulty of reconciling a condemnation of racism and genocide with the prevalent concern of many anthropologists that Western values not be imposed on the Third World (see Renteln, 1988b). More recent efforts have centered on the protection of (mainly but not exclusively primitive) cultures whose survival is threatened (see for instance Downing and Kushner, 1988).

4   Les droits de l'homme impliquent une conception de l'homme en dehors de toute détermination culturelle specifique . . . un homme a-culturé, en somme" (Berthoud, 1989). This belief is not unlike that found in Rawls' discussion of distributive justice. In the "original position," individuals stripped of all their cultural and political heritage and placed behind the "veil of ignorance" would rationally select the same principles (1971).

5   It is worth noting that how rights are categorized does in fact depend a great deal on the context to which they are applied, so that what may in one situation be classified as a derivative right will in another instance qualify as a basic right.

6   There is a wide range of views on the notion of complementarity, with some Muslims emphasizing the physical, intellectual, and emotional inferiority of women (e.g., Qutb, 1964) and others stressing that "natural" differences are not inconsistent with equality (e.g., AbdulRauf, 1977). For a discussion of the notions of complementarity in Islam, see Sha'rawi, 1982, Qutb, 1964, Stowasser, 1987a and 1987b.

7   Useful categorizations of Muslim positions regarding the status of women are provided by Stowasser, 1987a, and Bowen, 1992). The major groups are the conservatives, the activists/Islamists, and the reformers/feminists.

8   See the analyses of gender and state in Tunisia and Iran in Obermeyer (1994), in Malaysia in Ong (1990), and the general discussion of women, Islam, and the state in Kandiyoti (1991).

9   Bowen argues that if shari'a is considered broadly, then the system that it defines is equitable for the community as a whole; if however, the "pieces" are examined separately from the point of view of individual roles, gender disparity is apparent (1992:16–17).

10 The primacy of revelation over reason is most dramatically illustrated by the expression "the closing of the gates of *ijtihad"* (independent judgment). It has been argued that since the crushing of the *mu'tazila* in Basra, rationalist thinkers in the region have been on the defensive (see Laroui, 1978).

11 The notion of equality between man and woman is thus profoundly threatening to the traditional Muslim established order because woman is seen as embodying "uncontrolled desire, undisciplined passions, [and] is precisely the symbol of heavily suppressed individualistic trends. . . . We will not understand the resistance of Muslim society to the change in women's status and rights if we do not take into account the symbolic function of women as the embodiment of dangerous individualism" (Mernissi, 1987; see also Mernissi 1985, 1992).

12 For instance, Hashmi (1992) suggests that in Islam all moral standing is invested in the *umma*, and the state has little moral authority.

13 Although there are in fact diverse tendencies within the feminist movement in the West (liberal, Marxist, and cultural feminist tendencies are some examples of this diversity), this chapter does not attempt to make distinctions among these groups.

14 In the Qur'an, the general term for believers, *mu'minun,* is frequently used, and there are a number of statements that specifically address women as believers *(mu'minat)* (e.g., IX:71, XXXIII:35).

15 In particular, according to An-Na'im, much of the shari'a is based on the group of verses known as the Medinan Suras, while the earlier and more universalist Meccan Suras are deemed to have been superseded and abrogated (1990).

16 Not surprisingly, the Sufis have historically been regarded with suspicion by the religious establishment.

17 In fact, different translations of the texts have not yielded the same English equivalents.

18 A right that they had long before Western countries recognized similar rights for women.

19 This is true not only of outside observers but also more generally of societies of the Middle East, where women may sacrifice their rights to property and to their share of inheritance in favor of their male relatives. The rationale is often expressed in terms of conflict avoidance and as a tacit agreement that relatives will care for them in the future if necessary.

20 The issue of consent is one that has received much attention from feminists from a variety of points of view, and it is not possible to do it justice in a broad review such as this. How consent is determined is of course the most difficult part, whether it has to do with consent to sex (as is apparent in the West from the dilemmas surrounding definitions of the new sexual ethics), consent to marriage (how does one establish consent in marriage from a young uneducated individual?), or informed consent concerning medical procedures.

21 Indeed, in the mystical tradition sex is considered one of the ways to know God and get nearer to Him.

22 It is worth noting, however, that in recent months, there has been a hardening of this position. This change was noticeable during the International Conference on Population and Development in September 1994, when representatives of Muslim countries affirmed that abortion was unacceptable, except under extreme circumstances.

2

The Fertility Transition in Turkey: Reforms, Policies, and Family Structure

Cem Behar

The relative precociousness of the Turkish fertility transition, which started as early as the late nineteenth century in the larger cities of the former Ottoman Empire (Istanbul and Izmir) is unique to the region (Duben and Behar, 1991). The Turkish modernization process is certainly the oldest in the Middle East and the one that has had the deepest roots and the greatest impact. The process has been strongly backed by all Republican elites, irrespective of the political party in power. In addition, Turkey is distinguished among Islamic nations by several legal reforms with respect to the emancipation of women. The legal and civil reforms of the 1920s and 1930s were crucial to Turkey's transformation, along with the secularization of the Family Law, the commitment to improve women's education levels, and the fast economic growth and urbanization of recent decades. Indeed, in terms of demographic impact, these factors seem to outweigh the influence of the post-1965 national family planning program.

Turkey's transition occurred in a social environment defined by strong economic development and weak family planning programs (Kabeer, 1992). Factors of demand played a more important role in fertility reduction than those of supply. In other words, societal and structural factors—which enhanced women's status, improved children's health and education, and began to eradicate poverty—

appear to have created a demand for fertility control. This demand was far more important in promoting planned parenthood than the efforts of official family planning policies and the subsequent supply of contraceptives.

Reality, however, does not match this rather simple supply–demand dichotomy. This paper seeks to assess the relative weight of the factors that explain the uniqueness of the Turkish demographic transition.

THE FERTILITY TRANSITION IN TURKEY: HISTORICAL BACKGROUND

Fertility decline had an early start in Turkey in Istanbul and the larger cities, and the fertility transition was well under way before the founding of the Republic (1923). The Ottoman censuses of 1885 and 1907 give cross-sectional total fertility rates (TFRs) of 3.5 and 3.8 respectively for Istanbul. These levels were reached only in the late 1980s for Turkey as a whole, and are far below the normal range of TFRs of pre-industrial European populations. The lowest rates in Europe before the onset of industrialization (around 4.1) were those of Sweden, Norway, and Denmark in the 1770s (Coale and Watkins, 1986). The fertility decline in Turkey seems to have been contemporaneous with that in many parts of western and northern Europe during the last decades of the nineteenth century.

The decline started, therefore, at a time when no modern methods of family planning were available, and it represented a progressive democratization of traditional methods such as withdrawal, douche, and abortion. These traditional methods of birth control were well known to people in the cities, who felt that there was no important religious or moral barrier to their extensive use. Withdrawal, especially, was widely practiced. The Muslim population of Istanbul was, to the best of our knowledge, the first sizable Muslim group to have systematically and extensively practiced family planning.

Istanbul's crude birth rate in 1907 was 29.4 per thousand. Clearly, it was already on a downward trend, since it eventually reached 18.7 per thousand in the early 1940s (Duben and Behar, 1991; Shorter and Macura, 1982). A useful indication of limitation of marital fertility is given by the age of women at the birth of their last child. In the absence of birth control, the mean age would be about forty, so any age below thirty-six is an indication of a significant degree of parity-oriented family limitation (Coale and Watkins, 1986). Not only is the mean age for 1851–55 in Istanbul around thirty-four but it also shows a continuous downward trend, reaching levels below thirty for women born around the turn of the century. The relatively low fertility rates in Muslim Istanbul were, by the end of the nineteenth century, widely diffused through the social fabric of the city, and the variation between social strata within Istanbul was much less than that within the same stratum in different locations.

The considerable fall in total fertility was due not only to a decline in marital fertility, but also to significant changes in nuptiality rates. The mean age at first marriage for Muslim women in Istanbul rose from about twenty at the turn of the century to over twenty-three in the late 1930s. The singulate mean age at marriage for women was 20.5 in 1907. It had probably been rising for some time, since it was 19.1 in 1885. The shortening of the average period of childbearing which ensued accounts for almost half the fertility decline. Age at marriage for men in 1907 was around thirty, and showed no perceptible trend. Almost a third of men married after age thirty-five, and this had important implications for patterns of household formation.

These ages at marriage are high by Islamic or Middle Eastern standards. Increasing female age at marriage meant a narrowing of the age gap between spouses from about ten to about six or seven years—a prerequisite for a more companionate form of marriage. Marriage was late, but was still almost universal. By age twenty-five, 75 percent of women were already married, and all but two percent of women eventually got married before age forty-five. Only 5 percent of men remained single. Though polygyny was the focus of much attention, it was practiced by a small minority (around 2 percent of adult males), and corresponded to only a limited stage in the course of marital life (Behar, 1991).

Women in the late nineteenth and early twentieth centuries, according to all available indicators, were better educated than before and occasionally entered into the work force, especially after World War I. There were notable late Ottoman and early Republican efforts to improve the position of women in society. Public opinion was increasingly opposed to polygyny and concubinage, and increasingly sympathetic to personal choice in marriage for both men and women.

This account applies exclusively to large Turkish cities—Istanbul in particular. Married couples in the big cities were pioneers of the fertility decline within the Islamic world. In the 1930s, however, national fertility in Turkey was determined by high fertility levels in rural areas, which held 85 percent of Turkey's population (the high rural rate of 7.7 brought the national average to 7.1, in contrast to the urban rate of around 3.9) (Shorter, 1985). The high overall fertility rate persisted in Republican Turkey well into the 1960s, when a more generalized fertility transition process started taking shape.

In recent decades, the decline in Turkish fertility has been rapid (see Table 1), and faster than that of many similar countries of the Middle East. In 1960, Turkey had fertility levels similar to those of Egypt, Morocco, Iran, and Sudan. Thirty years later, the Turkish TFR is 20 percent lower than that of Egypt, and 40 percent lower than that of Iran, although fertility has been on the decrease in those two countries as well. Recent estimates for 1993 place Turkey's national TFR at about 2.7 (DHS, 1993).

The percentage of married women between the ages of fifteen and forty-nine regularly using contraception has risen from 38 percent in 1973 to 63 percent in 1993 (DHS, 1993) and is now higher than in other Middle Eastern countries (Table 2). The fertility transition in Turkey has in fact been progressing faster than expected. All population projections made for Turkey in the 1960s and 1970s have therefore proven to be overestimates. Further declines are expected (see Table 3), as regional differentials tend to recede, and as migrant families to urban areas usually adopt new reproductive models within less than a generation.

Table 1
The demographic transition in Turkey

Period	Crude birth rate	Crude death rate	Rate of increase	Total fertility rate
1945–50	46	27	1.9	6.9
1950–55	48	24		6.5
1955–60	47	20	2.7	6.5
1960–65	43	16	2.7	6.1
1965–70	39	14	2.5	5.6
1970–75	35	12	2.3	5.1
1975–80	32	10	2.2	4.3
1980–85	31	9	2.2	4.1
1988–89	28	8	2.0	3.4

Sources: Behar, 1993; Duben and Behar, 1991

Table 2
Percentage of married women (aged 15–49) currently using contraceptives

Country	1973	1988
Egypt	26	38
Tunisia	31	50
Morocco	20	38
Turkey	38	63

Source: Greenhalgh *et al.*, 1992

Table 3
Future fertility and mortality projections (1990–2010)

	Crude birth rate	Crude death rate	Rate of increase	Total fertility rate	$e_{(0)}$ [a]
1990–1995	27	7	20	3.3	68
1995–2000	24	7	17	2.9	69
2000–2005	21	6	15	2.5	71
2005–2010	17	6	11	2.1	72

Source: Özbay, 1993
[a] Life expectancy at birth

The fertility decline that has occurred in Turkey in the last decades has, however, been far from uniform throughout the country. Regional differences are quite substantial. The eastern and southeastern regions are lagging far behind. For instance, the crude birth rate (28 per thousand for Turkey in 1989) is between 23 and 28 in all regions of the country, except the east and southeast, where it stands at 37 per thousand. The same relationship holds true for the TFR, which is now down to 2.4 in the three largest cities (about 20 percent of the population), but is around 5.6 in the east and southeast. In the last decade (1980–90), the national TFR decreased by 22 percent, but the decrease was only 11 percent in these two regions. As a consequence, the eastern and southeastern TFR, which was only 45 percent above the national average in 1978, now exceeds it by almost two-thirds (see Table 4). In response, the priorities of the national family planning program are already shifting towards qualitative improvement and a regional redistribution of services.

THE NATIONAL FAMILY PLANNING POLICY

Since 1965, the official population policy, which is supported by a number of non-government organizations, has aimed at slowing down

Table 4
Total fertility rate in Turkey (by region)

	1978	1989
Aegean Coast and Marmara	2.89	2.63
Mediterranean Coast	3.77	3.02
Central Anatolia	4.26	3.07
Black Sea Coast	4.99	3.48
East and Southeast	6.31	5.65
Turkey (total)	4.33	3.39
of which:		
Rural	5.06	4.03
Urban	3.67	2.84

Sources: HIPS, 1989; SIS, 1991

population growth. With the Family Planning Act of April 1965, a General Directorate of Population Planning was created within the Ministry of Health to be responsible for policy implementation. This directorate was merged in 1983 with the maternal and child health (MCH) services of the same ministry, and the program began to emphasize greater integration of reproductive health in family planning.

Supply of MCH services in specialized clinics as well as distribution of contraceptives generally went hand in hand. The initial emphasis of the program was based exclusively on the insertion of intra-uterine devices (IUDs). The supply and distribution of oral contraceptives and of condoms in family planning clinics was introduced just a few years later, in 1968. The distribution of condoms, however, met with little success at first, was soon interrupted, and was resumed only in the middle of the 1980s. The production, import, and distribution of oral contraceptives, IUDs, and condoms was, in the meantime, almost totally liberalized.

The integration of family planning education within the general educational system was declared a first degree priority (Üner and Levine, 1978). Until the middle of the 1980s, however, this objective met with little success, except in schools for medical and paramedical personnel. Abortion on demand (to be performed by a gynecologist before the tenth week of pregnancy), as well as male and female sterilization, were not legalized until 1983. So far, however, the number of male and female sterilizations has been negligible, and there are no reliable figures on the number of abortions performed yearly.[1]

The initial demographic objectives of the national family planning program (set by the General Directorate of Population Planning) were quite high. The directorate aimed at reaching 5 percent of Turkish married women of childbearing age every program year. This meant a yearly rate of more than three hundred thousand new acceptors of contraception in the 1960s and 1970s. The crude birth rate was supposed to decrease by 25 percent within five years. The national family planning program hoped to reach all Turkish women of childbearing age, directly or indirectly, within ten years. These women were to become direct contraceptive acceptors or to be sensitized to the issue by educational activities, with the goal of making contraception an accepted part of Turkish family life.

Besides being overambitious, the program (which shared all the classical defects of first generation population planning programs) considered Turkish women only in terms of their childbearing function, and saw therefore the implementation of family planning policy as a purely mechanical and logistical problem. Fertility reduction at all costs was the only objective. This nearsightedness and obsession with figures and immediate palpable demographic results continued well into the 1980s. For example, a broader reproductive health program (or an MCH program) was not included in the agenda until the 1980s. But by then, Turkish fertility had already fallen considerably—though for reasons largely independent of program implementation itself.

No serious program effort aiming at method diversification and at expanding women's contraceptive choices was undertaken until 1985–86. All methods except pills and IUDs were systematically qualified as secondary (because of their supposedly lesser demographic efficiency), and were usually only distributed when there were complaints about the secondary effects of oral contraceptives and IUDs. The negative side effects of IUDs were not seriously taken into consideration either. Follow-up studies (of both oral contraceptives and IUDs) were insufficient, and the responsibility of coping with the side effects of these new contraceptive technologies and their risks was left almost entirely to women. Women, therefore, bore the heaviest burden of responsibility. During its first two decades, in fact, the program operated as though all contraceptive acceptors and users were women, and yet was generally insensitive to women's reproductive health and safety.

The concrete results of the national family planning program soon started to fall short of its overly-optimistic expectations. Only 1 percent of married Turkish women of childbearing age was reached on average every year. The total number of new acceptors (both oral contraceptives and IUDs) numbered just five hundred thousand during the first ten years of the program (1965–74). About 80 percent of these were IUD insertions. Besides, rates of attrition (by method, age, region, and so on) were never carefully calculated by program evaluators. Between 1975 and 1980, the yearly number of new contraceptors stabilized at around sixty-five thousand.

The program picked up after 1984, since both the family planning methods proposed and their distribution channels were diversified. Men were directly addressed for the first time as family planning decision-makers. They were given family planning training in the army and in educational programs organized by labor unions. The distribution of condoms through official channels was sped up. The spread of Aids and the echoes this caused in the Turkish media were influential. Still, the official program failed to reach more than 25 percent of the targeted population (Ministry of Health, 1991a).

It must also be added that the budgetary resources devoted to implementing the family planning program were frankly insufficient from the very start. The budget of the Directorate for Population Planning, for instance, decreased steadily in real terms throughout the 1970s. The proportion of the total budget of the Ministry of Health allotted to the operations of the directorate was at its highest in 1969, at 3.02 percent. It declined thereafter, until reaching about 0.65 percent just before the directorate merged with the maternal and child health services of the Ministry in 1983. The combined budget of these two central organisms was from 2 to 3 percent of the total budget of the Ministry of Health throughout the 1980s (Ministry of Health, 1991a). This figure compares badly with Indonesia's 32 percent, Taiwan's 7 percent, and the Philippines' 12 percent in the late 1970s (Nortman and Hofstatter, 1978). Though the government did give more frank and open support within the last decade, the paucity of financial resources allocated could be seen as an indication of the absence of a strong and endurable political will to implement the national family planning policy.

The program did not take into account the fact that until a few decades years ago, most available methods of contraception were male methods, which are usually cheaper, safer, and simpler to use. It also overlooked the fact that the demographic transition in the larger cities in the late nineteenth century and the early Republican period was achieved mainly through the widespread use of withdrawal (Duben and Behar, 1991). Turkey was indeed—and largely still is—a country with a strong tradition of male methods and initiative in contraception. In 1988, more than half of regularly contracepting Turkish couples were using either strictly male methods (withdrawal, condoms) or methods requiring male knowledge and participation (rhythm) (see Table 5). The corresponding proportion for developing countries as a whole was not above 25 percent in the 1980s (Kabeer, 1992). Seven percent of married Turkish men were regularly using condoms in 1988, a higher number than in any other Islamic or Middle Eastern country at the time.

The Turkish national family planning program did not choose to promote, between 1965 and 1985, a greater involvement of men in the responsibilities of planned parenthood. Efforts to diversify available methods and present couples with a broader contraceptive choice were made only in the second half of the 1980s. The national program was indeed quite late in trying to complement a strictly demographic and quantitative focus on family limitation with a greater concern for maternal and child health and contracepting women's well-being and general follow-up.

Looking only at the crude demographic figures, however, it may seem that the official family planning policy has been quite successful. Turkey's TFR has been halved within twenty-five years. It went down to 3.4 in 1988, and to 2.7 in 1993 (DHS, 1993), and by 1988 about two-thirds of married couples regularly used contraception. In the western parts of the country, the TFR is down to 2.0, and in the three biggest cities (Istanbul, Ankara, and Izmir, comprising more than 20 percent of the total Turkish population), it is just 2.4 (DHS, 1993). A closer look at the data, however, shows that the direct impact of this policy on the fertility decline has been far from decisive.

In terms of the demographic efficiency of the program (on which so much hope was placed at the beginning), the results were quite disappointing. Models devised by Nortman (Nortman *et al.*, 1978) were used to measure the net effect (difference between observed fertility in the presence of the program and fertility that would have prevailed without it) of the family planning program on Turkish fertility for the period 1965–80 (Behar, 1980). The study concluded that the official family planning program accounted for less than 10 percent of the effective fertility decline during that period.

In a recent article, Bongaarts, using a regression procedure incorporating non-demographic variables, has evaluated the net impact of the program at 31 percent of the total fertility decline in Turkey during the 1980s (Bongaarts, 1993). This percentage, though the lowest among the countries of the region, seems to be an overestimation. An indirect indication of this overestimation is given by some of the latest figures on sources of contraception in Turkey. In 1991, 82 percent of married women regularly using oral contraceptives were served by the private sector, and only 18 percent by the maternal and child health clinics. The proportion is around 50 percent for regular IUD users and 77 percent for condom users in the cities. These users are served by private hospitals and clinics, doctors, pharmacies, midwives, nurses, and so on (Ministry of Health, 1992). Bongaarts' overestimation is also indirectly confirmed by the fact that more than half the couples regularly using contraception in Turkey in 1988 were still using traditional methods (see Table 5). In fact, the proportion of married couples regularly using traditional contraceptives has steadily increased in Turkey over the last two decades.

Table 5
Family planning methods used by married women of reproductive age in 1988 (as a percentage of total married couples)

Modern methods	
Intra-uterine device	14
Condoms	7
Oral contraceptives	6
Vaginal methods	2
Voluntary sterilization, female	2
Voluntary sterilization, male	0
All modern	31
Traditional methods	
Withdrawal	26
Abstinence	4
Other	2
All traditional	32
All users	63

Sources: HIPS, 1989; SIS, 1991

Traditional methods (mainly withdrawal and douche) were used by more than 30 percent of married couples in Turkey in 1988. This figure should be compared to the 6 percent of couples protected by traditional methods in Morocco, the 8 percent in Jordan, and 9 percent in Tunisia (Robey, Rutstein, and Morris, 1992). Despite the promotional efforts of the official program to exclusively promote modern female methods, male methods of contraception are still predominant.

In 1988, although almost all Turkish women knew about oral contraceptives and IUDs (94 percent for each, as opposed to 85 percent for withdrawal and 76 percent for condoms), the method most frequently used by Turkish couples was withdrawal (see Table 5). Moreover, the number of those not using contraception that year was probably the lowest among comparable countries in the region (19 percent) (Robey, Rutstein, and Morris, 1992). The contraceptive gap in Turkey has now almost disappeared, and differentials by residence and education are gradually narrowing (see Table 6). It is highly improbable, however, that this state of affairs is due exclusively to the direct or indirect effects of the official national family planning program.

REPUBLICAN REFORMS AND THE LEGAL EMPOWERMENT OF WOMEN

The weakness of the family planning program strongly suggests that the speed of the fertility transition in Turkey in recent decades was due to favorable demand-side conditions rather than a supply-side policy

Table 6
Use of family planning by characteristics of women
(1988 percentage of married women aged 15–49)

Residence	
Urban	66
Rural	53
Education	
None	47
Primary completed	64
Some Primary	56
More than primary	74

Source: HIPS, 1989

mix. Indeed, crucial changes took place that further support the notion of a demand-driven transition, including the transformation of the Turkish household structure, the improvement of women's education and position in society, and new intra-family gender relationships. Government policy has enhanced women's legal and economic status, improved children's health and education, and tried, however insufficiently, to eradicate poverty.

The legal and political reforms of the Kemalist period, which deeply affected the status of women, were introduced soon after the proclamation of the Republic in 1923. The 1926 Civil Code, which included reforms enhancing the legal status of women, was almost entirely adapted from the Swiss Civil Code. This new civil code secularized all aspects of civil law and liberties, including the laws and procedures concerning marriage, divorce, custody of children, the provisions concerning polygyny, and the sharing of inheritances. Women were granted equal rights in all of these areas. Polygyny was prohibited and repudiation was abolished. Women were allowed to sue for divorce on an equal footing with men and were legally entitled to an equal share of inheritances. For the first time in the Ottoman Empire and Turkey, the law stipulated a minimum legal age for marriage: eighteen for men, and seventeen for women.[2]

Equality of legal rights applied to basic areas such as the legal person of women, their responsibility and liability, their capacity to testify, to trade, to inherit, or to make a contract, their age at legal majority, and so on. The new civil code wholly superseded the centuries-old shari'a and shari'a-related local customs. Turkey is the only country in the region that has abolished the Islamic provisions concerning marriage, divorce, and family law, and entrusted these areas to the secular state. The 1934 Law on Family Names required Turks to adopt family surnames, as was the practice in Europe and other parts of the world. In 1937, secularism was given the status of a fundamental and unchangeable constitutional principle.

Political rights for women and the granting of full citizenship soon followed suit. Women were granted the vote at local elections in 1930, and at national level in 1934. As an immediate consequence, eighteen women (totaling 4.5 percent of the National Assembly) were elected to the ruling Republican People's Party of the Kemalist regime at the 1937 Parliamentary elections. The veiling of women was never legally banned, but a vigorous propaganda effort, led by Mustafa

Kemal Atatürk himself, exhorted women in the 1920s and 1930s to adopt modern styles of dress.

The militant institutionalization of the new legal system and enforcement of the new laws was fully backed by successive political elites, regardless of the government in power. Dixon-Mueller rightfully argues that the existence of a tradition of a strong central government in Turkey facilitated the unhindered implementation of an equal rights policy for men and women (Dixon-Mueller, 1993).

The adoption of a new family code and the legal enfranchisement of women were part of a broader struggle to liquidate the theocratic institutions of the Ottoman Empire and legitimize a state ideology for the new Turkish Republic. The emancipation of women was part of the transition from a multi-ethnic empire to an Anatolian nation–state and part of a broader political project of nation-building and secularization. The new woman of the Kemalist era was an important symbol for the political break with the Ottoman, Islamic, and imperialist past (Duben and Behar, 1991; Kandiyoti, 1991).

The legal empowerment of women during the Kemalist era paved the way for more substantive later developments in women's status. But the inclusion of women as citizens was dictated above all by the transition from monarchy to populist republic and by the dominant nationalist discourse. The process leading to the legal empowerment of women was therefore essentially an ideological lever designed to serve a quite different cause. As a consequence, we cannot agree with Dixon-Mueller's interpretation that the imposition of non-discriminatory laws and policies in Turkey was an attempt to destroy patriarchal relations (Dixon-Mueller, 1993:25).

The economic and familial options available to Turkish women remained unchanged for quite a long time. The equal rights policy did not foster public concern with reproductive choice. Indeed, the nationalist Republic was strongly pro-natalist in its first four decades (Behar, 1980). Until 1965, there was no question of providing couples with either material means or information enabling them to exercise reproductive choice.

The authoritarian Kemalist regime supported feminism, but it also defined and strictly controlled the feminist movement. Kemalist Turkey did not tolerate any economic or political pressure groups— including autonomous women's groups (Kandiyoti, 1991). An independent feminist movement could not therefore make itself heard in

Turkey until the 1980s. Moreover, the legal empowerment of women did not lead to quick and noticeable progress in the autonomy of Turkish women. But although the reforms did not lead to the destruction of patriarchal relations (Dixon-Mueller, 1993), they have, nevertheless, provided a meaningful setting in which later women's movements could take hold.

Full legal rights are essential, but women can only exercise these rights effectively with accompanying social and economic resources. For example, Republican policy has ensured access to education and employment for women, but in practice families often did not send their daughters to school (especially in rural areas). In the last few decades, nevertheless, there has been considerable progress in the general educational level of women in Turkey (see Tables 7 and 8). An encouraging recent study showed that 93 percent of parents living in urban areas, and 83 percent of those in rural areas want their daughter to pursue her studies beyond the five-year compulsory primary education (SPO, 1993).

While the changes in the labor force participation rates of women have not been as dramatic—the proportion of unpaid family workers

Table 7
Literacy rates in Turkey (population aged 10+)

	Men	Women
1935	29.4	9.8
1950	45.3	19.3
1960	53.6	24.8
1970	70.3	41.8
1980	79.9	54.6
1990	90.1	71.2

Sources: SIS, 1991; Tekeli, 1990

Table 8
Percentage of men and women within each educational level (1986/87)

	Men	Women
Primary	47	53
Secondary	43	57
Technical	32	68
University	32	68

Source: Tekeli, 1990

went down from 92 percent in 1955 to 75 percent in 1985 (Tekeli, 1990)—recent public opinion polls show increasing support for the notion of female employment. Forty-five percent of Turks (58 percent of women and 39 percent of men) believe that the best way for a woman to be independent is to have a job of her own. Only 13 percent strongly disagreed with this idea. Fifty-five percent strongly believed that a working woman can be as good a mother as a housewife. The proportion was about the same for interviewed men and women. Only 11 percent strongly disagreed with this opinion. A very high propor-tion of the interviewed sample (86 percent) believed that both husband and wife should contribute to the household budget (TÜSİAD, 1991).

MEN, FERTILITY DECISIONS, AND HOUSEHOLD STRUCTURE

One of the most striking aspects of the Turkish fertility transition concerns the role of men. The exceptionally high male initiative, responsibility, and participation is perhaps the most salient feature of the fertility decision-making and implementation process in Turkey. In 1988, over one-half of contracepting Turkish couples with a wife between fifteen and forty-nine years old were using male methods. These were either family planning methods relying exclusively on direct male initiative (withdrawal, condoms), or they were methods requiring male knowledge and/or participation (periodic abstinence, other traditional methods) (see Table 5).

The contraceptive practice of withdrawal has a long history in Turkey, and was instrumental in bringing about most of the fertility decline in the larger cities of the Ottoman Empire (Duben and Behar, 1991). In the past, contraception in urban areas was almost exclusively a male initiative. It is still predominantly so, but now in both cities and countryside. The Turkish case fits a southern European pattern, as stressed in a recent article by G. Santow (1993). Men in Turkey have a long history of marrying quite late—especially in cities. Urban males were not considered 'fit' for marriage before they were well established in life and able to support a family (Duben and Behar, 1991). Men have traditionally borne the greater responsibility (moral, legal, and financial) for providing for children. The progression toward the nuclear family in recent decades has probably reinforced this historical tendency because nuclear families must shoulder the entire burden of costs of children, rather than sharing them with a larger kin group.

If we take only the married women of childbearing age in 1988, 63 percent of these were currently contracepting. Of these, 40 percent were using male methods, and only 33 percent were using female methods. Couples most frequently used withdrawal (26 percent), as opposed to those using IUDs (14 percent), the second most frequently used method (HIPS, 1989). Despite the heavy emphasis the official family planning program has always put on female and modern methods, the percentage of regular users of withdrawal rose from 22 percent in 1978 to 26 percent in 1988. The IUD seems, however, to be picking up in the last decade and its regular users have increased from 9 percent in 1978 to 14 percent in 1988 (HIPS, 1989).

Of the women using the traditional (mostly male) methods, 31 percent declared that these methods were "simple, straightforward, cheap, and had no side effects." Sixteen percent of the women said that they preferred them for health reasons. Whether these statements reflect the real opinion of women, or whether they are the product of the internalization or rationalization of male opinions does not alter the fact that the decision to use a specific method is well-perceived as a common decision. Of the respondents, 20.5 percent declared they use traditional methods (mostly withdrawal, but also rhythm and douche) because "their husbands preferred it." 'Common decision' or 'male initiative and female consent/agreement seem to have produced the same result (HIPS, 1989). The Director of the MCH and family planning services of the Ministry of Health recently said: "Turkish families are now better informed about modern family planning methods, but they choose to use the most inefficient ones, those which do not require the help of qualified medical personnel" (Ministry of Health, 1992).

It is not surprising to see that in Turkey male knowledge of family planning methods and general male attitudes and preferences concerning family size and ideal number of children (or of sons) are not significantly different from those of women. The Turkish Value of Children study confirms that the difference between men and women is negligible, and also that men are as well-informed as women on several family planning methods (Kağıtçıbaşı, 1981). In a more recent survey, the ideal number of children was measured to be almost the same for men and women. The average figure, in 1989, was 2.7 for married men and 2.6 for women (SIS, 1991a; Özbay, 1993).

Men in Turkey are as acutely aware of the burden of children as women. The difference between men's and women's preferences for children was somewhat larger in the past, though not as large as one would expect to see in a social setting traditionally qualified as male-dominated. In 1963, the average number of children desired was 3.7 for married men and 3.1 for married women (Özbay, 1993). There seems to be a tacit inter-gender agreement on these matters within Turkish families. The main division on preferred family size seems to run now between urban and rural areas and/or younger and older generations, instead of between men and women. The decision to use contraception is probably in most cases a common decision, whether vocal or implicit.

It is therefore no surprise either that there is no significant male opposition to family planning in Turkey. A recent survey research conducted in 1990 by the Ministry of Health on a representative sample of three thousand women in eleven of the seventy-four Turkish provinces calculated the proportion of non-contracepting married and fertile women who did not want to have any more children. The unmet need for contraception amounted to only 19.4 percent of the total number of women (Ministry of Health, 1991a).

When these non-contracepting women were asked why they were not using family planning methods although they wanted no more pregnancies, only 15.4 percent of them mentioned their husband's opposition as the reason. Besides, 14.8 percent of the women said they had been "neglectful," 13.7 percent were breast-feeding at the time of the survey, 18.1 percent did not have access to family planning, 5.5 percent had gynecological problems, 5.5 percent thought it was a "sin," and so on (Ministry of Health, 1991a). This means that only about 2.5 percent (that is, 15.4 percent of 19.4 percent) of all married and fertile Turkish women were kept from using means of contraception by their husband's opposition.

Withdrawal has always been presented as a simple but inefficient method, which has a high rate of failure. A recent study, based on the data of the 1988 Population and Health Survey shows that this is far from being true in Turkey (Glasgow, Hancioğlu, and Ergöçmen, 1991). Insofar as measurements are trustworthy, the present-day efficiency of withdrawal in Turkey may be above that of some other, more modern methods, and also probably above its use-efficiency in other countries.[3] In general, just as the critical factor in adopting contraception is not linked to access to highly effective or 'scientific' methods, the continued use of withdrawal cannot be wholly attributed to a lack of alternative methods.

The widespread and prolonged use of withdrawal raises the question of whether couples or husbands continue to use this method because they know that abortion is readily available if they fail. Abortion before the tenth week of pregnancy was legalized in 1983, but as indicated above, there are still no reliable figures on the number of abortions performed yearly. A plausible estimate puts the yearly figure at about half a million (HIPS, 1989). It is also estimated that only about one-fifth of these are performed in public hospitals (Bulut and Toubia, 1994). In a hospital study of 550 women who had an abortion in Istanbul, almost all the women said that they became pregnant "by accident" or "by mistake," and 27 percent attributed the mistake to their husband. A vast majority (81 percent) had practiced withdrawal in the past, but only 30 percent had ever used oral contraceptives, and 28 percent had used IUDs. Sixty-four percent of them became pregnant while practicing withdrawal, while 28 percent were not contracepting at all at the time of pregnancy, and eight percent were using either oral contraceptives or the IUD. Questioned about their previous use of contraception, 24 percent of the women having an abortion mentioned their "husband's opposition" to the use of a method other than withdrawal.

Turkish husbands seem to expect to take charge of contraception, just as they usually expect to initiate sexual activity. Whether they do so in order to protect their wives and children, or simply because they want to control reproduction is not clear, however. It seems, therefore, that a standard sequence (withdrawal–abortion–IUD) could be taking place. Indeed, 41 percent of the women surveyed had IUD insertions during the six months following the abortion. However, according to a follow-up study, another 37 percent returned to the practice of withdrawal and to dependence on their husbands for pregnancy protection. Intra-couple communication on these matters is still far from being perfectly fluid, and systematic study on the dynamics of this communication is seriously lacking. But men's participation and responsibility-sharing in family planning continue to be an important structural characteristic of Turkish family planning attitudes and practices, although the Turkish national family planning program failed at first to recognize and capitalize on this important historical asset.

REFERENCES

Behar, C. 1980. *Türkiye'de nüfus planlaması politikasının nüfussal etkinliği: 1965–1980* (The demographic impact of the Turkish population planning policy). Istanbul: Boğaziçi University.

————. 1987. Evidence on fertility decline in Istanbul (1885–1940). *Boğaziçi University Research Papers*. 87/07.

————. 1991. Polygyny in Istanbul (1885–1926). *Middle Eastern Studies*. 27/3:477–86.

————. 1993. Recent trends in the Turkish population. Paper presented to the *Conference on change in modern Turkey: Politics, society, economy*. University of Manchester, May 1993.

Bongaarts, J. 1993. *The fertility impact of family planning programs*. New York: The Population Council, Research Division Working Papers, no. 47.

Bulut, A. and N. Toubia. 1994. *Hastanelerde Gebelik Sonlandırma Hizmetlerinin İşlerliği ve Etkinliği* (Pregnancy termination services in hospitals and their efficiency). Istanbul: İstanbul Üniversitesi Çocuk Sağlığı Enstitüsü.

————. n.d. Efficiency and effectiveness of public sector abortion services in Istanbul and their suitability to women's needs. Report, The Population Council (New York) and University of Istanbul Institute of Child Health/ Family Health Unit.

Coale, A. and S. C. Watkins, eds. 1986. *The decline of fertility in Europe*. Princeton: Princeton University Press.

DHS. 1993. *Demographic and health survey Turkey*. Ankara: Hacettepe Institute of Population Studies.

Dixon-Mueller, R. 1993. *Population policy and women's rights: Transforming reproductive choice*. Westport, Conn. and London: Praeger.

Duben, A. 1985. Turkish families and households in historical perspective. *Journal of Family History*. 10/1:75–98.

Duben, A. and C. Behar. 1991. *Istanbul households: Marriage, family and fertility, 1880–1940*. Cambridge: Cambridge University Press.

Glasgow, I., A. Hancioğlu, B. Ergöçmen. 1991. Contraceptive failure rates in Turkey. *The Turkish Journal of Population Studies*. 13:3–11.

Gökçay, G. and F. Shorter. 1993. Who lives with whom in Istanbul. *New Perspectives on Turkey*. 9, Fall:47–75.

Greenhalgh, S., T. Hull, A. Jain, C. Lloyd, M. Nag, J. Phillips, F. Shorter, J. Townsend. 1992. *Population trends and issues in the developing countries: Regional reports*. New York: The Population Council, Research Division Working Papers, no. 35.

Hacettepe Institute of Population Studies (HIPS). 1989. *The 1988 Turkish population and health survey*. Ankara: HIPS.

Kabeer, N. 1992. From fertility reduction to reproductive choice: Gender perspectives on family planning. *University of Sussex Discussion Paper no. 229.* Institute of Development Studies, University of Sussex, Brighton.

Kağıtçıbaşı, Ç. 1981. *Çocuğun değeri* (The value of children). Istanbul: Boğaziçi University Publications.

Kandiyoti, D., ed. 1991. *Women, Islam and the state.* London: Macmillan.

Kiray, M. 1964. *Ereğli: Ağır sanayiden önce bir sahil kasabası.* (Ereğli: A coastal town before the advent of heavy industry). Ankara: State Planning Organization.

Ministry of Health. 1991a. *Türkiye'de ana çocuk sağlığı ve aile planlaması çalışmaları* (Mother and child health and family planning activities in Turkey). Ankara.

———. 1991b. *Gelişmede ikinci derece öncelikli 11 ilde AÇS ve aile planlaması: Durum saptama araştırması* (Mother and child health and family planning in 11 provinces: Research on the present situation). Ankara.

———. 1992. *Türkiye'de aile planlamasının yarını: Yeni yaklaşımlar, yeni hedefler* (The future of family planning in Turkey: New approaches, new goals). Ankara.

Moreno, L. and N. Goldman. 1991. Contraceptive failure rates in developing countries. *International Family Planning Perspectives.* 17/2:44–49.

Nortman, D. and E. Hofstatter. 1978. *Population and family planning programs: A factbook.* New York: The Population Council.

Nortman, D., R. Porter, S. Kirmeyer, J. Bongaarts. 1978. *Birth rates and birth control practice.* New York: The Population Council.

Olson-Prather, E. 1977. *Family planning and husband–wife relationships in contemporary Turkey.* Ph.D. Thesis, University of California at Los Angeles.

Omran, A. 1992. *Family planning in the legacy of Islam.* London: Routledge.

Özbay, F. 1988. Türkiye'de aile ve hane yapısı: Dün, bugün, yarın (Household and family structure in Turkey: Yesterday, today, tomorrow). *Mübeccel Kıray'a armağan* (Essays in honor of Mübeccel Kıray). Istanbul: Marmara University Publications.

———. 1993. Changing roles of young men and the demographic transition in Turkey: From nation building to economic liberalization. Unpublished paper. Istanbul.

Robey, B., S. Rutstein, L. Morris. 1992. The reproductive revolution: New survey findings. *Population Reports,* M/11. Johns Hopkins University.

Santow, G. 1993. Coitus interruptus in the twentieth century. *Population and Development Review.* 19/4:767–92.

Shorter, F. 1985. The population of Turkey after the war of independence. *International Journal of Middle Eastern Studies.* 17:417–41.

Shorter, F. and M. Macura. 1982. *Trends in fertility and mortality in Turkey, 1935–1975.* Washington, D.C.: National Academy Press.

State Institute of Statistics (SIS). 1991a. *The 1989 Turkish demographic survey*. Ankara: SIS.

———. 1991b. *The 1990 census of population: Administrative division*, Ankara: SIS.

State Planning Organization. 1993. *Türk aile yapısı araştırması* (Research on Turkish family structure). Ankara: SPO.

Tekelı, Ş., ed. 1990. *Kadın bakış açısından 1980'ler Türkiyesinde kadınlar*. (Women in Turkey in the 1980s from a woman's perspective). Istanbul: İletişim Publications.

TÜSİAD (Turkish Industrialists and Businessmen's Association). 1991. *Türk toplumunun değerleri* (Values in Turkish society). Istanbul: TÜSİAD.

Üner, S. and N. Levine. 1978. *Population policy formation and implementation in Turkey*. Ankara: Hacettepe University Publications.

NOTES

1 Several researchers have attempted to estimate the number of abortions performed in Turkey. Estimates have been wide-ranging, from 18 per 100 pregnancies (DHS, 1993) to 35 per 100 pregnancies (Omran, 1992; Hacettepe, 1989), and some have suggested that the rate of unreported abortions is probably four times higher than the official statistics state (Bulut and Toubia, n.d.). Clearly, it is difficult to obtain reliable numbers or rates of abortions for the country as a whole.

2 The total figure may even be a slight overestimate, since women who stayed within the national program but chose to switch from IUDs to oral contraceptives, or vice versa, were probably counted twice (Behar, 1980).

3 There were at least two unsuccessful attempts, in 1917 and 1924, at devising a compromise between the classical Islamic provisions on women and the family and secular European legal systems.

4 In 1938, however, these minimum ages were lowered to seventeen and fifteen for men and women, respectively.

5 Surprisingly, the rate of failure of regular withdrawal users was also found to be lower in rural areas (10.1 percent) than in the cities (16.1 percent) in Turkey. Moreover, the higher the husband's level of education, the higher the rate of failure for rhythm and withdrawal. Perhaps couples who have less access to modern methods are more skilled in the use of withdrawal.

3

State, Women, and Civil Society: An Evaluation of Egypt's Population Policy

Saad Eddin Ibrahim

The international debate on population policy has for a number of years fostered opposing camps—one promoting the provision of family planning services and another backing overall socioeconomic development as favored strategies for population growth reduction (Dixon-Mueller, 1993). But the fortunes of a population policy may be no better or worse than other public policies in a given country at a given time. What contributes to the overall competence of the state in formulating and implementing public policies? Which groups in society reinforce policy objectives and which act as 'saboteurs'? To address these questions, this paper examines Egypt's population policy over three decades to locate where, how, and why it may have succeeded or failed. We do so by assessing the different roles of a number of relevant actors operating in the public space bearing on human reproduction.

Egypt's demographers and social scientists noted the country's population problem as early as the mid-1930s: an exponential population growth at rates outstripping the country's capabilities to expand its resource base. Yet it was only in 1960 that the Egyptian state would formally adopt a population policy, and a vague one at that, to slow the rate of population growth and speed up the rate of economic development. While the growth of real income per capita may have kept pace, financing Egypt's economic development has led to a heavy external and internal public debt. The persistent high rate of population growth is often cited as the culprit, and the population policy is judged to have fallen markedly short of its objectives.

While population policy in theory concerns mortality, fertility, and migration, in Egypt the policy focus has been predominantly on fertility reduction (NPC, 1994). Population policy (like all public policies) is formulated at the upper echelon of the state. The middle and lower echelons oversee its implementation by targeting families, with the objective of reducing births and achieving longer spacing between them. Whether or not these echelons have been equally committed to the policy, and whether the institutional channels and the proper inputs have been adequately provided by the state are one set of variables to be evaluated.

However, as important as state-related variables are, those bearing on the targeted group of individuals are even more critical. The intimate decisions of men and women are made within families and a community of peers, neighbors, and friends. Increasingly, and especially in Egypt's urban areas, formal and semi-formal associational networks have become powerful intermediaries in shaping, sifting, and sorting an individual's world view bearing on reproductive behavior. In other words, the state's messages and actions pass through many filters before they affect individuals' attitudes and behavior. Those layers of non-state actors are what we loosely refer to as 'civil society.' They include some obvious actors, such as religious leaders, and other less obvious groups such as politically mobilized professional unions. An evaluation of Egypt's policy performance thus necessitates an assessment of the degree of concordance or discordance among civil formations and protest formations like the Islamic activists and between those groups and the state's population policy.

EGYPT'S POPULATION POLICY: THE RUMBLINGS OF THE 1930S AND THE TIMID ENCOUNTER IN THE 1950S

In 1932, Abbas Ammar, a social geographer at Cairo University, and Wendel Cleland, a professor at the American University in Cairo (Cleland, 1936; Darwish, 1989; Mahran speech, 1994; Abdel Hakim,

1994), triggered the first alarm bells over Egypt's population problem. By then, trend statistics were available, as Egypt had conducted at least four consecutive ten-year censuses since 1897. If estimates of the country's population by Napoleon's experts of the French expedition a century earlier (1798–1801) were accurate at around four million, then Egypt must have doubled its population in one hundred years— to about nine million. By 1932 the country was already approaching one half of the second doubling, to about fifteen million in less than thirty-five years. In 1937, a conference of Egyptian physicians called publicly for national programs to curb population growth.

Only a few non-governmental organizations and small groups of Egyptian scholars and intellectuals took the warning seriously.[1] They began studying and advocating the need for something to be done. Among their proposals was a reform of the conditions of the Egyptian peasant in rural areas, and even—a daring suggestion—a redistributive measure to reduce the flagrant concentration of land ownership. This was an early, if vague, awareness of a link between the population problem and socioeconomic development. These early rumblings did not result in a formal population policy as such. But they led the government to establish a special "Peasant Affairs Department" (Maslahat al-Fallah) in the mid-1930s, which would quickly evolve into the Ministry of Social Affairs in 1939. World War II and nationalist aspirations pushed the population problem to the margins of Egypt's public space until well into the 1950s.

Once the 1952 Revolutionary Free Officers established themselves at the helm of government, they began to look seriously into Egypt's socioeconomic problems. In 1953, two Permanent Supreme Councils were established, one to promote production, the second to promote services. A National Committee for Population Affairs (NCPA) was formed to address population. The genesis of the current debate on the best approach for coping with rapid population increase was ignited in the NCPA. The majority opinion, backed by the Free Officers, was that equitable socioeconomic development was bound to curb population growth in time. The minority opinion held that Egypt should not wait until the fruits of such development make their impact on demographic trends, because the growth rate itself could derail economic growth (NPC, 1994).

Some observers at the time suspected that Nasser, himself a father of five children, felt that bigger population gave Egypt much greater weight in Arab, Middle Eastern, and international affairs. Some of his public statements seem to substantiate this suspicion (*Al-Ahram*, 1955). However, Nasser would change his views on the matter several years later.

AN OBJECTIVE WITHOUT A POLICY IN THE 1960S AND A POLICY WITHOUT OBJECTIVES IN THE 1970S

Nine years after Nasser came to power, he articulated his general vision and proposed an agenda for the country in a famous document titled "The National Charter." It was widely representative of the views of all major social forces at the time. Of interest to us is an unequivocal statement asserting that "high growth rates represent the most dangerous obstacle that hinders efforts to raise the standard of living of the Egyptian people" (Egypt's National Charter, 1961). Since then, every Egyptian government has reiterated this assertion.

However, it took four more years after the issuing of the charter before the assertion was operationalized in a concrete objective. In 1965, the Egyptian government declared its first population target objective, "aiming at reducing the crude birth rate by one per thousand per annum" (NPC, 1994). It also declared its support for family planning efforts, pledging to prepare a network of family planning service delivery outlets. However, because the government was preoccupied at the time with pressing economic and military concerns, it invested little other than rhetoric during this period. The 1967 military defeat in the third Arab–Israeli war engulfed the country even further in other concerns. Nevertheless, the mobilization of one million Egyptian soldiers along the Suez Canal for the following seven years helped to achieve the government's objective of slowing down the rate of population growth. It was an achievement by default, however, and not the result of a policy.

Shortly after the 1973 October war and demobilization of troops, the first true national population policy was formulated, with a ten-year implementation plan (1973–82). Both the policy and the plan were couched in the most general of terms. They emphasized the links between population growth and socioeconomic development, and reiterated the majority opinion of the NCPA of exactly twenty years earlier. The policy took as an article of faith that "demand for family planning services hinges critically on the level and nature of development efforts" (NPC, 1994). This would include the expediting of several factors in advance of explicit demographic variables including: raising the standard of living; mechanizing agriculture and industry; upgrading education; improving the status of women; extending coverage of social security programs; reducing infant and child mortality; adopting relevant information, education, and communication programs; and upgrading family planning services.

This list of "desirables," however commendable, got the population practitioners nowhere. However, in a policy re-articulation in 1975, four dimensions of Egypt's population problem were clearly identified: rapid growth, spatial maldistribution, low level characteristics (indicators of development), and uneven structure (NPC, 1994). Though noted by many observers for decades, the dimension of spatial maldistribution appears for the first time in an official document as a policy concern. It would continue to be so in the following policy statements. A definite advance over previous governmental documents, the 1973–75 National Population Policy still lacked measurable targets and resource commitments equal to the magnitude of the task (NPC, 1994).

THE 1980S AND 1990S: CLARIFYING POLICY AND CONSOLIDATING
IMPLEMENTATION

A second national population policy was issued by the Egyptian government in 1980. It was titled "National Strategy Framework for Population, Human Resource Development, and the Family Planning Program" (NPC, 1994). In this and related documents, we see for the first time clear objectives or targets, and definite measures for their achievement according to a specified time-schedule. One target was to reduce the crude birth rate by 20 per thousand by the year 2000—i.e., 1 per thousand per year from 1980 on. A mark of this commitment was the holding of the National Population Conference in 1984, and the establishment of the National Population Council (NPC) shortly afterward to replace a succession of lower-level governmental bodies. The president himself headed the NPC board in its early years, and in 1986, the NPC formulated the third national population plan. It was far more advanced than previous plans in its clarity of targets and programmatic implementability, and in fact, many of the objectives of the third plan were achieved on time or even before the set dates.

Reflecting the lessons learned from more than three decades, the plan put greater emphasis on "free choice" of citizens to control or plan their families, and their right to migrate internally or externally. All the fashionable principles and development catch phrases are to be found in the plan document—for example, grass-roots participation, empowerment of women, education for all, environmental concerns, and a decisive role for the NGOs. Equally significant is the fact that the third population plan was integrated in the National Five-Year Plan of 1987/88–1991/92 for the first time ever. This meant, among other things, a parliamentary debate enacting it into law, and specific allocation of budgetary resources for its implementation.

It is significant that on October 14, 1993, a new cabinet position, the minister of state for population and family welfare, was created.[2] This represents considerable elevation from the first governmental body dealing with population in 1953, when it was merely the National Committee for Population Affairs. The evolving symbolism reflects the increasing importance of the issue at hand in the priorities of the Egyptian state. Perhaps of even greater policy importance was the presidential decree naming the new prime minister, also in October 1993. Seven national priorities were charged by President Mubarak for attention from the new government. For the first time ever, the population problem was among them. Thus, in symbolism and substance, and at the highest state level, population has become a paramount policy issue in the 1990s.

EVALUATING EGYPT'S POLICY

Egypt's population policy entails, in theory, more than family planning. In the mid-1970s, two other goals were formulated: a more balanced distribution of population over the territory, with the aim of reducing the high density of some urban areas; and enhancing the overall status of the population—including women's status—through national development.

Success in reaching these two goals has been limited. According to both the Population Plan and the National Five-Year-Plan 1987/88–1991/92 for Socioeconomic Development, Egypt was to build some twenty new cities in desert and border governorates between 1987 and 1992. But despite the large public and private investments that were made in these projects, they have not attracted more than 7 percent of the targeted population. The highly dense governorates have grown even more between the 1976 and 1986 censuses. The four border governorates of the New Valley, Matruh, the Red Sea, and Sinai have remained with nearly the same thin density.

Egypt has made some progress on other indicators of socioeconomic development. In the health area, there has been marked improvement, as indicated by the fall in the infant mortality rate from about three hundred to about sixty of every thousand live births between the 1960s and 1990s. Between 1960 and 1990, the number of those who obtain safe drinking water rose from 50 to 90 percent, calorie intake increased from 90 to 127 percent of the daily human requirements, adult literacy rose from 30 to about 50 percent, primary and secondary school enrollment rose from 55 to 89 percent of those eligible, and the per capita share of GDP (adjusted for purchasing power) increased from $500 to $1,934 (UNDP, 1992: table 4). But such changes cannot be attributed to Egypt's population policy as such. Indeed, despite the formulation of other goals, slowing down the rate of growth has been the primary focus of Egypt's policy, and the distribution of birth control methods in family planning clinics has continued to be the principal method of implementation.

Available statistics suggest that the success of Egypt in reducing fertility has been mixed. There has been an increase in the age at marriage. During a quarter of a century, the percentage of women sixteen years of age and older who were never married rose from 12 per thousand to 20 per thousand. Egypt's Demographic and Health Survey (EDHS) data for 1988 and 1992 indicate that the medium age at first marriage has increased by about 2.5 years during the last quarter of a century. There has also been a rise in the percentage of women using contraceptives. The percentage of women reporting contraceptive use has risen from about 25 percent in 1980 to slightly over 47 percent among currently married women. The biggest net increase between 1988 and 1992 was in Lower Egypt (11.3 percent), followed by Upper Egypt (9.3 percent), and the urban governorates (3.1 percent). But total fertility remains high at 3.9 children per woman (DHS, 1993), despite increasing levels of female education and rising standards of living. To understand the factors behind this limited success, we need to consider the processes underlying the official policies, as well as the impact of these policies on their intended audience.

A SMALL-SCALE SURVEY

With these objectives in mind, a survey was conducted of nearly seven hundred individuals who in one way or another are 'stake holders' in family planning programs and fertility reduction. The sample included senior national decision-makers, top and middle executives on the governmental level, family planning service providers, local community leaders, and women aged 15–49 who are the potential users of family planning services.[3] Communities included in this survey were purposely selected from among low-income urban neighborhoods in the capitals of nine governorates, as well as village communities in nearby rural areas. The nine governorates included three in Upper Egypt, three in Lower Egypt, one remote region, and two urban governorates. The doctors, social workers, and community leaders, both religious and civic, were drawn from the same neighborhoods as the larger sample of women (a breakdown of the number of respondents in each category is shown in Table 1). The subsample of women were drawn from current clients at sampled family planning clinics, and one or more of their female neighbors. The fact that this was a relatively small sample of convenience suggests that the findings from this survey should be seen as indicative and informative, rather than as representative of Egypt as a whole.

Table 1

The population issue in the consciousness of Egypt's relevant actors

	Percentage who		
	Spontaneously mention the issue	Mention after probing	Deny the issue after probing
Senior national executives (n=22)	18.2	27.3	54.5
Middle executives (n=45)	24.4	26.7	48.9
Family planning practitioners (n=54)	40.7	11.1	48.2
Physicians (n=36)	25.0	8.3	66.7
Social workers (n=18)	72.2	16.7	11.1
Community leaders (n=72)	34.7	19.5	45.8
Civic (n=36)	58.3	30.6	11.1
Religious (n=36)	11.1	8.3	80.6
Women 15–49 (n=503)	14.1	48.7	37.2
Total (n=696)	19.1	40.7	40.2

Source: Ibn Khaldoun Survey Data (1993)

EVALUATING MAJOR POLICY ACTORS: THE PRESIDENCY AND TOP-LEVEL DECISION-MAKERS

It took President Nasser (1952–70) nearly ten years in office before recognizing the serious impact of Egypt's rapid population growth, which is first mentioned in the National Charter only in 1961. President Sadat (1970–81) hardly paid any attention to the problem. In fact, Sadat acted as a negative role model by arranging one of his daughters' marriages before she reached the legal age of sixteen. President Mubarak (1981–present) spent four years in office before he paid serious attention to the issue. Mubarak agreed to chair the newly created NPC in its first three years (1985–88), but his interest seemed to have waned when he relegated the chairmanship to the prime minister, who convened the NPC executive board only once, though holding periodic consultations with the NPC's secretary general. In the last three years, however, President Mubarak has taken a direct and renewed interest in the population issue.

Why did both Nasser and Mubarak come to believe well into their presidencies that population issues deserved greater attention? In Nasser's case, it appears that radical fervor and single-minded belief in his economic reforms became tempered over time by the intractable nature of poverty in the country. Similarly, Mubarak appears to have concluded that his policies of economic liberalization were not going to lift Egypt's fortunes on their own. Both men were faced with the stark demographic reality that population growth was swallowing up gains on the socioeconomic front.

According to a top presidential aide, Mubarak has taken more interest in the population issue since 1991. The informant attributed this to several factors: the implementation of the IMF agreement for economic reform in the spring of 1991; the repeated attention given to population issues by high-level foreign visitors, especially Western aid donors; and the International Conference on Population and Development (ICPD) hosted in Cairo (September 1994). This growing presidential interest has recently been reflected on several occasions, the last of which were the establishment of the Ministry of State for Population and Family Welfare in October 1993 and the president's address to the parliament on November 11, 1993 (*Al-Musawwar*, 1993; *Al-Ahram*, 1993).[4]

However, Mubarak has yet to devote a public speech to population as one of the country's pressing economic and political issues.

Population policy is usually mentioned in the context of broader policy statements and along with many other issues. While there is presidential recognition of the importance of Egypt's population problem, it is not perceived as warranting top attention. Moreover, the presidential perception of the issue has narrowly focused on family planning, as an element best handled by technocrats, especially MDs. Only recently, in late 1993 and early 1994, the president began to make proclamations about a "national strategic project," referring to efforts to develop and settle Sinai and the Red Sea governorates.[5]

The interviews with top executives also suggest a mixed degree of commitment to a strong population policy. For the purpose of this paper, twenty-two cabinet level executives were interviewed—eighteen ministers and four governors.[6] The interview typically started by asking about Egypt's major problems and/or challenges at present and in the near future. No specific mention was made of the population issue by the interviewer (a former cabinet-level official himself). The results of these interviews are summarized in Table 1. Only four out of the twenty-two officials (18 percent) spontaneously mentioned the population question on their list of major problems/challenges. None of the four listed it in first or second place. Two mentioned it as third and tenth. The top executive who had the longest list of problems (fourteen) mentioned population as number thirteen. Problems which had primacy, or were more frequently mentioned, included economic, political, social, and religious problems. Extremism and terrorism were equally high on the executives' lists. Governmental inefficiency, lack of coordination, and shortage of state resources were also mentioned. Aside from the four who mentioned it spontaneously, our interviewer probed with the question of whether the respondent would include population as a "problem." Out of the eighteen, only six conceded that it was; another eight thought overall development would take care of it; and four said population was merely an excuse for other state failures!

These testimonies were unexpected, given that Egypt's current population plan has assigned specific roles to many of the state institutions over which these top executives preside. The five-year plan specifically mentions at least nine ministries responsible for programs and activities bearing on the three policy objectives. All pertinent ministers (current or former) were among our sample of top executives. Such a weak commitment to the state's population policy by a decisive majority of Egyptian decision-makers immediately below the president may well help to explain why so few of the objectives have been achieved. Even those who either mentioned the population problem on their own or conceded its existence felt no direct responsibility for policy implementation. Their view was that only the NPC, Ministry of Health, and Ministry of Social Affairs were responsible for implementation. Given Egypt's political culture, we expect that the president's recent forceful statements on population and the international attention on Egypt surrounding the UN Population Conference will have a marked effect on the views of cabinet level decision-makers.

THE IMPLEMENTERS: MIDDLE EXECUTIVES, PHYSICIANS, AND SOCIAL WORKERS

Forty-five high-level executives were interviewed in nine governorates; each had direct responsibility for some aspect of population policy implementation. In each governorate, they included the directors general of health, social affairs, education, and information and the senior representative of the NPC. Our interviewers used the same format as with the cabinet members—that is, a general question asking about Egypt's major problems, followed by questions on the importance of the population issue and their views on the effectiveness of various societal actors in addressing the population problem. Their responses are also summarized in Table 1.

Only eleven executives (out of the forty-five) put the population problem on their list (that is, 25 percent), and these included seven of the NPC senior representatives. When they were probed, twelve more of them agreed, bringing the total to twenty-three, or 51 percent. One NPC representative in Upper Egypt did not mention population spontaneously, and denied it was a significant problem even when the interviewer specifically probed him about the population issue. When told in effect that population is the raison d'être of his work, he responded that it was "just a job."

Among the 49 percent of respondents at this high technocratic level who did not mention population on their problem-list, the most frequently mentioned problems, in order, were the following: unemployment, absence of democracy, terrorism, poor public educational system, backwardness of women, corruption in high circles, the growing gap between

government and the people, weak sense of belonging among people
(especially youth), poverty, governmental neglect of Upper Egypt and
urban slum areas, weakness of social and religious values, and loss of
credibility and confidence in the state and its media.

It is striking that directors general of health, social affairs, and
education in six out of the nine governorates did not include population in their problem list. When probed about it, they persisted in
denying its seriousness. Many of them thought the main problem was
one of underdevelopment and spatial distribution. Our research team
interviewing at this level concluded that a majority of the leading state
technocrats, in all nine governorates, are not supportive of the population policy, and that many of them are outright hostile toward it.
They may comply with directives from their respective ministries in
Cairo, but they do not really accept or support the policy. At any rate,
as we saw earlier, the higher-level executives did not display any
better profile on the issue.

The next level of public workers interviewed were doctors and
social workers in the local family planning units, including maternal
and child health clinics. Some fifty-four respondents in this category
were interviewed: two-thirds MDs and one-third social workers.
These field practitioners are the ones having direct contact with
women who are the potential end-users of family planning. Ten to
twenty years younger than their superiors discussed above, the field
practitioners nonetheless display fairly similar attitudes.

On the first, open question about Egypt's problems and challenges,
only 41 percent of the field practitioners mentioned population in their
problem-list, as shown in Table 1. However, separating MDs from
social workers reveals a more disturbing pattern. Fully three-quarters
of the thirty-six MDs practicing family planning did not mention
population as a problem, whereas among social workers, three-
quarters did so. Aside from the tension that this asymmetry may create
among practitioners of different professions in the same work place,
it suggests a variable 'world-view,' possibly resulting from early
college training. The interviewers also observed that many of the
young male doctors were bearded, and nine of the seventeen female
doctors were veiled, which suggests a religious orientation among
these young physicians. This was further substantiated by content
analysis of the problem-lists of young doctors. "Corruption" and "lack
of religious values" were among the most frequently mentioned

problems. Another problem (hardly encountered in the lists of higher state functionaries) was that of "Western conspiracies" to keep Muslims weak. Other problems were similar to those mentioned by other groups—unemployment, inflation, illiteracy, social injustice, lack of competent leadership, and heavy-handed bureaucracy.

With the second round of questions specifically probing the population issue, very few of those who had not mentioned it initially would consider it as a serious problem. Only six more respondents added it to their problem-lists—three MDs and three social workers, to bring their percentages to 33 percent and 89 percent, respectively. In other words, some 67 percent of the MDs, whose work is to inform and help women with family-planning decisions, persisted in rejecting the notion that population is a problem in Egypt today.

The research team also observed some markedly overt hostility among field practitioners toward the government and its population policy. When asked to evaluate the role of the state in dealing with the population issue, more than 60 percent of the respondents in this category ranked its performance as weak or very weak. The other 40 percent gave the state a less harsh evaluation, but none ranked it as good or very good. The practitioners were more positive in their evaluation of the role of NGOs; misgivings expressed about NGOs were either because of the foreign connections of some or because they yield to governmental restrictions. This overall profile of state criticism and ambivalence toward the goals of the program in which they are key service providers suggests several possible explanations. One is that doctors' education has emphasized technical training at the expense of broader societal problems and issues. Another possibility is that some public-sector physicians have been influenced by the anti-state and anti-Western ideology of Islamist political groups, who are known to be active within Egypt's medical profession.

COMMUNITY LEADERS: CIVIC AND RELIGIOUS

As part of our sample, we targeted religious and civic community leaders—seventy-two respondents, evenly divided (thirty-six each). Respondents were selected from middle- and low-income areas, in or near localities where a family planning service existed.

In our category of religious community leaders were the imams (preachers) of state and non-governmental mosques (eighteen in each sub-category). Only four out of the thirty-six imams mentioned population in their problem-list. When the other thirty-two imams were probed specifically about population, another three added it to their problem-lists, in all seven out of thirty-six, or 19.4 percent. These seven were imams of governmental mosques, or state employees. The other twenty-nine Imams (80.6 percent) were adamant in denying that a population problem exists in this country—or any Islamic country for that matter. For them, it is all "Western propaganda." While the government imams would not preach openly against family planning, they were as unequivocal as their non-governmental counterparts in condemning "birth control" *(tahdid al-nasl)*, a phrase our interviewers and our questionnaires did not use. But for most imams, "family planning" *(tanzim al-usra)* was synonymous with "birth control," which is tampering with God's will.

The non-governmental imams were overtly against the government policies in general and that of population in particular. They all indicated that they preach in mosques and advise in private against "birth control" of any kind. When asked what large families with limited means or mothers with poor health and four or five children should do, about 75 percent of all imams said "there will always be divine providence" and other "compassionate Muslims" to help. The other 25 percent would counsel such parents to "persevere and be patient."

In addition to religious leaders, thirty-six notables (well-regarded officers of at least one active NGO) from the communities surveyed were targeted for interviewing. Actually, eighteen of those inter-viewed (50 percent) had multiple membership in NGOs, all of them in urban communities.

Table 2 compares the responses of religious and civic leaders on a number of pertinent issues. More than 58 percent of the civic leaders readily mentioned population in their initial problem-list, compared to only 11 percent of the religious leaders. As a matter of fact, with the exception of family planning social workers, the civic leaders were more concerned about the population problem in Egypt than any other category among the nearly six hundred respondents. Even among those who had not spontaneously mentioned it in their problem-list (30 percent), many readily added it under probing, to bring their total to 81 percent, compared to 19 percent of the religious leaders.

With these civic leaders, there was more than recognition of and concern about the population problem. As shown in Table 2, the

Table 2

Comparison of religious and civic community leaders on population issues (percentage; n=36)

	Civic leaders	Religious leaders
Government efforts on population issues		
Positive ranking	53.1	6.2
Negative ranking	46.9	93.8
NGOs' efforts on population issues		
Positive ranking	71.9	12.5
Negative ranking	29.1	68.8
No response	0.0	18.7
Citizens' cooperation on population issues		
Positive ranking	56.3	31.3
Negative ranking	43.7	37.5
No response	0.0	31.3

Source: Ibn Khaldoun Survey Data (1993)

proportion among them who have something positive to say about governmental efforts is greater (53 percent) than among their religious counterparts (6 percent); it is also greater than among government service providers of family planning (40 percent; see Table 1 under family planning practitioners). When it came to evaluating NGOs, civic leaders were even more positive (72 percent). While there may be biased responses by civic leaders toward like-minded NGOs, we observe that on this score both religious leaders and grumbling MD practitioners tended to be more positive in evaluating NGOs' efforts compared to those of the government. NGOs were evaluated as more efficient and less corrupt. Equally significant is the fact that civic leaders seem to be generally more positive (56 percent) in their perception of citizens' cooperation in dealing with the population problem. With the religious leaders, the question must have been perplexing. "Citizens' cooperation" for some of them must have been understood as defying the government population policy. Disregarding the seven imams who were supportive of that policy, we observed a negative evaluation (38 percent) or simply no answer to a question on citizens' cooperation.

We found several areas in which community leaders, both civic and religious, seem to hold common views, even if for different reasons. Many criticized the state for the ambiguity and weakness of its public policy on population and education. The next most common opinion with regard to population was a demand for "more forceful spatial redistribution." Many civic leaders, however, complained that the state has so far failed in obtaining a definitive opinion from authoritative religious sources "legitimating" family planning. The civic leaders feel that much of the government effort, regardless of efficacy, is undermined by conflicting signals about the religious legitimacy of family planning.[7] One other misgiving many civic leaders expressed was over the government's undue restriction of and interferences with the efforts of NGOs. They feel on the whole that these organizations do a good job in the field of family planning, and would do much better if they were not over-regulated by the state.

In sum, our research team found that of all the categories encountered in the course of their field work, the community civic leaders are the most concerned about the population issue. While critical, they are not hostile toward the state, and are appreciative of some of its efforts. Likewise, while wishing for a more positive response from fellow citizens in their respective communities, they maintain a higher level of confidence in people's cooperation. It may be appropriate to recall that it was civic leaders and NGOs who issued the earliest warning about Egypt's population problem some sixty years ago, a full thirty years before the state would take serious note of the issue. It was also Egypt's NGOs that took concrete action nineteen years before the first state-sponsored family planning service was set up. That long tradition among Egypt's NGOs is highly regarded in the community, but needs greater recognition at official national levels.

WOMEN'S VIEWS OF POPULATION ISSUES

Since the early 1960s, women of reproductive age (15–49) have been the primary target of the family planning policy of the state. Here we take a closer look at those who are the ultimate measure of success or failure—the women who make reproductive choices.

We interviewed over five hundred women in their reproductive years, from nine of Egypt's twenty-six governorates (four in Upper Egypt, four in Lower Egypt, and a border governorate). They all had children, and their age distribution approximated that of the national population (34 percent from fifteen to thirty; 49 percent from thirty to forty-five; and 17 percent from forty-five to forty-nine). The sample was somewhat tilted in favor of rural women and urban women in poorer and lower middle-class areas.

As Table 3 indicates, nearly all the women in our sample know about family planning methods, both modern and traditional, which is consistent with the results of recent surveys. Radio and television were mentioned by almost all women (92 percent) as sources of this knowledge, followed by relatives and neighbors (55 percent), and family planning centers and health clinics (24 percent), while other sources of information were mentioned by fewer women in the sample (15 percent). As shown in section C of Table 3, television and radio (which in Egypt are state-controlled media) are highly regarded by most of those exposed to them; however, as many as 15 percent of our sample considered the media messages on population and family planning useless or "sheer propaganda."

Exposure to family planning knowledge obviously affects women's attitudes—93 percent of them expressed supportive attitudes. A somewhat lower proportion have ever used a family planning method (85 percent), and an even lower proportion are regular users (about 40 percent). Those who once used but stopped to have more children are 27 percent. As many as 20 percent stopped because of religious, moral, or health reasons, or husband's disapproval or other family-related reasons. There was occasional dissonance between expressed attitudes and actual family planning practices. Some of the women who were favorable to family planning did not practice it. And some who thought negatively of family planning, for religious or moral reasons, are nevertheless practicing it. The two groups of dissonant cases were a minority of about 21 percent in our sample. As with other groups in our survey, we started the women's interviews with two open questions about personal or family concerns and Egypt's problems nowadays. More than the other groups, women's problem-lists were replete with the immediate and concrete—on both the personal and national levels.

Of significance to our analysis is where the population issue figures in their problem-lists. Some 14 percent of the women mentioned it spontaneously without probing. Many of them stated it in simple terms—for example, "too many people crowding everything." When probed with the standard question ("What about population, which some think of as a problem?"), 63 percent readily agreed. This suggests that women, being immediately responsible for bearing and raising children, may more easily appreciate the burdens of high population.

Table 3

Selective indicators of knowledge, views, and practices of reproductive women (n=503)

Indicator	%
A Knowledge of family planning methods (FPM)	
Modern methods only	76.7
Traditional methods only	2.0
Both modern and traditional methods	21.3
B Sources of knowledge of family planning methods mentioned[a]	
Radio and/or television	92.4
Relatives and neighbors	55.3
Family planning centers	12.9
Health clinics	11.9
Newspapers and magazines	7.4
Rural social workers	4.6
Lectures, conferences, and seminars	3.2
C Opinions of T.V. and radio family planning information	
Very informative	70.8
A constant reminder of proper use	12.2
Useless propaganda	15.1
Unexposed to it	2.9
D Attitudes toward family planning	
Definitely supportive	93.2
Definitely opposed	6.8
E. Ever practiced family planning	
Yes	82.9
No	6.8
F Reasons for not practicing family planning at present (n=301)	
Husband or family disapprove	51.0
Religiously or morally repugnant	31.0
Fear of side effects	9.0
Other reasons	9.0
G Frequency ranking of current personal and/or family concerns[a]	
Limited income and high cost of living	71.0
Educating the children	44.3
Unemployment of a family member	38.0
Crowded or substandard housing	29.2
Raising too many children	24.8
Rising health and medication cost	20.3
H Frequency ranking of Egypt's problems[a]	
Inflation and low incomes	38.4
Housing	35.6
Terrorism	31.8
Unemployment	20.0
Too many people	13.8
Declining morality	10.5
Corruption	9.0

Source: Survey Data Files, Ibn Khaldoun Center, 1993

[a] Totals are more than 100 percent because categories are not exclusive. The figures indicate the percentage of women in the sample who mentioned each item.

STATE, CIVIL SOCIETY, AND WOMEN: CONVERGENCE OR DIVER-
GENCE OF INTERESTS?

National decision-makers responsible for Egypt's population policy
have often formulated sweeping and well-intentioned programs to
serve the policy objectives—including those bearing on women's
education, training, employment, and public participation. But the
overall coordinator of the policy (the Ministry of Population) has no
real control over other organs of the state that implement those
programs, not to mention the society at large. We have seen from this
field study how little interest or commitment was shown by most
cabinet-level decision-makers, technocratic executives, and MD field
practitioners toward family planning. While this is only one component in Egypt's larger population policy, clearly it is the most important from the state's viewpoint.

Likewise, intra-governmental rivalries have undermined the effective implementation of much of Egypt's population policy. For
years, there has been a three-way conflict among the Ministry of
Population (and its predecessors), the Ministry of Health, and the
Ministry of Social Affairs. The intensity of the conflict frustrated
President Mubarak to the point of removing himself from the chairmanship of the NPC executive board, and delegating the job to his
prime minister. The power struggles at the top are often devolved to
the governorate level or all the way down to the field units. We saw
how divergent were the views of MDs (mostly with the Ministry of
Health) and the social workers, who are mostly with the Ministry of
Social Affairs or the NPC.

Moreover, because the implementation of Egypt's population
policy is multi-level and multi-sectoral, the plethora of agencies and
activities[8] makes it difficult to determine where true accountability for
results rests within the system. The problem has been compounded by
recent efforts to decentralize responsibility for population targets.
Thus a new layer of governmental actors—the governors and local
officials—are added into the picture.

The more serious cleavage in Egypt today, which undermines
many public policies, and especially that of population, is a three-way
conflict among the state, civil society, and the militant religious
groups. We saw how divergent, for example, were the views of
community civic and religious leaders. All three actors are fighting for
a share of Egypt's public space. Both the state with its centralized

hierarchic traditions and the religious groups with their absolutist dogma want full control of that space, and with it full control of the intention and reproductive behavior of women. For their part, organs of civil society are valiantly trying to expand their minute share of Egypt's public space.

Each of the three actors has its own, albeit unequal, arsenal of communication weapons to deploy in this conflict. The state has the powerful official media, institutional and financial resources, some four thousand mother and child health clinics, and twenty thousand government mosques. However, its fighting forces are not in the best shape: having been demoralized by bureaucratic inertia, they may comply with orders but with little enthusiasm. The Islamic activists have at least one opposition paper *(al-Sha'b)*, forty thousand non-governmental mosques, and activists to distribute hundreds of thousands of cassette-tapes, with messages often attacking family planning programs as external plots against Muslims. Their fighting forces are single-minded zealots who have managed in some cases to penetrate the state agencies, at least as we have seen at the field practitioner level. Civil society has some twenty thousand trade and professional unions, political parties, PVOs and NGOs, cooperatives, youth clubs, and business associations. Only a fraction are directly involved in family planning per se, though most are generally committed to empowerment and freedom of choice for all, including women. But civil society is outgunned by the state through over-regulation and by the Islamic activists' through powerful local organization. However, in the specific battle of family planning, civil society has become an uneasy ally of the state, and is credited for effective family planning services. Unfortunately, the state's insistence on over-control has kept the potentials of civil society substantially unrealized to date.

Another potential threat to the policy, however, comes from other actors: MD field practitioners in some of the state family planning and maternal health centers, and religious community leaders. Implicitly or explicitly, these two groups are presently quite hostile to state policies in general and to the population policy in particular. Their pro-natalist attitude is a function of a radical Islamic ideology that has been spreading among young, educated Egyptians, especially in medical schools where they are not exposed to any social science training. Curiously enough, a similar radical socialist ideology was in vogue from the mid-1960s to the mid-1970s, and was equally pro-natalist. It was that ideology which propagated overall development and social equity as a substitute for family planning and contraception services. Different as they are on many other societal issues, and doggedly competing in Egypt's public space, the two radical ideologies see eye-to-eye on the population issue. They were partly responsible for setting back Egypt's population policy after a promising start (1961–66).

With this state of affairs in Egypt in recent years, it is perhaps surprising that the country has moved to a contraceptive prevalence rate of 47 percent. Part of this progress must be attributed not so much to official harmony of effort, but to the individual decisions reached by women and couples far from the political struggles.

CONCLUSION

Despite the zigzagging and ambiguity, Egypt's population policy seems to be taking shape and proceeding on a well-defined track. A review of Egypt's long history of public concern over population issues reveals a number of important lessons.

First, starting in the early 1930s, it took three full decades of warnings from Egypt's civil society and non-governmental organizations before the Egyptian state issued its first public declaration on the population problem in the early 1960s. In the interim, the country's population had already doubled. Even the delayed state response was hampered for over two additional decades by competing paradigms of what to do about the problem, by oscillating commitments of the top leadership, and by conflicting bureaucracies over how it was to be done and who was to do it. In the interim, Egypt's population doubled again. Out of the three decades of state concern, only the first and the last five years witnessed a forceful joint action by the state and civil society in pursuing the primary objective of the policy—the reduction of the growth rate.

While still short of the performance of the first five years, the results of the last five years are quite impressive. But they are potentially threatened by a number of factors and counter forces. The renewed presidential commitment to the three-pronged population policy (reduction of growth rate, spatial redistribution, and upgrading population characteristics) is not matched by many cabinet members, or top and middle state executives. The pro-natalist attitudes of radical

Islamic activists, presently in vogue especially among young MDs, are consistent with deep-seated traditional values and reproductive norms in rural and poorer urban areas. Nevertheless, and powerful as they are, such counter-forces to the state population policy are not in full monopoly of Egypt's public space. The state has several actual and potential allies. Part of the state bureaucracy and nearly all civil society organizations are committed to Egypt's population policy. Because of raised consciousness, health reasons, or socioeconomic pressures, most of Egypt's women have become positively disposed to family planning, and nearly one half are current users. Approximately another one-fourth are willing or eager to try it if proper conditions are created—e.g., husband and family approval, easier access, and quality medical care or assurances against side-effects.

The battle over the future of the country's population policy—indeed over Egypt's destiny—is contingent on a forceful commitment to educating and empowering women, achieving sustained commitment at the highest level of decision-making, and increasing the margin of freedom of Egypt's civil society organizations.

REFERENCES

Abdel Hakim, M. S. 1994. An interview on the genesis of Egypt's population policy. Ibn Khaldoun Center, Cairo, January 11, 1994.
Al-Ahram. 1955. July 24.
Al-Ahram. 1993. Interview with President Mubarak, November 12.
Al-Ahram. 1994. December 27, December 29, January 6.
Al-Musawwar. 1993. Interview with President Mubarak, September 24.
Cleland, W. 1936. *The population problem in Egypt: A study of population trends and conditions in modern Egypt.* Lancaster, Penn.: Science Press.
Darwish, Y. 1989. *Mu'tamar al-tanzimat al-ahliya al-'arabiya.* In the proceedings of the Conference on Arab Non-governmental Organizations held in Cairo, October 31–November 3, 1989.
DHS. 1988. *Egypt demographic and health survey, 1988.* Cairo: National Population Council.
DHS. 1993. *Egypt demographic and health survey, 1992.* Cairo: National Population Council.
Dixon-Mueller, R. 1993. *Population policy and women's rights: Transforming reproductive choice.* Westport, Conn. and London: Praeger.
Egypt's National Charter. 1961. Cairo: Department of Information.
Mahran, M. 1994. Egypt's population policy: Past, present, and future. Presentation at Ibn Khaldoun Center, Cairo, January 6, 1994.

National Population Council (NPC). 1994. Egypt national report on population. Draft submitted to the International Conference on Population and Development, 1994. Cairo: National Population Council.

United Nations Development Programme (UNDP). 1992. *The human development report.* New York: Oxford University Press.

World Bank. 1993. *World development report.* Washington, D.C. and New York: Oxford University Press.

NOTES

1 Notable among these were three Egyptian NGOs: al-Nahda (Renaissance), al-Ruwwad (Pioneers), and the Egyptian Feminist Union. For details, see Darwish, 1989:74–85.

2 In Egypt, power is highly centralized and concentrated in the executive branch of the state. Egyptians have learned to take their clues of the relative importance of policies, issues, events, and persons from a number of political symbols. The designation of a governmental organization as a 'committee,' a 'commission,' a 'council,' or a 'ministry,' carries with it progressive prestige and importance. Dr. Maher Mahran, who had been the Secretary General of the National Population Council since 1986, was appointed as the first minister of state for population and family welfare.

3 Absent from these target groups are husbands and male heads of households, to whom very little attention has been given by official policy.

4 On these and other recent occasions, the president placed population as number four on a six-point national agenda for the remainder of the 1990s.

5 See briefing on a series of presidential meetings with the Cabinet and the ruling National Democratic Party (NDP) (Al-Ahram, 1994).

6 Some have since left their positions in a recent cabinet reshuffle (October 14, 1993).

7 This view is in fact incorrect, as the religious authorities of al-Azhar have, as early as the 1930s, promulgated fatwas (official opinions) affirming the acceptability of family planning.

8 For example, the third policy objective of population redistribution is the responsibility of five ministries: the Ministry of Reconstruction and New Settlements, the Ministry of Defense, the Ministry of Tourism, the Ministry of Land Reclamation, and the Ministry of Industry. Each of them is to generate plans, programs, projects, and activities to lure people away from the overcrowded Nile Valley and Delta toward new communities in the desert and border governorates (the Red Sea, Sinai, Matruh, and the New Valley). Likewise, the Ministry of Manpower and Training is in charge of reducing unemployment among men and increasing paid employment for women, through targeted training and retraining. Along with upgrading education and health, this task is to contribute to the policy objective of improving population characteristics.

4

Fertility Transition in the Mashriq and the Maghrib: Education, Emigration, and the Diffusion of Ideas

Youssef Courbage

POPULATION POLICIES IN EGYPT AND MOROCCO

Egypt and Morocco are far apart in terms of population, geography, and history. Egypt, with 57 million inhabitants in 1992, is far ahead of Morocco, with 25.5 million (CAPMAS, 1992; Direction de la Statistique, 1993). Egypt is the geographic heart of the Arab world, its center of gravity, and has remained for centuries its cultural matrix. Morocco, on the other hand, is doubly off-center: by nature of its location on the borders of the Arab world, and by its history, which separated it very early from the Arab heartland. But dramatic demographic growth over the long term characterizes Morocco as much as Egypt. Egypt was the most populous Arab country at the beginning of this century, with 10 million inhabitants. It was twice as large as Morocco, which counted less than 5 million. In the nine decades that have passed, these populations have each multiplied by more than five.

Concern with population growth began relatively early in Egypt, and several decades later in Morocco. During the 1920s, Egyptian demographic growth raised many worries. With the support of the highest spiritual authorities, the political leadership began to attempt to regulate population in the 1930s, well before many other Third World countries. In Morocco, on the other hand, French and Spanish colonial authorities viewed their protectorate as an underpopulated area. They opened the floodgates wide to European immigrants, and imposed a half million additional inhabitants on their Moroccan protégés.

The 1960s marked a turning point in population policies in Egypt and Morocco. Laissez-faire policies were renounced, less pro-natalist legislation was adopted, and family planning programs were initiated. Egypt, suffering from both high growth and overpopulation, took these steps with conviction. Morocco, which had to deal only with high growth, did so more timidly. Thirty years after the first expressions of concern about overpopulation in Egypt, the government took action in 1964, drawing ambitious population programs with quantitative objectives for the reduction of the birth rate. Two years later (in 1966), Morocco followed its example.

The vigor of Egyptian programs as compared to those of Morocco is hardly surprising. In Egypt, the population is crowded into thirty-six thousand square kilometers, and density of habitable land is a record sixteen hundred inhabitants per square kilometer. In Morocco, which has more cultivable land (eighty-three thousand square kilometers) and a lower population density (three hundred inhabitants per habitable square kilometer), the pressure on land is less acute. In the past, both countries—but especially Egypt—have experienced increases in net import of foodstuffs and food shortages even in the best of times. Today, however, Morocco has become a net exporter of agricultural products (exporting twice as much as its imports in 1991), whereas in Egypt the deficit is still increasing rapidly (from less than US$ 100 million in 1976 to US$ 200 million in 1989).

In the 1960s, when population reduction programs began to take shape, Egypt's fertility rate was 6.7, which was lower than that of the rest of the Arab world except Lebanon, and notably lower than Morocco's (7.2). In the first five years of the program, a decline in fertility was resolutely underway in Egypt. President Nasser, at his death in 1970, could present at least one positive achievement: the success of his population policy. The birth rate had dropped by five points between 1965 and 1970, exactly in line with expectations. The situation in Morocco, by contrast, was quite gloomy, since the fertility rate had increased to 7.4 in 1973 (CERED, 1991).[1]

Since then, the trajectories of fertility in the two countries have followed a course unimaginable twenty years ago. The level of Egyptian fertility[2] remained virtually static above 5.0 until 1988, oscillating between a low of 5.41 in 1982 and a high of 6.15 in 1979, and dropping below 5.0 only as late as 1989.[3] In Morocco, a very fast drop in fertility from 7.4 to 5.9 occurred between 1973 and 1977. The five-year plan for 1968–72 aimed at a birth rate of 33 per thousand in 1986, but the actual rate was in fact lower (31). This trend continued smoothly afterwards, as fertility declined below 5.0 in 1983 and approached 4.0 in 1989. The results are clear: the pace of the fertility decline in Morocco has been much faster than in Egypt, despite factors that would have appeared to favor Egypt.

PROXIMATE DETERMINANTS OF FERTILITY IN EGYPT AND MOROCCO

A comparison of the proximate determinants of fertility—patterns of marriage, contraceptive use, and breast-feeding—can help focus on key differences between the two countries.[4] Marital fertility is practically identical in the two countries,[5] although available data would suggest that the two principal determinants of marital fertility—contraceptive practices and maternal breast-feeding—should result in a lower level in Egypt than in Morocco. This is due to the fact that traditional methods of limiting births—which are less effective—represent an appreciable portion in Morocco (6.9 percent in Morocco compared to 2.3 percent in Egypt), even though the use of birth control is as widespread in Morocco as it is in Egypt (35.9 percent in 1987 in Morocco; 37.8 percent in 1988 in Egypt).[6] However, the level of education has greater impact on the practice of contraception in Morocco than in Egypt: in Morocco, among illiterate women, 30.8 percent practice contraception; among women with primary education the figure is 57.4 percent; and among those with secondary education it is 65.6 percent. In Egypt, the equivalent figures are 27.5 percent, 42.5 percent, and 52.6 percent.

In both countries, the average duration of breast-feeding (a period when the woman is somewhat protected against the possibility of pregnancy) lasts more than a year, but Egyptian women breast-feed their babies longer than Moroccan women do (17.3 months, as opposed to 14.4 months). In addition, the level of education has a strong influence over the duration of breast-feeding in Morocco: 15.4 months among illiterate women, 10.3 months among women with primary education, and only seven months among those with secondary education. In Egypt, breast-feeding varies very little according to education level: 18.1 months among illiterate women, 16.8 months among those with primary education, and 17.5 months for those with secondary education. So one would expect fertility, *ceteris paribus*, to be lower. The fact that it is not may be due to variations in behavioral factors which compensate for the reductive effect of contraception and maternal breast-feeding.[7]

An estimate of the effect of these variables indicates that the combined fertility reduction effect of all variables except marriage is the same in Egypt as in Morocco and that nuptiality patterns constitute the key factor that differentiates fertility in Egypt and Morocco.[8] Thirty years ago, the average age at marriage was low in Egypt (twenty years) and very low in Morocco (17.3 years). Since then it has increased by eight years in Morocco (twenty-five years in 1992), whereas in Egypt its rise, slower to begin with, stopped altogether at 22.4 years in 1992. Between twenty and thirty-four years, the time of life when women are at the peak of their fecundity and give birth to the majority of their children, marital statistics vary greatly: 57 percent of women are already married at 20–24 years in Egypt, compared to only 44 percent at the same age in Morocco. The proportions among ever married women diverge even more with increasing age: of Egyptian women aged 25–29 years, 87 percent are ever married, compared to 66 percent of Moroccan women; and of Egyptian women aged 30–34 years, 95 percent are ever married, compared to 86 percent of Moroccan women.

Such differences account for the largest part (about two-thirds) of differences in fertility. All the other determinants together—contraception, maternal breast-feeding, post-partum amenorrhea, abortion, sterility, fetal mortality—explain only one third of fertility differences. In order to further understand the reasons for the different patterns in the two countries, we need to examine their indirect determinants.

INDIRECT DETERMINANTS OF FERTILITY IN EGYPT AND MOROCCO

In a previous analysis of fertility trends in the Arab world (Courbage and Khlat, 1993), we assessed the role of the economic or social determinants that affect fertility through their effect on 'proximate' factors. These include infant mortality, urbanization, standard of living, literacy among adults (particularly among women), children's education, and the participation of women and children in the work force. When indicators of development or of standard of living are high or on the rise, we expect lower fertility than when conditions are less favorable. The following analysis of indirect determinants in Egypt and Morocco demonstrates, however, the extent to which the path taken by fertility may be resistant to traditional explanations of the demographic transition.

The evolution of child mortality and fertility demonstrates significant differences between the two countries (United Nations, 1993). The rate of child mortality was higher in Egypt than in Morocco until around 1986, when the levels converged. From 1960 to 1972, fertility decline was faster in Egypt than in Morocco, in spite of a high incidence of infant and child mortality (40 percent higher in Egypt), which did not decline significantly over this time period. But since 1972, infant and child mortality declined much more rapidly in Egypt, while fertility decline slowed down in Egypt and picked up speed in Morocco. Thus, trends in fertility and child mortality and their patterns are substantially different in the two countries.

Another key factor relates to urbanization. Since the beginning of this century, Egypt has been more urbanized than Morocco.[9] The major cities of Egypt comprise a more important segment of the population (35 percent) than did cities of equivalent rank in Morocco (28 percent). Greater Cairo comprises 20 percent of the country's population, while only 16.8 percent of Moroccans live in the megalopolis which stretches along the Atlantic coast from Casablanca to Kenitra. In both Egypt and Morocco, the majority of the population is rural. But the Egyptian qaria (there are approximately four thousand such villages in the country) has little in common with the Moroccan douar (which number 31,500). Extremely concentrated in space, the villages of the Nile Valley gather more than 6,700 inhabitants each on average and should be seen more as provincial towns than as villages stricto sensu. In Morocco, on the other hand, the rural world is made up of small *douars*, each with only 370 inhabitants on average (eighteen times less than in Egypt). The distances between these rural localities and between the localities and the city are enormous when measured on the Egyptian scale, where the exigencies of land use preclude wide open spaces, and where the village is always close to the city. The conditions in the Egyptian countryside—densely-populated localities, pressure on agricultural space, proximity to the city, rapidity and intensity of communications—could be expected to lead to a reduction in fertility. And yet the rural Egyptian woman gives birth to one more child on average than does the Moroccan woman in a similar situation (6.93 compared to 5.97).

The recent deceleration of urban growth in Egypt (World Bank, 1993)[10] is partly the result of a slowdown in rural exodus. The head of a rural household is now able to find work in the city without necessarily living there. The network of transport and the narrowness of the country facilitate a daily pattern of migration which has little effect on the pattern of family formation. In Morocco, on the other hand, where the exodus of entire families to the city is still persistent, the fertility of migrants aligns itself with that of city-dwellers,[11] thus lowering the national average.[12] Rural exodus also further reduces Moroccan fertility, as urban/rural differentials in fertility are more marked than in Egypt: 55 percent in Morocco, 30 percent only in Egypt.[13]

Fluctuations in income and fertility in Egypt and in Morocco do not tally with the economic theory of fertility (see also Simon, 1976; Repetto, 1979). Until the middle of the 1970s, fertility fell in Egypt and stayed approximately the same in Morocco. The rhythm of economic growth, however, was similar in the two countries. Since then, Egyptian economic growth has been particularly rapid without bringing down fertility, while in Morocco slow economic growth and a decrease in fertility have gone hand in hand.[14]

Similarly, standard of living and the distribution of wealth would seem to be somewhat more favorable in Egypt. Expressed in terms of gross national product per capita (adjusted for parity of purchasing power),[15] the standard of living in Egypt (US$ 2,440 in 1991) is 22 percent higher than that of Morocco (US$ 1,993) (INED, 1993). During the last two decades, vigorous economic growth in Egypt exceeded demographic growth by 3.9 percent per year; in Morocco, on the other hand, economic growth and demographic growth followed each other closely, allowing only a modest elevation of 1.9 percent in the standard of living per inhabitant. Finally, inequities in the distribution of wealth are less marked in Egypt than in Morocco.

Given that economic factors contribute little to our understanding of the differences in fertility trends in the two countries, we now move

to a consideration of differences in educational levels and their
fertility correlates.

EDUCATIONAL ACHIEVEMENT IN THE TWO COUNTRIES

School attendance and the increase in literacy began earlier in Egypt than
in Morocco; in 1960, 43 percent of Egyptian males could read and write,
compared to only 22 percent in Morocco. Moroccan women were
practically all illiterate (96 percent), far behind Egyptian women (84
percent). For the current generation in both countries, illiteracy has
declined but has not been eradicated. Although a minority phenomenon for men in both Egypt (23 percent), and Morocco (42 percent),
illiteracy is still the norm for Moroccan women (64 percent), but is less
prevalent among Egyptian women (41 percent). Interestingly, however, the decrease in illiteracy runs parallel to the decline in fertility in
Morocco, whereas in Egypt, illiteracy has diminished without a concomitant
decline in fertility. If we consider the level of instruction of women of
childbearing age (15–49 years old), the handicap of Morocco is even more
marked: 63 percent of Moroccan women are illiterate, as opposed to 40
percent in Egypt. Furthermore, among educated Egyptian women, 54
percent have had secondary schooling or higher education, as opposed to
38 percent in Morocco. One might assume that fertility would be 20
percent higher in Morocco than in Egypt. In reality, however, the
relationship between the two countries is exactly reversed.

In Egypt, reproductive behavior varies less according to all determinants than it does in Morocco. This is particularly true in the case
of education. A few years in primary school for Moroccan women
translate into a decrease in fertility of over 50 percent, but the
comparable decline for Egyptian women is only 11 percent. Access to
secondary education is associated with a decrease in fertility of nearly
60 percent in Morocco (where female students are still rare). In Egypt,
however, where the female presence at the secondary level is stronger,
the corresponding figure is only 33 percent. Female education has a
greater effect on fertility in Morocco than in Egypt. The age of
marriage rises 2.4 years for women with primary education in Morocco, but only 1.1 year in Egypt, and the use of contraception rises by
27 percent in Morocco, as opposed to 15 percent in Egypt.[16]

School attendance of children has always been greater in Egypt
than in Morocco, no matter what the sex of the child or the level of

education: primary, secondary, or higher. Today, Egypt has close to universal school attendance for its children under 16 (89 percent), while Morocco is far behind (50 percent). Furthermore, there is less educational inequity between the sexes in Egypt, where eighty-two girls are in school for every hundred boys, than in Morocco (sixty-nine girls for every hundred boys). Investment in education, which is closely connected to adult literacy, is as marked in Egypt (6.1 percent of the GNP) as in Morocco (6.9 percent of a lower GNP). Students are a more important segment of the Egyptian population (22.6 percent) than of the Moroccan population (18.6 percent).

Contrary to generally accepted ideas, the costs per student are almost the same in the two countries. Adjusted for parity of purchasing power in dollars, the Egyptian and Moroccan costs of education are each about US$ 200 per student per year. Although education is free in both countries, parents must bear the incidental costs of their child's attendance in school (educational tools, clothing, transportation, and so forth), as well as the loss of the benefits of the child's labor. In Egypt as well as in Morocco, the agricultural sector often depends on family members (children particularly) as a labor pool. In both countries, child labor is essentially a rural phenomenon (more than 80 percent). In Egypt, only 5 percent of the working population is between six and fourteen years of age (7.4 percent in rural areas), compared to about 9 percent in Morocco (14 percent in rural areas). In Morocco, reliance on child labor and fertility rates have both decreased along with rising education levels. But in Egypt the rising education levels and lower reliance on child labor were accompanied by stable fertility.

OTHER SOCIOECONOMIC DETERMINANTS OF FERTILITY: FEMALE EMPLOYMENT AND STATE REVENUES

On the basis of all the factors we have thus far examined—land, economic indicators, standard of living, overall education, female education, gender inequity in education, and child labor—one would predict that Morocco would be at a disadvantage with respect to fertility decline. And yet the fertility transition in Morocco has been faster and more sustained than in Egypt. Three factors can explain Morocco's success: female employment, the relation of the citizen to the state, and international migration.

In Egypt as well as in Morocco, large numbers of women work in the agricultural sector, where there is no split between the home and the work place. Time-budget surveys (rather than census reports, which have less to say on the subject) clearly demonstrate that unpaid female family workers have work days as heavy as men's work days (Fergany, 1991; Direction de la Statistique, 1988). These female agricultural workers, however, have the same reproductive behavior as housewives.[17] The absence of constraints on raising a child (entrusted to siblings or to older relatives) and limited exposure to the world beyond the family encourage the maintenance of high fertility.

Since 1960, when the two countries were similar in having low female participation in non-traditional sectors, the proportion of women in the work force has increased slowly in Egypt, but quickly in Morocco. Women now make up 14 percent of the non-agricultural work force in Egypt, and over a fourth of the work force in Morocco. In both countries, the presence of women in the work place is a prime factor accelerating fertility decline, but the effect is greater in Morocco than in Egypt: remunerated work reduces fertility by 50 percent in Morocco, but only by 37 percent in Egypt.

The financial relation between the citizen and the state is another factor that may partly explain differences in the two countries' fertility transitions. This relation has gone through different paths in the two countries, the 1970s marking a turning point. After the 1973 Arab–Israeli war, Egypt recovered almost simultaneously the west bank of the Suez Canal, its oil fields in the Sinai peninsula, and the loans and grants of the richest Arab countries—the main sources of non-fiscal revenues of the state. Meanwhile, the expenditures due to the war decreased significantly. The household's contribution to the functioning of the state, through direct and indirect taxes and import duties, has decreased from its high level in the 1960s and beginning of the 1970s. At the beginning of the 1980s, taxes contributed to a third of the Egyptian GNP, and about 24 percent of GNP in 1989 (UNESCO, 1991; World Bank, 1993).

In Morocco in the same period, the state lost one of its main sources of non-fiscal revenues, the export of phosphates (Morrison, 1991), at the moment when it was compelled to raise its military expenditures after the Green March of November 6, 1975, and the beginning of the Sahara war (Leveau, 1993). When the price of phosphates tripled in 1974, the government used the windfall profits to finance new spending programs. Public investment more than tripled, government employees received a pay raise of 26 percent, and food prices were subsidized. But in 1976, the phosphate price slumped again, falling 47 percent from its level in 1975. State non-fiscal revenues counted for one-third of the state budget when Morocco relied heavily on phosphate exports, which have since fallen to 17 percent. Fiscal pressure, which was very low at the beginning of the 1970s—less than 700 dirhams (at 1987 constant prices)—increased abruptly in 1975 to over 1,000 dirhams, and is today over twice its earlier value. Taxes, which constituted less than 14 percent of the GNP, increased to 20 percent in 1975, and have remained at this high level (with some annual fluctuations) until today.

The sudden reversal of the economic and fiscal condition of Moroccan households is related to the sharp drop in fertility, which diminished by 20 percent from 7.3 to 5.9 children in just four years. Moroccan families instantly faced an unprecedented situation, in which most educational, social, health, and military expenditures had to be based on their own personal budgets rather than on the windfall profits of the state. While socioeconomic factors (urbanization, literacy, female activity) show a gradual effect on demographic indicators, the year 1975 marks a clear turning point in Moroccan demography, precisely as a result of changing financial relations between state and citizen.

As striking as these contrasts are between the two countries, they cannot be accounted for by endogenous causes alone. To explain why the decline in fertility is stalling in Egypt and continues in Morocco, we must look beyond limited models of fertility decline. Openness to the outside world and notably to extra-national models introduced through international migration no doubt contribute to explaining fertility's divergent paths.

INTERNATIONAL MIGRATION AND THE DEMOGRAPHIC TRANSITION

During the 1960s in Morocco, and a decade later in Egypt, migration abroad became a major demographic and economic force shaping the two societies (Courbage, 1993). Recent estimates indicate that in the mid-1980s 2.3 million Egyptians and 1.2 million Moroccans (CAPMAS, 1989; Belguendouz, 1987) were living abroad, provisionally or permanently. In each country, the cumulative weight of international migration corresponds to almost 5 percent of the total population, and approximately 10 percent of the working population. The savings which Egyptian and Moroccan migrants send home are astronomical: US$ 3 to 4 billion a year in Egypt, US$ 2 to 2.5 billion in Morocco. This manna has become the principal item of the balance of trade, financing imports and often wiping out the deficits of the commercial balance.

But the exchanges between the Egyptian and Moroccan expatriate workers and their countries of origin are not simply monetary. Emigrants are decisive agents of social, familial, and demographic change due to their economic influence in their communities.[18] The benefits of migrant savings not only assure the survival and improve the daily life of the migrant's nuclear family, they also affect a wider network of kinship and neighborhood relations.[19] The migrant has a profound effect on consumption habits by encouraging aspirations toward upward mobility and a reevaluation of the costs and benefits of having a child. In villages and urban lower-class neighborhoods in Egypt or Morocco, where few look beyond the horizon of family life and the upkeep of a large family, a change in consumer habits can transform family choices.

There are important implications of the geography of migration flows in the Maghrib and Mashriq. In the mid-1980s, Egyptian emigrants tended to travel to Arab countries: 95 percent went to Saudi Arabia, Iraq, and Libya, while 87 percent of Moroccan emigrants went to Europe. With the exception of Yemen and Jordan, all of the countries where Egyptian emigrants go have vast resources and small populations. They are also countries whose governments have declared that their rate of population growth was too low (Saudi Arabia and Iraq) or satisfactory (Kuwait, Bahrain, Qatar, Oman, and Libya). In general, societies to which Egyptians have emigrated are strongly pro-natalist and encourage, for diverse reasons, large families. Thus, Egyptian emigrants may find themselves unwitting carriers of pro-natalist values, which they bring from the depths of Arabia to the banks of the Nile—even though these very banks cannot tolerate any increase in population. By contrast, the Moroccan emigrant is immersed in a European society, where small families are the norm. As a result, there is a progressive adaptation to the norms and values of the anti-natalist host society, manifested in a rapid drop in the fertility of Moroccans abroad. In the 1960s, Moroccan migrants continued to have large families (6.5 children, almost as many as in Morocco during the same period). But by 1990, the figure had dropped to 3.5 children. This change in the fertility of Moroccans abroad preceded and may have contributed to the acceleration of the transition to a lower birth rate in Morocco.

The transfer of values through Moroccan migration is likely to increase with the coming of age of a second generation of young Moroccan men and women. Born and educated in Europe, they nonetheless maintain contact with their country of origin and may play an important role in fertility decline. Emigration from Egypt, by comparison, is much more recent and there is no equivalent group of Egyptians raised abroad.

It may be noted that international migration is a more powerful vector of cultural contacts than other vehicles such as foreign-style education and mass communications. In Morocco, as much as in the other Maghrib countries, the school system and curricula are still deeply influenced by the French system. These countries also benefit from direct access to foreign media and are major consumers of European satellite television. Both foreign-style education and a large access to overseas media might influence life-styles, ways of living, and therefore fertility, but it is the existence of large numbers of migrants that strengthens the impact of these foreign lifestyles, as migrants act as brokers of these new ideas.

In its train, Moroccan international migration has brought an acceleration of rural–urban migration. The emigrant's family often leaves the village for the city in order to benefit more quickly from the money sent from abroad. Contact with the city tends to influence the reproductive behavior of these internal migrants, bringing them more into line with urban behavior. In Moroccan cities, as opposed to the countryside, almost all children of both sexes go to school (Direction de la Statistique, 1992).[20] Thus, the Moroccan migrant indirectly influences children's education (especially for girls) through the process of urbanization, which in turn influences female fertility at a later stage.

MAGHRIB AND MASHRIQ—DIFFERENT PATHS TO LOWER FERTILITY?

Our discussion of Egypt and Morocco demonstrates the uncertainty of demographic projections. No one could have foreseen the slower fertility decline in Egypt and its relative acceleration in Morocco, because the evidence suggested exactly the opposite. Twenty years ago, the United Nations predicted that fertility today in Egypt would be 3.91, while that of Morocco would still be higher than 5.0 (United Nations, 1977). At the beginning of the 1990s, and with a latitude of a few decimal points, it seemed that actual fertility had evolved in exactly the reverse manner.

The limited effect that education has had on fertility in Egypt seems to be evident in other countries of the Mashriq as well, where increases in levels of female education have not precipitated a decline in fertility.

The persistence of high fertility despite rising education is clearly illustrated by the case of Syria, where fertility stabilized at a high plateau for three decades or more (until 1986) of 7.8, despite the substantial achievements of the school system and the concomitant reduction of illiteracy. The censuses of 1970 and 1981 show fertility increases for all women within educational strata:[21] instead of a reduction in fertility for each educational sub-group, the data show an increase of fertility within sub-groups (see Table 1).

The explosion of the school-age population, which has doubled every fifteen years, explains why priorities were set to accommodate the largest numbers, rather than to improve the quality of education. Due to budget constraints and sometimes to high military expenditures, both the average expenditure per student and the average salary of the teachers have undergone drastic cuts with the expansion of the school system. These pressures may also explain the greater emphasis on learning to read, sometimes at the expense of writing. Given that the acquisition of writing is considered to be essential for promoting mental changes (see Furet and Ozouf, 1977), the comparative neglect

Table 1
Trends in fertility by education level, Syria 1970–81

	Proportion of women		Total fertility rate	
	1970	1981	1970	1981
Illiterates	75.7	56.4	8.12	8.34
Below primary	10.9	14.6	6.47	6.95
Primary	7.6	14.4	5.19	5.86
Intermediate	3.3	8.0	3.73	4.41
Secondary	1.5	4.2	3.10	3.46
Vocational	0.6	1.6	3.25	3.72
University	0.3	0.8	2.24	2.46

of writing is a possible factor behind the limited impact of increasing schooling on fertility. Another possible explanation is the changing role of the school teacher, once a respected opinion leader, and today facing a profound moral crisis.

Comparisons between Arab countries also show that the reduction in fertility expected from a rise in the level of education is weaker when one is dealing with a population with overall high levels of education. Thus in Jordan (with one of the highest levels of education among Arab countries), where 70.3 percent of women are literate, differences in fertility between educational strata are much smaller than in Morocco, where 27.9 percent of women are literate. The total fertility rate is 6.92 for illiterates, 6.0 for women with primary education, 5.39 for those with secondary education, and 4.1 for university-educated women. It is as if education, when it is the prerogative of a certain social class, is associated with a reduction in fertility, but as soon as it spreads throughout the population, it has a lesser effect.

Another crucial implication of our comparison is that mass education cannot be translated into significant fertility decreases unless it is accompanied by broadening female employment opportunities. The persistence of high fertility in the Mashriq is in part a result of the wide discrepancy between the access of females to the school system and their participation in the labor market.

In the Maghrib countries of Morocco, Tunisia, and Algeria, by contrast, fertility reductions are the result of both the restructuring of the female population of reproductive age and the incidence of an intrinsic fertility decrease specific to each educational stratum. In Morocco, educated women had on average 3.83 children in 1981–83, but 2.36 in 1989–91 (a fall of 38 percent in seven years). Higher levels of education are associated with very low fertility, lower now (2.03) than replacement level. This model of small families is rapidly spreading even to the segment of the population that was kept out of the school system; the fertility of illiterate women has diminished by one child from 5.84 in 1981–83 to 4.86 in 1989–91. Similarly in Tunisia, fertility reductions are also observed across all educational strata. There is therefore a high potential for further fertility reductions both under the impact of restructuring of females population in fertile age-bracket by educational achievements and because of education-specific fertility decreases. Fertility projections by educational levels show that replacement level (2.1 children) would be reached in about ten years in Morocco (by 2005–2010). Tunisia's completed fertility transition should appear five years earlier, Algeria's ten years later.

CONCLUSION

Very recently, national fertility has begun to fall in Mashriq countries, both as a result of the restructuring of the female population of reproductive age and under the effect of a true fertility decrease. This is true of Egypt, where fertility has recently decreased for all Egyptian women, whatever their level of education, including illiterates. In Syria, where national fertility remained at world record levels until the middle of the 1980s, current changes are dramatic. The Syrian national fertility level was cut by almost half in less than a decade: from 7.7 at the beginning of the 1980s to 4.2 at the beginning of the 1990s. The fertility decline included all women, and especially illiterates, whose fertility level dropped from 8.3 to 5.3 during the same period (Courbage, 1994a and 1994b). There is no doubt, however, that the tempo of fertility transition in the Mashriq has been relatively slower than in the Maghrib, and this is probably due to a complex mix of factors: endogenous ones related to female labor force participation, impact of education, and fiscal systems, and exogenous ones, mainly patterns of international migration.

Figure 1
Total fertility rate in Egypt and Morocco, 1960–90

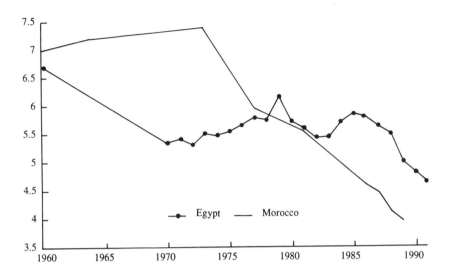

Figure 2
Female singulate mean age at marriage in Egypt and Morocco, 1960–90

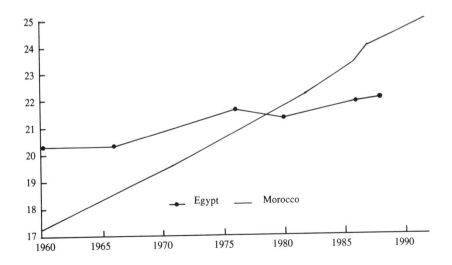

Figure 3
Infant mortality rate (per 1000) in Egypt and Morocco, 1952–87

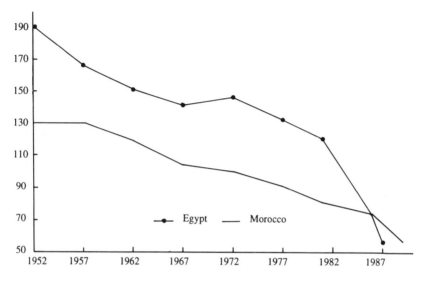

Figure 4
Percentage of population living in the largest cities in Egypt and Morocco, 1960–85

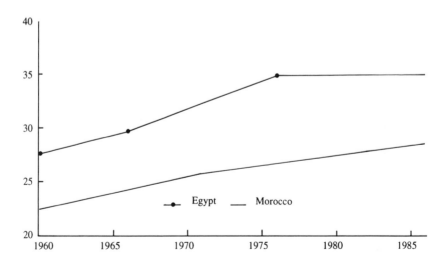

Figure 5
GDP per capita at constant price in Egypt and Morocco, 1969–90

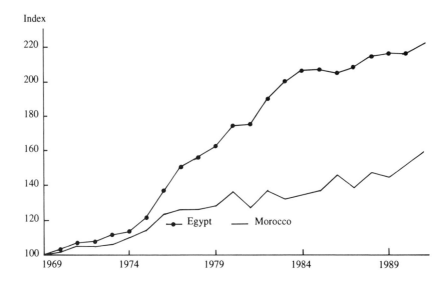

Figure 6
Female illiteracy in Egypt and Morocco, 1960–91 (percentage of illiterate females age 10+)

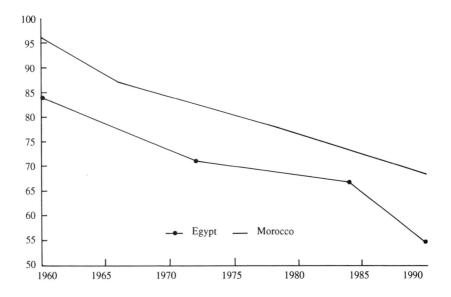

Youssef Courbage

Figure 7
School enrollment rate (primary and secondary) in Egypt and Morocco, 1975–90
Percentage of children <16, both sexes

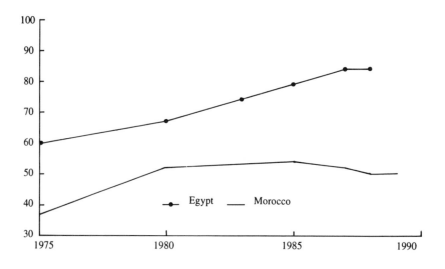

Figure 8
Percentage of females in non-agricultural labor force in Egypt and Morocco, 1960–90

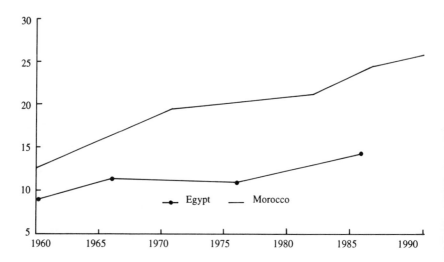

Figure 9
Share of taxes in Egypt and Morocco as percentage of gross national product, 1970–90

Morocco

Egypt

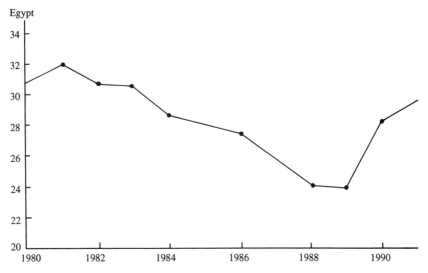

REFERENCES

Belguendouz, A. 1987. L'émigration des travailleurs marocains. *La grande encyclopédie du Maroc*, vol. Géographie humaine. Rabat: Grande Encyclopédie du Maroc.

Bendiab, A. 1986. Femmes et migration vers les pays du Golfe. In G. Beauge and F. Buttner, *Les migrations dans le monde Arabe*. Paris: Centre National de la Recherche Scientifique.

Bongaarts, J. 1978. A framework for analyzing the proximate determinants of fertility. *Population and Development Review*, 4/1.

Boustani, R. and P. Fargues. 1990. *Atlas du monde Arabe—géopolitique et sociétés*. Paris: Bordas.

CAPMAS. 1962. *Census of population 1960*. Cairo: Central Agency for Public Mobilization and Statistics.

———. 1980. *Egyptian fertility survey 1980*. Cairo: Central Agency for Public Mobilization and Statistics.

———. 1986. *Census of population 1984*. Cairo: Central Agency for Public Mobilization and Statistics.

———. 1989. *Statistical yearbook Arab Republic of Egypt 1952–1988*. Cairo: Central Agency for Public Mobilization and Statistics.

———. 1991. *The characteristics of the household and the role of Egyptian women in the family*. Cairo: Central Agency for Public Mobilization and Statistics.

———. 1992. *Statistical yearbook Arab Republic of Egypt, 1952–1992* Cairo: Central Agency for Public Mobilization and Statistics.

CERED and Direction de la Statistique. 1991. *La fécondité marocaine 1973*. Rabat: Centre d'Etudes et de Recherches Démographiques.

Courbage, Y. 1993. Demographic transition among the Maghrib people of North Africa and in the emigrant community abroad. In Peter Ludlow (ed.), *Europe and the Mediterranean*. London: Brassey's UK.

———. 1994a. L'imprévisible fécondité égyptienne. *Population*, 1.

———. 1994b. La politique démographique en Egypte et son évaluation: que nous apprennent les enquêtes recentes? *Population*, 4.

———. 1994c. Fertility transition in Syria from implicit population policy to real economic crisis. *International Family Planning Perspectives*. 20/4:142–46.

Courbage, Y. and P. Fargues. 1992. *L'avenir démographique de la rive sud de la Méditerranée*. Sophia-Antipolis: Plan Bleu.

Courbage, Y. and M. Khlat. 1993. Population structure and growth in the Arab world: Recent trends. Paper presented at the Arab Population Conference, Amman, April 1993.

DHS (Morocco). 1988. *Enquête nationale sur la population et la santé—rapport préliminaire*. Rabat: Ministry of Public Health.

———. 1992. *Enquête nationale sur la population et la santé—rapport préliminaire*. Rabat: Ministry of Public Health.

DHS (Egypt). 1988. *Egypt demographic and health survey, 1988*. Cairo: National Population Council.

———. 1993. *Egypt demographic and health survey, 1992*. Cairo: National Population Council.

Direction de la Statistique. 1984. *Characteristiques socio-economiques de la population, d'apres le recensement general de la population et de l'habitat de 1982*. Rabat: Niveau National.

———. 1988. *Population active rurale, 1986–1987*. Rabat: Ministry of Planning, Direction de la Statistique.

———. 1992. *Niveaux de vie des ménages, 1990–1991*. Rabat: Ministry of Planning, Direction de la Statistique.

———. 1993. *Annuaire statistique de Maroc 1993*. Rabat: Ministry of Planning, Direction de la Statistique.

Fergany, N. 1991. *Final report overview and general features of employment in the domestic economy*. CAPMAS, Labor information system project. Cairo: Central Agency for Public Mobilization and Statistics.

Furet, F. and M. Ozouf. 1977. *Lire et écrire—l'alphabétisation des Français de Calvin à Jules Ferry*. Paris: Les Editions de Minuit.

Groupe d'Etudes et de Recherches Appliquées (GERA). 1992. *Etude des mouvements migratoires du Maroc vers la communauté européenne*. Brussels/Rabat: Commission des communautés européennes.

Handwerker, W. P. 1986. Culture and reproduction: Exploring micro/macro linkages. In W.P. Handwerker (ed.), *Culture and reproduction: An anthropological critique of demographic transition theory*. Boulder, Col.: Westview Press.

Institut National d'Etudes Démographiques (INED). 1993. Tous les pays du monde. *Population et Sociétés*, 282.

Képel, G. 1992. *Le Prophète et Pharaon—aux sources des mouvements Islamistes*. Paris: Seuil.

Leveau, R. 1993. *Le sabre et le turban—l'avenir du Maghrib*. Paris: Bourin.

Morrison, C. 1991. Adjustment, income and poverty in Morocco. *World Development*, 19/11.

Ministry of Public Health. 1984. *Enquête mondiale sur la fécondité et la planification familiale au Maroc, 1979–1980*. Rabat.

PAPCHILD. 1991. *Egypt maternal and child health survey*. 1991. Cairo: Central Agency for Public Mobilization and Statistics.

———. 1994. Syria 1993: Results from the PAPCHILD survey. *Studies in Family Planning*, 25/1:248–52.

Repetto, R. 1979. *Economic equality and fertility in developing countries*. Cambridge: Harvard University Press.

Service Central des Statistiques. 1964. *Resultats du recensement de 1960: 1, nationalité*. Rabat.

Simon, J. 1976. Income, wealth and their distribution as policy tools in fertility control. In R. Ridker (ed.), *Population and development.* Baltimore: Johns Hopkins University Press.

Stauht, G. 1991. Réémigration et changement social—prospective pour les pays du Moyen-Orient exportateurs de main-d'oeuvre. In G. Beauge and F. Buttner, *Les migrations dans le monde Arabe.* Paris: Centre National de la Recherche Scientifique.

Syrian Central Bureau of Statistics. 1988. *Results of the population census in the Syrian Arab Republic 1981.* Damascus.

Syrian Ministry of Planning. 1982. *Census of population 1960 in the Syrian Arab Republic.* Damascus: Directorate of Statistics.

United Nations. 1977. *World population prospects as assessed in 1972.* New York: United Nations Population Division.

———. 1993. *World population prospects, the 1992 revision.* New York: United Nations Population Division.

UNESCO. 1991. *Statistical abstracts.* Paris: UNESCO.

World Bank. 1993. *World tables.* Washington, D.C.: World Bank.

NOTES

1   Notably, Sheikh Abd al-Magid Salim of al-Azhar authorized the faithful to resort to contraception with the fatwa of 1937.

2   The Moroccan Fertility Survey of 1980 (Ministry of Public Health, 1984) gives a somewhat lower estimate of 6.9 for the period 1970–74.

3   For Egypt, we have relied upon civil registration and estimates of intercensal population to compute fertility. We did so because surveys generally tend to underestimate fertility. For a methodological comparison of sources, see Courbage and Fargues, 1992.

4   In 1994, according to projections of the 1992 DHS survey, the total fertility rate would be even lower, at close to 3.5 children, probably as a result of the weighting of the survey, which tends to underestimate urbanization. The figure we use here for the five-year period 1987–91 is based on a revised weighting of urban and rural women of fertile age which explicitly takes into account the rapid pace of urbanization.

5   Except where otherwise indicated, the figures presented in this section are calculated from the following sources: for Egypt: CAPMAS, 1989 and 1991; DHS (Egypt), 1988 and 1993; for Morocco: DHS (Morocco), 1987 and 1992.

6   The total marital fertility rate (for the last years observed) is 8.92 in Egypt, 8.9 in Morocco.

7   The last available figures show a contraceptive prevalence of 47.6 percent for Egypt (DHS (Egypt), 1993) and 42 percent for Morocco (DHS (Morocco), 1992).

8   Such factors include induced abortion, sexual abstinence, and separation of couples. Biological factors such as fetal mortality, sterility, and age at

menarche and at menopause are not believed to account for substantial differences in fertility. According to limited and unofficial sources, induced abortion may be widespread in Morocco.

9   This was done following Bongaarts' method (Bongaarts, 1981). Average ages at marriage are calculated from population census data for the two countries.

10   According to current statistics, Egypt in the 1960s was more urbanized than Morocco (38 percent in Egypt as opposed to 29 percent in Morocco), but recently lost this advantage, since it is now 45 percent urbanized, as opposed to 48 percent in Morocco (UN, 1993). These statistics, however, are not comparable, because in Egypt, urban localities are designated once and for all, whereas in Morocco reclassification is frequent, so current statistics give an inexact vision of the levels and rhythms of urbanization.

11   Between 1976 and 1986, the rate of annual growth in major cities fell to 28.5 per thousand, and that of Greater Cairo fell to 26.9 per thousand, a rate close to that of natural growth.

12   Between 1971 and 1986, the rate of growth of the major cities was 32.7 per thousand, while that of the Casablanca–Kenitra axis was 34.5 per thousand—clearly more than the rate of natural growth. Furthermore, rural–urban migration concerns not only adult men, but also women and children (INED, 1993).

13   There are insufficient data to compare precisely the respective situations of middle-sized and small cities. It is certain that Morocco has known an explosion in urban population in cities with less than one hundred thousand inhabitants (4.7 percent average growth between 1960 and 1988), while in Egypt the growth rate has diminished (1.6 percent). However, these divergences—growth in Morocco and decrease in Egypt— have only a minor influence on the transition in national fertility. These cities include only a small proportion of the population (9 percent in Egypt, 14.8 percent in Morocco).

14   Author's calculations based on Egypt's population censuses of 1976 and 1986.

15   Between 1973 and 1988, the GNP per capita doubled in Egypt, and went up by just a third in Morocco (UNESCO, 1991).

16   This is different from the GNP per capita, in that it adjusts for differences related to the cost of living and the exchange rate. These calculations were prepared by the Centre d'Etudes et de Prospectives Internationales in Paris.

17   Sources of educational statistics cited in this section are: censuses of 1960 for the two countries, Demographic and Health Surveys for the two countries (DHS, 1992 and 1992b) and UNESCO, 1991.

18   The inertia of Egyptian fertility at the national level conceals another less obvious trend: the recent rise in fertility for each educational stratum. For Egyptian fertility to have remained stable at the national level, in spite of the

social restructuring of the last decades (urbanization and increase of literacy), means that it has risen for a large proportion of the female population.

19 Between 1975 and 1989, the rate of school attendance (primary and secondary for the two sexes) rose by 48 percent in Egypt, in spite of an already high level in 1975 (60 percent). In Morocco, the level of this rate was low in 1975 (37 percent) and grew a modest 35 percent from 1975 to 1989.

20 For Morocco, this conclusion is based on somewhat dated figures drawn from the census report of 1982. It is likely that the situation has since changed. For Egypt, the lack of difference between housewives and unpaid family workers is based on the 1988 DHS.

21 Since the implementation of *infitah* (President Sadat's 'Open Door' policy) and the resulting new sources of state revenue, Egypt has gone through a process comparable to that which took place in the oil-producing countries, where "far from questioning the structure of the society, namely through the access of women to the labor market, oil wealth brought on the contrary the financial means to realize traditional goals, mainly the large family" (Boustani and Fargues, 1990).

22 Since then, their contribution has increased again.

23 Fiscal pressure is defined as the annual amount of income taxes, indirect taxes, and import duties on a per capita basis.

24 In 1987, the average monthly sum transferred by a Moroccan emigrant was 2,200 dirhams (about US$ 275), three times the minimum salary in that country. In Egypt, the figures are similar or higher.

25 There is increasing literature concerning transfer of values from the receiving countries to the sending countries via emigrants. However, this literature mainly addresses indirect determinants of fertility—standard of living, marriage patterns, school-attendance of female children, women's emancipation and participation in the labor market—rather than fertility itself (for Egypt, see Képel, 1992; Stauht, 1991; Bendiab, 1986. For Morocco, see GERA, 1992).

26 For Moroccans aged seven to thirteen in 1990, the rates of urban school attendance were 88 percent for boys and 85 percent for girls, as compared to 58 percent for boys and 30 percent for girls in the countryside.

27 For more on the relation between education and fertility in Syria, see Courbage, 1994c.

28 In the past, school teachers have been non-traditional opinion makers, adhering to the values of the small family.

29 For education-specific fertility projections, see Courbage and Fargues, 1992.

30 One has to be cautious in interpreting the results of the 1992 DHS survey in Egypt, which tends to underestimate fertility by as much as 10 percent compared to the more reliable civil registration of births. For a critique, see Courbage, 1994a and 1994b.

5

Population Policy and Gender Equity in Post-Revolutionary Iran

Homa Hoodfar

The development of population policy in the Islamic Republic provides fertile ground for reexamining the widely-held assumption that Islamic ideology is the antithesis of modernity and incompatible with feminism. By analyzing strategies the Islamic Republic has adopted in order to build public consensus on the necessity of birth control and family planning, this paper draws attention to the flexibility and adaptability of Islamic ideology to political and economic realities.

Assuming that women's input in family planning decision-making is closely associated with women's socioeconomic status in society and their autonomy and security within conjugal bonds (higher status parallels smaller families), we examine the response of both middle- and low-income women to the call for birth control. Women's adoption of smaller families is crucial to the success of the population program because the Islamic government, in line with a world trend, and contrary to earlier practice, has shifted the responsibility for birth control from men to women. Thus an increase in women's economic and public involvement will not only improve women's position within marriage but will also enhance their role as family planners. The required changes, however, constitute a fundamental challenge to the government because they contradict gender roles—especially the idea of female domesticity—advocated by the Islamic regime as a cornerstone of their envisaged Muslim society. An important focus of the paper is therefore to examine the degree to which official institutions reconcile these two different sets of requirements.

For their part, Iranian women, both individually and collectively, have questioned prescribed gender roles and the male interpretation of the proper 'Islamic' role for women. A theme throughout the paper is the process through which Islamist women activists have used the ambivalent and sometimes contradictory ideological positions of the government to launch their woman-centered interpretation of the Islamic position of women. Adopting new and creative interpretations, they have given new meaning to familiar Islamic concepts and social institutions. They have encouraged the government to introduce reforms in the areas of marriage, divorce, and education, and are agitating for further improvement in the legal and social position of women.

RESEARCH METHODOLOGY

The data presented in this paper are based on an ongoing comprehensive research project on women and law in Iran. The fieldwork to investigate reproductive rights and family planning commenced in February 1993 and was based primarily on participant observation and the analysis of radio and television programs, major public speeches of political and religious leaders, women's magazines, and national newspapers. The team carried out informal interviews in four major public hospitals of Teheran, several smaller health centers in the outskirts of Teheran, and informal interviews with a core sample of 120 women. In addition, a total of twenty-five nurses, doctors, and hospital managers have been individually consulted on their views and impressions regarding family planning. Data collected by the research center of the Family Planning Board for the provinces of Teheran and Markazi, as well as several other works on family planning published in Iran, provide a larger context for the anthropological data.

POPULATION POLICY IN IRAN PRIOR TO 1979

In 1967, the Iranian government launched its first official population control policy, and in 1970 announced the ambitious goal of reducing the population growth rate to 1 percent within twenty years. Thus in

1973, the regime legalized induced abortion during the first trimester with permission of the husband (Aghajanian, 1991b; Mossavar-Rahmani, 1983; Khan, 1975). Through a network of family planning clinics, the Ministry of Public Health provided contraceptives to the public. The national women's organization, along with other associations, became involved in promoting and distributing contraceptive devices, primarily oral contraceptives. Along with the pill, other techniques and contraceptive devices such as the IUD, tubal ligation, vasectomy, menstrual regulation, and injection were introduced. However, as resources were not allocated to make these procedures widely available, the pill became, by default, the nationally-advocated contraceptive.

The urban public proved to be very receptive to the use of contraceptives, as there was already considerable demand, particularly among the middle-income groups, who wished to limit the size of their families but were dissatisfied with traditional methods. There was little effort to extend family planning to the rural population; nonetheless, nationally, an estimated 11 percent of women of childbearing age used some form of contraceptive (Aghajanian, 1991b:708).

Despite considerable improvement in the GNP and per capita income, the infant mortality rate remained very high, even in comparison with poorer countries in the region such as Egypt and Turkey, due to the inequitable distribution of public services. However, several changes to improve women's status within the family and in the public arena accompanied the population policy. Substantial efforts were made to include women in the labor market (Aghajanian, 1991a). The legal age of marriage for women was increased to eighteen,[1] and in 1975 marriage and divorce law was reformed to limit men's arbitrary right to divorce and to curb the right of men to enter into polygynous marriages without the consent of the first wife. The court also demonstrated greater flexibility in granting the custody of children to the mother; this was extended to the age of two years for boys and five years for girls. Although the implementation of many of these changes—especially the family protection law—was problematic, the symbolic value was considerable. These moves conveyed to women and the general public that women's rights were officially recognized, and that attempts were being made to remove the traditional discrimination against them.

THE DEVELOPMENT OF POPULATION POLICY IN THE ISLAMIC REPUBLIC

With the downfall of the shah and establishment of the Islamic regime, the family planning program fell in disarray. The new regime did not formulate an explicit population policy. On the question of the use of contraceptives, many conservative leaders continued their pre-revolution stance that these devices had been developed by Western powers in order to subjugate the oppressed nations and limit the number of Muslims. Some leaders, including former prime minister Sayed Hussein Mussavi, considered a high population the sign of a strong nation (Obermeyer, 1994). The family planning clinics which had been set up in major urban areas in the pre-revolution period were effectively dismantled. Many employees were transferred to other government agencies; the rest were reassigned to school health visits and similar tasks.[2] Moreover, the government adopted a policy of encouraging early and universal marriage and enacted a law to lower the minimum age of marriage. As a result of the regime's opposition to family planning, contraceptives became difficult to obtain as the stock of modern contraceptives (which were primarily imported) was allowed to be depleted. Within a few months of the revolution, the price of contraceptive pills shot up from 50–100 rials to a minimum of 1,000 rials, and even at that price they were sometimes impossible to find. The side-effects of contraceptive pills and IUDs on the health of women became a popular subject of discussion, particularly in women's religious gatherings *(sofreh)*, where issues of marriage, family, and parenthood were traditionally discussed.[3] Given all these factors, therefore, it is not surprising that the fertility level increased immediately after the revolution (Aghajanian, 1991b).

The result of the 1986 national survey, which estimated the population at over fifty million, had a sobering impact on the more politically-astute members of the government, forcing them to revise the regime's pro-natalist policies. The high birth rate and increase in population, together with the depressed economy and massive migration from the war zones to Teheran and other major cities, placed considerable demands on the government to provide jobs and basic amenities.[4] The government of the *mustazafine* (oppressed or powerless people), as it portrayed itself, had committed itself ideologically and constitutionally to the provision of basic amenities such as health care, education, and equal opportunity for all in order to move toward a just Islamic society. Moreover, the leadership also recognized that failure to meet basic needs in the cities could have severe political consequences for the government, particularly after the Iran–Iraq war, which weakened the country's economy and infrastructure. The government had no real choice but to introduce and carry out an effective, and Islamic, population control policy.

Pressure from more enlightened segments of the religious and political leadership resulted in an explicit pronouncement that the use of pills and other contraceptives which would temporarily stop the creation of a fetus was not *haram* (prohibited).[5] The announcement, justified in theological terms, was significant as it marked the beginning of a more conciliatory approach to questions of population control; the statement paved the way for the revision and reformulation of population policies in Iran within the next few years.

By 1988, the question of overpopulation and its dangers on the national and international scale had found its way into the political speeches of Iranian leaders at various levels, notably in the Friday sermons of imams in major cities. After Ayatollah Khamene'i discussed the necessity of introducing family planning in a Friday sermon, the government issued a national birth control policy which was ratified by Ayatollah Khomeini shortly before his death in 1989. The Family Planning Board, directly under the control of the minister of health, started its activities at once.

The population policy of the Islamic Republic and the government's strategies for its promotion differ from the pre-revolution program in many important ways, however. The Islamic Republic has achieved considerable success in convincing the population to both accept and practice family planning through a powerful consensus-building campaign and by putting in place an effective service network to provide affordable and reliable contraceptive means.

THE NATIONAL CONSENSUS-BUILDING CAMPAIGN: DEFINING
FAMILY PLANNING

The most striking difference between the family planning policy of the Islamic Republic and that of the shah is the way in which the present government has tried to raise general knowledge and understanding of the national population question, rather than limiting its focus to the use of contraceptives. With considerable coordination, political and religious leaders frequently discuss the importance of the population question and family planning in public. Major social issues are discussed and the government's political and ideological lines are publicly defined in nationally televised speeches, particularly in the Friday sermon.[6] The government has also provided support for scholarly research and publication on the question of population and Islamic family planning.

An analysis of these public speeches and the strategies of the government to raise public awareness on the question of family planning indicates that there have been three broad and overlapping themes in public debates.[7] Firstly, the international dimension: with the use of concrete examples drawn from China, the Philippines, India, Pakistan, and Bangladesh, as well as other developing nations, the talks question whether the world can continue to support an ever-increasing population. In addition, they examine the consequences of increased population for developing countries. In simple and accessible language, public talks examine domestic food production, and education and health-care costs. Invariably, they also point out that the result of high rates of population growth in developing countries with limited resources is inferior education and health care, whatever the ideology of their governments. In contrast, they argue that Western countries, with their low rate of growth and a much more balanced population pyramid, can provide good education and health care to their people and thus continue to reinforce their power over the rest of the world.[8]

Food dependency is also used to highlight the importance of population.[9] The West, with its small rate of population growth, has the highest food production, while Third World nations depend increasingly on the West for food, the most basic of human needs. Iranian public discourse therefore laments that Muslim nations are forced to beg food from North Americans. They conclude that to avoid a similar predicament, the Prophet and other ulema allowed Muslims to practice contraception in times of economic hardship. On several occasions our informants used this example, arguing that family planning is among the most *halal* (permitted) things any Muslim can do.

Iranian leaders sometimes use the claim that Islam permits contraception while sanctioning sexual pleasure to show that it is a superior and timeless religion (Sane'i, 1991). The history of Islamic discussion of family planning from medieval times to the present has been the subject of publications of the Islamic Republic's health ministry and several religious and university presses, as well as popular magazines.[10] An important aspect of medieval family planning was the tradition of herbal prescriptions, recorded by celebrated Muslim doctors (such as Ibn Sina and Razi) who were also respected for their religious knowledge. Thus, modern articles on this topic simultaneously promote Iran's Islamic heritage, nationalism, and family planning.

The second most frequent theme in these debates is the question of whether family planning, or, as it is referred to in Persian, *tanzim-e-khanevadeh* (family organization), is an issue for government or only an individual family concern. Using accessible examples, public speeches communicate that in Muslim society, individual decisions have always been taken with much concern for the public interest and, moreover, that the community tries to respect the rights of individuals. It is argued that just as no government can legitimately demand that its citizens not have any children at all, families cannot have as many children as they please since the government, and by implication the public, bears much of the expense from the time a child is conceived throughout his or her life. Therefore, if Iranians want to build an able, intelligent, educated Muslim nation they must find a balance between their individual desires as parents and what society can afford. Again these arguments are presented with specific comparisons of the Iranian case with those of other, more advanced nations, particularly Japan, which has come to represent a technological ideal to Iranians.

The official discourse asserts that all temporary means of contraception are in accordance with Islamic practice, and backs this opinion with references to various Shiite and Sunni texts and *fatwas* (official religious opinions). Tubal ligation and vasectomy are more controversial, as these procedures make an individual *aghim* (unable to bear children); and in Islam, any contraceptive which makes one aghim is argued to be haram. A number of ulema, however, have argued that if a reversal of the operation is possible then there is no Islamic barrier. Others have claimed that if a person already has children, he/she cannot be considered aghim, but if they are still young and do not have children they should not choose these methods. Despite some popular resistance, there is general agreement among religious leaders and administrators of government-run hospitals to perform the operations free of charge. The major complaint is that there are not sufficient specialists (particularly women) to meet the demand; consequently there is a long waiting list for the procedures.[11]

Abortion has been the most controversial and problematic issue of the birth control program. It remains officially illegal unless the pregnancy is judged detrimental to the psychological or physical well-being of the mother. In this respect, the woman's health is valued above the fetus, regardless of the stage of pregnancy. Ironically, Ayatollah Beheshti (an important conservative religious leader of the revolution) outlined a theological approach to abortion which was instrumental in liberalizing the abortion law in 1973. Under the current regime, if an illegal abortion takes place during the first 120 days, before the 'ensoulment' of the fetus is thought to occur, the person who caused the abortion should pay a *dieh* (blood money) to the fetus's lawful heirs, who are usually the parents.[12] After the time of ensoulment, abortion is equivalent to murder and is punishable, accordingly, by a higher blood price. Doctors who knowingly partici-pate in illegal abortions at this stage may be subject to three years of jail and removal of their license. In practice, medical certificates permitting abortion for the health of the woman are regularly signed and doctors are rarely prosecuted. When we asked our informants whether they thought abortion was widely practiced, all, including doctors and nurses, said that it was frequent. No one had heard of a single case of a doctor being reprimanded.

The third feature of the pro–family planning campaign is the consid-erable emphasis placed on the effects of numerous pregnancies on the health of mothers and their children. The Qur'an gives children the right to two years of breast-feeding and love and attention from parents. Closely-spaced births mean that older children do not get the attention they deserve, and, to alleviate their mother's burden, they are required to watch over siblings instead of enjoying their childhood.[13] Moreover, a mother should also have time to enjoy her children, as well as to protect her health and beauty. What does motherhood mean if a mother cannot enjoy her children's smiles and watch them blossom (Younecy, 1991; Ardestani, 1991)? By introducing medical 'facts,' religious leaders argue that the best age for women to have children is twenty to thirty-five; younger mothers may experience problems in giving birth because their bodies are still developing and older women are likely to give birth to unhealthy children. Older men are also advised not to have children, since their old age affects the health of their children; they are reminded of the possibility that they may not live to see the child to adulthood (Sane'i, 1991). These ideas are reflected in numerous radio and television programs that discuss the cost of pregnancy to women's health as well as the problem of having large families in modern times.[14] All conclude that the way to make a happy family and a successful Islamic nation is to have few, but educated, children.[15]

To the government's credit, it has worked relentlessly toward raising understanding of population issues as a personal, national, and international concern in order to create a broad consensus on family planning at the national level. Several widely-publicized national and international conferences on population have been held in Teheran. Along with the media campaign, there are plans to include population and the history of Islamic family planning in the national education curriculum at all levels. Similarly, there are plans to include information on family planning in adult literacy classes, many of which are held in the local mosques (Malek Afzali, 1992). The Ministry of Education is to receive extra funds in order to facilitate the design of this curriculum (Karimi, 1992).

Although not all of these goals have been realized, their existence indicates a comprehensive approach to family planning, one which is much more sophisticated than the pre-revolution population policy. At the moment, there are special family planning sessions for girls in the last years of high school. There are also similar segregated sessions for both male and female workers in larger industrial establishments. Following Chinese and Indonesian models, many large workplaces also include a health clinic, which provides contraceptives to employees. In rural areas and smaller communities, information and discussion sessions on population and birth control methods are held in 'health houses' (local clinics) or in local mosques where there is no clinic or its space is limited.

The government's explicit rationale for the family planning program is an important manifestation of its understanding of the complex web of variables that influence fertility levels. A holistic approach to the question in turn can indicate the chances of success and achievement of government-set goals. The Islamic Republic has focused on defining family planning in an attempt to prevent the criticism directed at the pre-revolution family planning program, and to combat the earlier apprehension that was nurtured among the general public by religious leaders in opposition to the shah's policy.

The current program is defined as improving families' and society's physical and social health by preventing unwanted pregnancies. The most important function/goals of family planning are spelled out as follows: creating suitable spacing between children; preventing transmission of genetic diseases; preventing the negative impact of frequent births on the mother's health; curing infertility; creating a suitable context for the psychological and physical health of members of the family and society; expanding social and health research for the advancement of these policy goals; creating harmony between social and economic development goals of the nation and population changes (Karimi, 1992). Several other documents prepared by the Ministry of Health underline the improvement of women's position within family and society as the cornerstone of success of family planning in Iran (Malek Afzali, 1992). The fact that family planning is presented as an encompassing program and a form of cooperation to achieve common goals of families and the government has made the program much more acceptable to the general public.[16] Therefore, it is not surprising that in the largest recent health survey in the central province around Teheran, 96.7 percent of women said they agreed with family planning.[17]

THE FAMILY PLANNING NETWORK

Thanks to political support, the Family Planning Board has managed to regenerate itself since 1989, when the Islamic Republic formulated its first population policy. It is now a major division of the Ministry of Health, directly under the control of the minister. Structurally, it is divided into three sub-divisions: a center for research on family planning, a center for studying the legal and ethical aspects of health regulation in relation to family planning and population control, and the family planning service, which is the largest and most important section. Apart from major hospitals and clinics in the urban centers, 'health houses' in the rural areas have resident nurses to provide family planning services and information, in addition to other services. In most regions, these centers have been established and are active, although their numbers still fall short of the ambitious health and family planning goals of the regime. The 16,654 existing health centers in the country provide for only 62.9 percent of the total estimated need, and about 21 percent of rural areas are not yet served

(Malek Afzali, 1992:19–20). In major cities, however, a lively private sector operates in addition to the government family planning sector.

Both the family planning campaign and its services are directed primarily at the low-income segment of the population. The unstated assumption is that more affluent clients can afford private services, and in any case, their children are considered less of a public burden. Quantities of contraceptive pills, IUDs, condoms, and several different injectable contraceptives have been imported and are distributed either free of charge or at a heavily subsidized price to those seeking birth control. Vasectomy and tubal ligation are legal and are available at major hospitals. Due to a lack of trained personnel, the adoption of the IUD in small communities is more problematic. More recently, the use of some methods, especially injectable contraceptives, has been curtailed because of the perception of substantial side effects. To offset the fear of side effects in women, much research is being directed toward identifying the varieties of contraceptives which have the least side effects.

Family planning clients are given a routine check-up and are advised on different contraceptive methods. The majority, particularly younger women, choose the pill. Women are provided with a monthly supply of pills or condoms and are expected to return every month for a check-up and to renew their contraceptive supply. Ostensibly, this procedure is to monitor women's health, but since their supply budget is limited, officials use this strategy to ensure that only those who are committed receive supplies. Particularly in remote areas, centers often run out of supplies, creating distrust among their intended clientele. Transportation and communication problems, as well as unexpected changes in household schedules, mean that women can't always control their own timetables. Thus, as many of our informants mentioned, women cannot always return to the clinic at the appropriate time.[18]

Despite much effort to disseminate information, the reliable and efficient use of contraceptives (particularly the pill) has not yet reached its optimum level, as indicated by several studies carried out by the Family Planning Board's reproductive research and information division. A 1991 study, for instance, mapped the prevalence of contraceptive use among all women between the ages of fifteen and forty-nine who were not pregnant among one thousand urban and one thousand rural households in the province of Teheran—where the public is assumed to have easier access to information. The study indicated that in both rural and urban areas, over 25 percent of participants, including a considerable number of literate women, took the pill either every other night or only before intercourse. Our data indicate that beyond lack of information there are other reasons behind inaccurate use of the contraceptive pill, which is the most frequently-used female contraceptive. These vary from hoping to reduce possible side-effects to trying to stretch the supply of pills (Ministry of Public Health, 1992b).

Data from various research projects on the prevalence of various forms of contraception carried out by the Family Planning Board deserve further analysis. For example, every major study in the province of Teheran and nationally indicates that in both rural and urban centers, *azl* (withdrawal, or coitus interruptus) is the most common method of contraception (Table 1 indicates the prevalence of use of different contraceptives among the population of Markazi province). Since there is no effort by the government to promote or advocate this method, its wide usage is indicative of an existing tradition of birth control practice (Musallam, 1983; Omran, 1992).

Both technical literature and government statistics indicate that men have played and continue to play an active and prominent role in preventing pregnancies.[19] Today, however, women are the primary target group of family planning campaigns. Clinics, publicity, information sessions, and radio and television programs are aimed at women. Coitus interruptus and vasectomy are rarely mentioned as alternatives. The common message of these media is that while family planning should be a joint decision made by a woman and her husband, the woman should implement the appropriate measures.

Table 1
Prevalence of different contraceptive use among women in Markazi province (percentage)

	Urban n=62	Rural n=46	Total n=108
Pills	21.0	30.4	25.0
IUD	8.1	4.3	6.5
Condom	11.3	8.7	10.2
Coitus interruptus	40.3	37.0	38.9
Tubal ligation	17.7	17.4	17.6
Others including vasectomy	1.6	2.2	1.8

Source: Reproductive information in three provinces of Iran, Health survey research project, Markazi province, Feb. 1992, p. 24.

Indeed, apart from coitus interruptus, men's participation in the use of contraceptives is limited. For instance, as Table 1 shows, 12.1 percent of men in the province of Markazi used condoms and vasectomy, compared with 49 percent of women who use the pill, IUD, or tubal ligation. That is not to say that men are not being addressed. Apart from public talks and media programs accessible to men, there are also formal information sessions targeted at men. Men appear to approve and relay the information to their wives. As Table 2 indicates, in rural and urban areas husbands were the single most important provider of information for their wives about contraceptives. However, only female forms of contraception are discussed. This indirectly conveys a message that the government holds women, and not men, primarily responsible for implementation of family planning. If we accept the premise that prior to modern methods, coitus interruptus and abstinence were the primary means of birth control, the data suggest that there has been a shift in responsibility for birth control from men to women. This indicates that the Islamic Republic, despite its own rich Islamic family planning tradition, has chosen to adopt 'Western' family planning strategies and methods along with their inherent gender biases.[20]

In the case of sterilization, Iranian specialists evaluate vasectomy to be easier and cheaper than tubal ligation, since men can be released from the hospital just hours after the procedure, and the possibility of successful reversal is relatively high. Yet men demonstrate a stronger resistance to vasectomy, even at higher ages and after having fathered several children. Research in Teheran province has estimated that the ratio of male to female sterilization (vasectomy versus tubal ligation) is less than 1:5 (Ministry of Public Health, 1992b). Although resis-

Table 2
Primary information source on family planning among women aged 15–49 in Markazi province (percentage of women who say they received information)

	Urban n=69	Rural n=59	Total n=128
Health professionals	3	19	10
Husband	35	30	33
Relatives	29	17	23
Public media	17	19	18
Others	16	15	16

Source: Reproductive information in three provinces of Iran, Health survey research project, Markazi province, Feb. 1992, p. 29.

tance to vasectomy appears to be a universal phenomenon in Iran, its low appeal despite the strong tradition of male methods and initiatives in contraception may be partially explained by the shift in responsibility for birth control from men to their wives.

Some of our women informants expressed outright hostility to the selfish attitude of men who expect women to have a tubal ligation after two or three children, so the male can have worryless sexual pleasure. In explaining why they thought men were reluctant to consider vasectomy, women frequently said men were worried that the operation may render them impotent. A few said their husband would do it if he were not worried that other men would make fun of him and call him "hen-pecked." A middle-class woman said the government and the religious leaders deliberately do not mention vasectomy as a safe and easy contraceptive method, because *their* wives might demand that they have the operation too.

The Islamic Republic's family planning campaign demonstrates other contradictions that will affect its success. Despite a concerted attack on individualism in government-produced school manuals, films, soap operas, and radio programs, and the explicit goal of perpetuating a culture of interdependence and connectedness between family and kin members, neighbors and community, population programs are directed exclusively at young couples and particularly at young women. We found, however, that women's decisions (especially among young women), are highly influenced by their social network. Mothers and mothers-in-law, in particular, have a very important voice in family planning decisions. The extent of such influence is clearly demonstrated in Table 2, where kin and neighbors are the most important sources of information on contraceptives, after husbands, in both rural and urban settings. Many of our informants expressed their desire to have only two or three children, but said their mothers and in-laws had pressured them to have more children. Fear of gossip and community disapproval, particularly in small communities, are strong deterrents against contraceptive use. In the right ideological context, on the other hand, their community could reinforce the use of contraception. The effectiveness of the family planning program would thus be enhanced by addressing older women directly and securing their support. It is ironic that a government that has made the preservation of traditional Iranian Muslim culture and its communal values a paramount goal has so far overlooked the importance of women's kin relationships and the central role that older women play in the lives of younger women.

POPULATION PROGRAM ACHIEVEMENTS

Despite its shortcomings, the Islamic Republic's population policy has been very successful thus far in slowing down the extremely high rate of population growth (see Table 3). Infant mortality rates and life expectancy, contrary to the general expectation that the Iran–Iraq war and the weak economy would result in a worsening of an already dismal record, have also improved considerably.[21] In 1991, the government stated its twenty-year goals as reducing the total fertility rate to 3.5 children per woman, reducing births to 28 per thousand, reducing the rate of population growth to 2.2 percent, and increasing the proportion of married women using contraceptives to 44 percent (Malek Afzali, 1992:62). However, the unprecedented success of these policies in the first five years has made some officials anticipate achieving these goals, particularly a total fertility rate of 3.5, by the year 2001.

The regime's officials and experts are aware that attaining such ambitious goals depends not only on careful project planning and implementation, but also on coordinating legal and social change in other areas of society. To this end, they have emphasized higher levels of education for women, improvement of the general level of health, and the enhancement of social and economic security of all citizens. The greatest importance, however, is placed on the social and economic integration of women and the improvement of their general

Table 3
Annual rate of population growth in Iran

Year	Population (millions)	Annual rate of growth (percentage)
1966	25.7	3.1
1976	33.7	2.7
1986	50	3.4[a]
1992	58[b]	2.7

Sources: For 1966, 1976, and 1986: Aghajanian, 1991b:704; for 1992: Malek Afzali, 1992:62; for 1994, United Nations, 1993.
[a]This figure excludes a net influx of approximately 2 million refugees from Afghanistan; the overall rate of population growth for this year is 3.8 percent.
[b]Iran's population is currently estimated at 60 million (see Introduction, this volume), although the United Nations (1994) cites a higher figure of 63 million

status both in society and in their domestic unit (Karimi, 1992; Ministry of Public Health, 1992a; Malek Afzali, 1992). The regime's enthusiasm for the plan has brought good coordination among its various organs. (For instance, in 1993 a controversial law cut benefits to fourth children, beginning in 1994.[22]) However, since the government advocates female domesticity, a cornerstone of the envisaged Muslim society, improving women's position through higher socioeconomic integration has posed the biggest challenge to the government (Moghadam, 1993).

WOMEN'S SOCIAL POSITION IN POST-REVOLUTIONARY IRAN

Women's status and their family planning decision-making are closely interrelated (Lloyd, 1991; Aghajanian, 1991a; Farooq, 1985). In the first phase of the revolution, women's status appeared to deteriorate in Iran due to the reversal of reforms initiated by the shah during the 1970s. Pressure from Islamist women activists and the demands of development, including population control, have encouraged the Islamic Republic to revise some of its views and adopt a more compromising attitude on gender issues. In this endeavor, both the Islamic Republic and women Islamists have demonstrated considerable creativity in their attempts to modernize their Islamic doctrine (Obermeyer, 1994; Ramazani, 1993). The new reevaluation, though short of the changes deemed necessary to improve women's status, indicates the considerable potential of Islam, like many other religions and social ideologies, to adapt to and accommodate diverse situations, including feminist values. In order to put into context women's responses to family planning, we next briefly examine the position of Iranian women with regard to education, the labor market, and marriage.

After the Islamic regime made the *hijab* compulsory, segregated classes at the university, and banned women from some engineering courses, opponents of the regime forecast that women's education in Iran would suffer a catastrophic setback. New statistics and research show that this has not happened. In fact, the pragmatic approach of the regime, particularly the more liberal wing, which has exercised greater power since 1989, has repeatedly linked women's education with the creation of an Islamic society. Ayatollah Khamene'i has repeatedly announced that Islamic society cannot tolerate even one illiterate person (Khamene'i, 1991). Government ideologues in various capacities frequently stress that Islam has recognized equal education rights for male and female children, and that biases are inherent in society and not in Islam. Thus, the advent of a true Islamic society should end such discrimination. Ayatollah Khomeini's daughter, who was known to have a very close relationship with her father, has a doctoral degree and is cited as living proof that the supreme leader of the revolution was a strong advocate of female education.

The Islamic Republic views education as an important vehicle for the construction of an Islamic society, and accordingly has placed great emphasis on reforming the educational system to reflect the regime's ideology. Education has also been allocated a generous portion of total government public expenditure, amounting to 21.9 percent of the budget in 1989 (United Nations, 1992). Although the gap between male and female illiteracy remains considerable, women's literacy has improved at a much faster rate than during the pre-revolutionary era (Mehran, 1991; Moghadam, 1993:182–84). At the university level, many institutions have reversed early barriers they had placed on women's participation in some disciplines, particularly law and engineering.[23] Although these improvements have sometimes been framed as the Islamic vision of society, officials also indicate a high demand for women doctors, nurses, and other professionals to respond to the needs of the female population, who, according to Islamic doctrine, should avoid non-related males. Medicine, the most prestigious discipline in Iranian universities, has become more open to women, and their admission in different medical fields is now on par with males.

The adult-literacy campaign has been very successful in attracting women. In 1988, 74 percent of literacy students who had completed their programs were women (Mehran, 1991:47), a reversal of pre-revolution trends. In addition to official figures, a large number of women participate in literacy and Qur'an classes run by volunteers in local mosques. Many urban women attend these classes, which are informal and have a more flexible schedule than government-sponsored literacy classes. A popular poster in these classes conveys a saying of the Prophet: "A Muslim should go as far as China [then the most distant civilization] in search of education." Therefore, although the regime's claim to a golden educational record is an exaggeration of the extent of their success, assertions that women's educational opportunities have greatly deteriorated are equally distorted. This indicates the contradictions that characterize women's status in general. At the same time as literacy is progressing, the values and ideology that it propagates through school texts indicate that the image of women is limited to the domestic arena, and that there is little, if any, encouragement for women to look beyond domestic life for fulfillment.[24] While encouraging women to participate in the revolution and support the regime, Iranian religious leaders saw domesticity as women's paramount role. This contradictory approach to the public role of women is also indicated in various legal documents, including the constitution of the Islamic Republic.[25]

Since the revolution, the government has adopted several strategies with the intention of reducing women's employment. These have included introducing compulsory hijab and different packages that enable women to retire after only fifteen years of work, or to resign and have their full salaries transferred to their husbands, or to work part-time only (see Moghadam, 1988, 1993, for more discussion). Such programs were ostensibly offered in order to ease women's lives and make it possible for them to attend to domestic responsibilities.[26] Consequently, women's public-sector employment is reduced by 2 percent each year. The systematic plan of the government to minimize women's employment and reduce their visibility in the government bureaucracy has been a major theme of criticism by women Islamists both within and outside the government.[27] Firuzeh Sharifi (1992) questioned policies that have resulted in women holding only 3 percent of senior government posts, although women employed in the public sector were relatively better educated than their male colleagues.[28] In a similar vein, Zahra Behrozy, a member of parliament, expressed her disappointment that only three women hold senior government managerial posts (*Zan-e-ruz*, 1991). Although women have not accepted this situation passively, and are challenging the government on many fronts, such a bleak picture of women's employment signals the government ideology concerning women's role.

POLICIES AFFECTING MARRIAGE PATTERNS

Immediately after coming to power, Khomeini and other religious leaders asserted their success over the Pahlavi modernist ideology by annulling the family code which had restricted men's right to polygynous marriages and had given women the right to file for divorce in some circumstances. Temporary marriage, which had been outlawed (although it continued to be practiced among more traditional social groups), was legally sanctioned once again (see also Haeri, 1989). The most dramatic change, however, was to lower the legal age of marriage for girls to nine years on the Hijra calendar, and to enshrine the law in the civil code.[29]

The pro-natalist ideology of the regime viewed marriage as the most important means of eradicating social ills. Not only did marriage and its advantages for society become a frequent subject of official speeches but the government also established the Marriage Foundation to help people, both men and women, find spouses within a strict Islamic code.[30] The foundation also provided some financial assistance in setting up new households. Consequently, the rate of marriage in the early years of the revolution increased rapidly (Aghajanian, 1991c).[31]

Within several years, however, newspapers, magazines, and sometimes even official radio began to carry reports of men who abused their power to divorce at will and threw their wives into the street, after years of marriage, without providing any support beyond the minimum three months' maintenance. Stories also circulated about child marriages and the health dangers of these marriages for young brides. More news accounts told of many poor young women who had entered into temporary marriages and now found themselves pregnant while the father of the child disappeared or totally denied his responsibility. Senior women activists and even women members of parliament raised questions about the meaning of Islamic justice for women. They demanded the introduction of laws preventing men who were either bad Muslims or whose understanding of Islam was questionable from causing injustice and misery in the name of religion.

The final result of this campaign was Ayatollah Khomeini's introduction of a new family law. Although this law did not go as far as many Muslim women activists had hoped, it represented one of the most advanced marriage laws in the Middle East (after Tunisia and Turkey), without deviating from any of the major conventional assumptions of Islamic law. Most Muslim schools of law, and certainly Shiite law, permit women to stipulate conditions in their marriage contract. Culturally, however, it is difficult to discuss these matters at the time of betrothal, when everyone hopes the couple will live happily together. Under the new law, the standard marriage contract includes eleven clauses, the two most important of which are that the first wife has the right of divorce should the husband take a second wife without her consent, and that wealth accumulated during the marriage is divided equally between the couple in the event of divorce.[32] The burden of negotiation is now upon the groom and his family, should they wish to remove some of the clauses; this in turn makes it easier for the bride's family to introduce their own conditions into the contract, including her right to continue education or work outside the home.

This partial victory for Muslim activist women has encouraged a new line of public debate and negotiation. They have produced woman-centered interpretations of Islamic law, challenged its conventional and conservative male-centered interpretation, and agitated for change.[33] A recent and successful case in point is the victory in winning wages for housework; this legal amendment protects women married before the reintroduction of the family law, which was not made retroactive. Housework wages must now be paid upon divorce, or on the woman's demand. Women Islamic activists argue that Islam does not require women to work in their husband's home, even to the extent that the husband is under obligation to pay his wife for breast-feeding her own child. This, they point out, indicates that real Islam does not want women to be exploited in any way, even for the sake of their own children, who are the dearest thing to any mother.[34] The controversial law was passed in December 1992, and despite difficulties in enforcement, it sends a clear message that the regime is responsive to women's voices.

These legal gains are not easily put into practice. Some men still find 'Islamic' excuses to divorce their wives unjustly and remarry, knowing that women have little recourse. Such actions render many women both economically and psychologically insecure. Islamist women are also campaigning to improve laws concerning polygyny, custody of children, and *nushuz* (the right of a husband to divorce his wife without recompense should she leave her home without his permission or against his wishes). Major newspapers and women's magazines debate these issues in an Islamic context, and some religious leaders have been very receptive. Speaking publicly, Ayatollah Sane'i has stated that men, having learned from the Qur'an that they may have four wives, know neither the historical circumstances of the law nor the conditions under which they have such permission (see also Damad, 1989, 1991). Observant Muslim women activists have managed to win many concessions from the government. These include the establishment of a Council of Women's Affairs, which reports directly to the president, a women's legal advisory office in the parliament, and the appointment of women advisors to aid judges in divorce and custody suits (though women cannot themselves be judges). Despite these gains, however, as Azam Talaghani has said in a personal communication, women still have a long way to go before they have undone the harm that has been caused by centuries of misinterpretation of Islam.

WOMEN'S FAMILY PLANNING GOALS

Within this socioeconomic and legal context, women as social actors assess their options and decide the size of their family. Our data clearly indicate that both marriage and financial insecurity are among the most important factors that influence women as they assess their alternatives. Since women are frequently many years younger than their husbands, most expect to be widows in the second half of their lives; 84 percent of all widowed spouses are women. In addition, other women are deserted or divorced at an older age, with little chance of remarriage. Data from the 1986 national survey indicated that 20 percent of divorces in the province of Teheran involve women of 36 years and older (*Statistical Yearbook*, 1992). Moreover, women's job opportunities, already typically lower-paying than men's, have decreased since the revolution. Therefore, women hope to have several sons, who can provide for them. Because they also try to protect themselves against the possible death or financial failure of an only son, women will generally have a larger family than they themselves or the government would advocate.

There are other reasons that women aim to have larger families. Many women have noted the contradiction between the government's demand that women have small families and the way women are treated legally and socially. They openly blame the legal permissiveness of the government toward polygynous and temporary marriages, which they feel put women in a more disadvantageous position than prior to the revolution. It is not clear what percentage of men actually contract polygynous marriages, as many of these marriages are not registered; nonetheless all our informants, both male and female, felt that the percentage of polygynous marriages has increased sharply. Such a perception strongly influences women's childbearing strategies and encourages them to choose larger families in order to consolidate their marriage ties.

To bring women's choice of family size into line with that envisaged by the government, the regime needs to enact substantial reforms and remove contradictory and ambivalent policies affecting women's roles. Recent reforms giving women the right to divorce if the husband marries a second wife are ideologically important, but of limited significance in practice. Few women actually exercise this right because their opportunities in the second-marriage market rarely offer them a life better than accepting a polygynous marriage. Therefore women opt for larger families to decrease the chance their husbands will decide to divorce them, even if they marry another woman. As one interviewee put it, many women in a polygynous union might accept looking after one or two children that are not theirs, but not many would want to look after several children who see them as usurping their mother's place.[35]

In a society whose ideological slogans and cultural values tell a woman that her role as mother is the most important element of her life, the fear of losing her children is constant. According to the Iranian interpretation of Islamic laws, when a woman divorces or dies, the father and agnates automatically receive the custody of children after the age of two for boys and five for girls (although in recent years under some circumstances a divorced mother may be able to keep the children for a longer time). In 65 percent of all divorces reported by our interviewees where children were involved, fathers had custody of the children. Unmarried divorced fathers often gave the children to their own mothers or other female relatives to help care for them. It is also very common that mothers are denied any visiting rights by the father. The remedy to this threat, according to many of our female informants, was to have many children and make it difficult for others—their mother-in-law, sisters-in-law, a co-wife, or stepmother—to take over their maternal responsibilities. Similarly, many women put up with unhappy and even violent marriages just to be with their children.

Clearly, women are planning their families and using contraceptives, but their assessment of preferred realistic family size does not always correspond with that of the government. Low-income women feel less competition for their husbands, particularly after having had several children, since, as one women put it, "poor husbands are not scarce, and one poor man is as good as the next one, but if one's husband is rich, then it is a different game." Financial insecurity and vulnerability in old age, however, encourage women to have more sons and give them the best training and education a household can afford, often at the cost of neglecting their daughters and reproducing traditional male biases. In parallel, middle-class women's strategy in the face of their even more vulnerable marriages is to opt for larger families.

SUMMARY AND CONCLUSION

The development of population policy in Iran indicates that contrary to its image in the West, the Islamic Republic has demonstrated much resilience and adaptability in face of harsh socioeconomic reality. Moreover, the regime has demonstrated a keen awareness that creating an informed public and building a broad consensus is important to the success of any development plan. A population program is particularly sensitive, since it touches upon the most intimate and day-to-day aspects of peoples' lives. Unlike the monarchy, the Islamic regime has popularized, by means of the Friday sermon and other media, the fundamental relevance of the population question to society. The government population policy is a considerable success thus far, because it combines Islamic discourse with modern population discussion in a very accessible format.

Common to both regimes is the official consensus on women's responsibility for birth control. Much of the Islamic debate on family planning has focused on *azl* (coitus interruptus). The research conducted on the prevalence of contraceptive methods by the Population Policy Board, both nationally and on a smaller scale, has indicated that azl is still very widely used. Now, however, women are being persuaded to adopt contraceptives and limit the size of their family. This transfer of responsibility, however, is not accompanied by a corresponding authority. Ethically, the use of contraceptives should be the subject of consultation and agreement between the husband and wife. Moreover, despite the government's claims of protecting Iranian Muslim culture from the evils of Western cultural imperialism and the advent of individualism, by directing their information campaign to younger women solely, the government has demonstrated little sensitivity to the significant role women's networks, particularly those of older women, play in the decisions made by younger women.

The most controversial issue of population policy in Iran, however, is the close association between women's socioeconomic position and fertility behavior. While the government has readily promoted education for women, other requirements, such as labor market participation, contradict the state vision of women's role. In returning to old Muslim ways, the regime legalized polygynous marriages, returned to men the unilateral and unconditional right to divorce, made the veil compulsory for women, and introduced policies to reduce women's labor market participation.

This particular vision and its corresponding legal changes contradicted the promise of a just Islamic society for all men and women. Furthermore, the government-envisaged gender role for women did not correspond with those of the Islamist women activists, many of whom are daughters, wives, and relatives of the political leaders. These women have pointed out that much of what is presented to women as Islamic is but patriarchy in 'Islamic' costume. The last decade of Iranian debate and discussion on the question of women, which is the most politicized subject, has been colored by a sharp contrast between this patriarchy and a woman-centered interpretation of women's rights in Islam. The advantages of the Islamist feminists over secular Western feminist activists is that they can challenge and reform the Islamic doctrine from within rather than imposing/advocating a Western model of gender relations. Islamist feminists have already managed successfully to change women's consciousness to distinguish between patriarchal tradition and 'Islam.' Ironically, the return to strict interpretations of the marriage institution and the role of women has turned women strongly against traditions. These arguments have also made it clear that many other issues besides population affect women's family planning goals, including women's rights and responsibilities.

Because of the establishment's eagerness to succeed in population policy and its awareness of the importance of women's socioeconomic status in this regard, it has introduced a conciliatory and accommodating attitude toward some Islamist women's demands. In their attempt to modernize their 'Islamic' doctrine, many conservative religious leaders have adopted some women's interpretations. However, given economic and unemployment pressures, there is little sign that the government will promote women's labor market participation. It also remains to be seen whether the establishment will legally and socially redefine marriage to make it a more secure social institution for women, and thus encourage a lower fertility rate.

Finally, the lively debates in Iran around the dynamics of the population program and women's rights and responsibilities prove that reproductive choices and strategies, whether the government's or women's, are not dictated solely by Islam, but by the political and economic realities of society.

AUTHOR'S NOTE

The data presented here are based on an ongoing comprehensive research project on women and law in Iran carried out under the auspices of Women Living Under Muslim Laws, an international network of women living in Muslim communities, established to promote debate and research for social change in the Muslim world.

I would like to thank Carla Makhlouf Obermeyer and Carolyn Makinson for their insightful comments on an earlier draft. I am indebted to Patricia Kelly for her many discussions and comments during the development of this paper.

REFERENCES

Aghajanian, A. 1991a. Socioeconomic modernization, status of women and fertility decline in Iran. In G. Gaburro and D.L. Poston, eds., *Essays on population economics*. Milan: CEDAM.

———. 1991b. Population change in Iran: 1966–86: A stalled demographic transition? *Population and Development Review*. 17:703–715.

———. 1991c. Women's roles and recent marriage trends in Iran. *Canadian Studies in Population*. 18/1:17–28.

———. (forthcoming). The status of women and female children in Iran: An update from the 1986 census. In M. Afkhami and E. Friedl, eds., *In the eye of the storm: Women in post-revolutionary Iran*. London: I. B. Tauris.

Anderton, D. and R. J. Emigh. 1989. Polygynous fertility: Sexual competition versus progeny. *American Journal of Sociology*. 94:832–55.

Ardestani, S. 1991. *Zan-e-ruz.* 1335:10–13, 56–57 (1370/1991).

Arowolo, O. 1981. Plural marriage, fertility and the problem of multiple causation. In H. Ware, ed., *Women, education and the modernization of the family in west Africa.* Canberra: Australian National University Press.

Betteridge, A. 1980. The controversial vows of urban Muslim women in Iran. In N. A. Falk and R. M. Gross, eds., *Unspoken worlds: Women's religious lives in non-Western cultures.* New York: Harper and Row.

Clignet, R. 1970. *Many wives, many powers: Authority and power in polygynous families.* Evanston, Ill.: Northwestern University Press.

Constitution of the Islamic Republic of Iran and its Amendment 1368/1990. 1992. Teheran: Ministry of Culture and Islamic Guidance.

Damad, Hojjatolislam. 1989. *Zan-e-ruz.* Issue 1253:9

———. 1991. *Zan-e-ruz.* Issue 1302:52

Etala'at. January 6, 1993.

Farooq, G. M. 1985. Household fertility decision-making in Nigeria. In G. M. Farooq and G. B. Simmons, eds., *Fertility in developing countries: An economic perspective on research and policy issues.* New York: St. Martin's Press.

Haeri, S. 1989. *Law and desire: Temporary marriage in shi'i Iran.* Syracuse: Syracuse University Press.

———. 1992. Temporary marriage and the state in Iran: An Islamic discourse on female sexuality. *Social Research.* 59/1.

Karimi, I. 1992. *Feshar-e-jam'iyat man' asasi dar tose-ye-iqtisadi, ijtima'i, va farhangi* (Population pressure as an obstacle to economic, social, and cultural development). Teheran: Family Planning Board, Ministry of Public Health, Health Education Division.

Khamene'i, Ayatollah. 1991. *Zan-e-ruz.* 1361:4 (1371/1992).

Khan, M. 1975. *Socioeconomic factors in the reduction of human fertility in the Islamic world with a case study of Iran.* Ph.D. dissertation, Stanford University.

Kitabi, A. 1986. *Nazariyat-e-jam'iyat shenasi* (Islamic theories of population). Teheran: University of Teheran Press.

Lloyd, C. B. 1991. The contribution of the world fertility surveys to an understanding of the relationship between women's work and fertility. *Studies in Family Planning.* 22/3:144–61.

Malek Afzali, H. 1992. *Vaziet-e-salamat-e-madaran va kudakan dar jumhuriyyeh islamiyyeh Iran* (The health status of mothers and children in the Islamic Republic of Iran). Teheran: Ministry of Public Health, Health Education Division.

Mehran, G. 1991. The creation of the new Muslim woman: Female education in the Islamic Republic of Iran. *Convergence.* 23:42–52.

Ministry of Public Health. 1992a. *Barname-ye-jam'iyyat va tanzim-e-khanevadeh dar sal-e 1371* (The family planning program in 1992). Teheran: Ministry of Public Health, Health Education Division.

————. 1992b. *Baresi-ye-karburd va sa'el-e-pishgiri az hamelegi dar manategh-e-shahri va rusta-e-ustan-e-Teheran* (The usage of contraceptives in urban and rural areas of the province of Teheran). Teheran: Ministry of Public Health, Health Education Division.

Moghadam, V. 1988. Women, work and ideology in the Islamic Republic. *International Journal of Middle East Studies.* 20/2:221–43.

————. 1993. *Modernizing women: Gender and social change in the Middle East.* Boulder, Colorado: Lynne Rienner Publishers.

Mossavar-Rahmani, Y. L. 1983. Family planning in post-revolutionary Iran. In G. Nashat, ed., *Women and revolution in Iran.* Boulder, Colorado: Westview Press.

Musallam, B. F. 1983. *Sex and society in Islam.* Cambridge: Cambridge University Press.

Obermeyer, C. Makhlouf. 1994. Reproductive choice in Islam: Gender and state in Iran and Tunisia. *Studies in Family Planning.* 25/1:41–51.

Omran, A. R. 1992. *Family planning in the legacy of Islam.* London: Routledge.

Payam-e-hajar (English edition). 1992. 1/1.

Payam-e-zan. 1993. 2:4, 16–17.

Ramazani, N. 1993. Women in Iran: The revolutionary ebb and flow. *The Middle East Journal.* 47:409–428.

Sane'i, Ayatollah. 1991. *Zan-e-ruz.* 1329:8–12.

Sansarian, E. 1982. *The women's rights movement in Iran: Mutiny, appeasement and repression from 1900 to Khomeini.* New York: Praeger.

Sharifi, F. 1992. *Mughayat-e-zan dar nizam-e-idariy-e-Iran* (The position of women in the public sector in Iran). *Zanan.* 2:4–9.

Statistical Center of Iran. 1978. *Population growth survey of Iran, final report, 1973–1976.* No.777:93 Teheran: Teheran Planning and Budget Organization.

Statistical Yearbook. 1992. Teheran: Statistical Center of Iran.

United Nations. 1990. *Investing in women: The focus of the nineties.* New York: United Nations Population Fund.

————. 1992. *Human development report 1992.* United Nations Development Program. New York: Oxford University Press.

————. 1993. *World population prospects 1992 revision.* New York: United Nations Population Division.

————. 1994. *World population prospects: The 1994 revision.* New York: United Nations Population Division.

Younecy, Hojjatolislam. 1991. *Zan-e-ruz.* Issue 1320.

Youssef, N. H. 1982. The interrelationship between the division of labor in the household, women's roles and their impact on fertility. In R. Anker, M. Buvinic, and N. H. Youssef, eds., *Women's roles and population trends in the third world.* London: Croom Helm.

Zan-e-ruz. 1991. 1304 (1370/1991).

NOTES

1   This law was repealed in 1978 under pressure from the religious right; the minimum age of marriage for girls reverted to fifteen. Sansarian (1982:96) notes that the minimum age of marriage was not enforced.

2   Nonetheless, a considerable number of experienced personnel remained within the system. Many of them saw this phase as temporary and were convinced that the situation would change. As one official told us, "I knew that sooner or later the government would realize that no country, certainly none with Iran's population and economy, can afford not to implement a population control policy and expect to progress."

3   I attended two of these gatherings in 1981. Women, particularly those who had not yet had children, were warned not to use the pill because it may render them permanently infertile. They were told that God would not listen to their complaints if their husbands divorced them because of their infertility. For a discussion of the *sofreh,* see Betteridge, 1980.

4   It was also clear that many war migrants were not going to return to their village or town, as there was very little left to go back to.

5   It was Ayatollah Beheshti's interpretation of the permissibility of these practices that made such a ruling possible.

6   These Friday sermons and many other official talks and interviews are also printed in major national newspapers and magazines, including women's magazines.

7   It is important to note that these are usually delivered in the form of questions and answers, the traditional way in which the ulema (religious scholars) delivered their sermons.

8   The population pyramids are discussed with clear comparative examples. For instance, 45 percent of Iran's population is under the age of fourteen, while in most industrialized countries this age group constitutes between 9 and 15 percent of the population.

9   This is a frequent subject of letters to the editor and radio programs. Even our informants brought up the topic of food dependency.

10 For examples of this line of argument, see Younecy and Ardestani (1991) and Karimi (1992).

11 Much of these writings is along the lines of Musallam (1983) and Omran (1992). The most widely circulated of these books is Ahmad Kitabi's *Nazariyat-e-jam'iyat shenasi*(Islamic theories of population)(Kitabi, 1986).

12 The Islamic regime would prefer tubal ligations to be performed by women, but due to shortages it is acceptable for male doctors to perform the operation.

13 If one of the parents has caused the abortion without the permission of the other, s/he would have to pay the other person's share of the blood money. If there is a doctor involved, he or she may be punished by lashing and payment of the blood money.

14 This issue is the subject of several beautifully designed posters by the Family Planning Board.

15 These issues are also incorporated in some soap operas and radio dramas. The television show *Ahlaq dar khanevadeh* (Morality in the family) frequently discusses these ideas as does the popular morning radio program *Khanevadeh* (Family).

16 The responses of the editors of women's magazines and women activists to family planning have been more subtle. Apart from *Payam-e-hajar*, a publication of the Islamic Institute directed by the widely respected Islamist activist Azam Talaghani, few magazines have ventured to publish articles written by women. In many cases, however, magazine editors have subtly emphasized (in headlines and side-bars) those speeches which are more liberal, and underscored issues directly relevant to women and those which give a more liberal interpretation of women's or marital issues (the choice of headlines and the selection of speeches emphasized in women's magazines are an interesting topic for analysis). *Payam-e-hajar*, which has been published since 1980, has printed articles discussing family planning as a basic human right and stressing the right of a woman to control her body and therefore her fertility (*Payam-e-hajar*, 1992).

17 The emphasis placed on curing infertility has had a definite impact on the credibility of the program.

18 For reproductive information in the three provinces of Iran, see Malek Afzali, 1992, figures 3–6.

19 Since irregular use decreases reliability of contraceptives, it may be more realistic for families to refill their prescription and have a check-up every two or three months.

20 Women had a more dominant role in deciding the fate of the fetus after conception. Like most aspects of women's history, we do not have much literature indicating the frequency of abortion. All Iranian women in this study, however, including older ones, knew of women who had aborted or attempted to abort, usually using methods and knowledge that stand outside the modern medical system.

21 Cem Behar's study of Turkey (this volume) indicates a similar finding regarding coitus interruptus, which has fallen into policy disfavor despite its prevalence. This phenomenon probably reflects the strong medical bias in most family planning programs.

22 The improvement of infant mortality rates, from about 100 per thousand for the period from 1973 to 1976 (Statistical Center of Iran, 1978) to 40 per thousand for the period from 1990 to 1995 (United Nations, 1993), is due to the government's commitment to providing a minimum level of primary health care (including vaccinations) in rural areas through health houses.

23 Although religious leaders have not directly discussed this matter, a rumor circulated that a fatwa was forthcoming that would declare the

conception of a fourth child under Iran's present socioeconomic condition haram. Interestingly, most criticism of the bill has come from doctors
and medical personnel who raised the ethics of denying medical care to
a fourth child who needs it (*Etala'at*, 1993).

24 Status here refers to indicators such as education, labor market participation, women's rights with respect to marriage, and divorce and custody
laws.

25 The 1986 census listed 2,259 women in engineering (Ramazani, 1993).

26 At a recent government reception, Zahra Shoja'i, advisor on women's
affairs to the home minister, criticized the pale image of women in
elementary textbooks, stating that references to men in school texts are
267 times more frequent than references to women. (*Payam-e-zan*, 1993)

27 Article 28 states: "Every person has the right to pursue the occupation of
his or her choice in so far as this is not contradictory to Islam and the public
interest or the right of others." (*Constitution*, 1992). This has been interpreted in the courts and by the public to mean that a husband has the
right to stop his wife from being employed outside the home (see also
Moghadam, 1993).

28 One should note that these policies were part of a plan to reduce unemployment, where the priority is given to employing men, and have also
been observed in other countries, for instance the United States during the
post–World War II era.

29 Zahra Behrozy, a member of parliament, openly criticized the patriarchal
Iranian culture that prevents full participation of women in the labor
market (*Zan-e-ruz*, 1991).

30 She notes that 18 percent of women in public-sector employment have
higher education, compared to only 6 percent of men.

31 The age of *bolouq* (coming of age) has been specified in the civil code,
article 1210, as fifteen for boys and nine for girls, on the Hijra lunar
calendar. This then has been taken to mean that the minimum age of
marriage for girls is nine. After some unfortunate cases in which young
girls suffered bodily harm because of early intercourse, the government's
position has been that the minimum age for consummation of marriage
is thirteen. However, no legal changes have been made except some
qualifications, such as that a girl should have had her first menstruation
before her first marriage. Nevertheless, if her father or her guardian
marries her off before then, they will not have committed an unlawful act.
Today, however, the Family Planning Board and the Ministry of Public
Health are campaigning to increase the minimum age of marriage for girls
to eighteen.

32 The Marriage Foundation existed on a small scale before the revolution,
because facilitating marriages was deemed to be *savab* (a good deed).
However, after the revolution it became a social pillar of the Islamic

regime, particularly after the war, since the foundation undertook the task of remarrying thousands of young war widows.

33 The percentage of married persons increased despite a sharp escalation in the divorce rate.

34 This is of paramount importance, because, according to religious law, Muslim women do not inherit much from their husbands, and couples keep separate title to their wealth. As a result, a woman who does not have an independent income will not have title to any of the marital property. However, the incorporation of the marital property clause in the official marriage contract has changed women's consciousness in this regard.

35 All six major women's magazines are full of these accounts; national newspapers, radio, and television also cover these interpretations, which are sometimes picked up by government officials and even religious leaders.

36 The gist of this argument is: How can Muslims justify the fact that a woman who marries a man and works hard, managing their money and pinching pennies to improve the material situation of her family, can be divorced and left in the street when she grows old? If Islam has given a man the right to divorce, although divorce is the act most disliked by God, surely the woman has been given the right to enjoy the fruit of her labor in her old age. Therefore, the husband must pay housework wages, as recompense for his wife's work, before he can exercise his right to divorce.

37 Also see Clignet, 1970, Anderton and Emigh, 1989, and Arowolo, 1981 for other discussions of the relationship between fertility behavior and polygynous marriages.

6

Women, Uncertainty, and Reproduction in Morocco

Rahma Bourqia

Despite the substantial decline of the fertility rate in Morocco during the last decade, this phenomenon remains specific to urban areas.[1] The rate of fertility in urban areas declined from 4.38 in 1977 to 2.5 in 1991, a decrease of 42.9 percent in fourteen years, whereas in rural areas it fell from 7.02 to 5.5 in the same period, a decrease of only 21.6 percent (DHS, 1992). These disparities parallel those that exist in levels of education, as the percentage of literacy is much higher in urban centers (63.3 percent) than in rural areas (28.2 percent) (Direction de la Statistique, 1992).

Data on regional differences in fertility levels indicate that for women in poor urban neighborhoods and in rural regions, who represent the majority of women, the fertility rate is still high.[2] A number of socioeconomic and service factors help explain this situation, such as household income, levels of education, and the inaccessibility of health care. In this chapter, I would like to stress the importance of women's perception of children and the social cost that a woman has to bear in exchange for adopting family planning, especially in a culture that defines womanhood as dependent on the reproductive function.

The value of children as a determinant of fertility decision-making has been the subject of a large number of studies carried out in developing societies. Gradual changes in modes of production and the resulting increase in the cost of living in general and the cost of children in particular contribute to our understanding of the demographic transition (Arnold and Fawcett, 1975). But it is clear that decision-making about children is not purely driven by economic considerations. The value of children is not only measured in economic terms but also has social and cultural dimensions (Lorimer, 1954; LeVine and Scrimshaw, 1983), and "economic ends cannot be divorced from social ends" (Caldwell, 1983). A great number of children might be perceived as costly for certain social groups, while for others, children constitute an economic investment. Studies on developing societies have pointed out the contribution of children in the labor force among rural and poor urban communities (Caldwell, 1977). Children carry out tasks in the process of production (Nag, White, and Peet, 1978). They are also perceived as a source of security for old age (Caldwell, 1983).

Moreover, while it has been repeatedly documented that fertility is higher in societies where women are economically dependent (Cain, 1984), it should be noted that the correlation between women's status and fertility is a complex phenomenon. The economic and social costs and benefits of children need to be examined in the context of the household and the community and in light of women's position in the family.

WOMEN FACING UNCERTAINTY

The ethnographic data used in this contribution derive from a study of women and reproduction in four poor neighborhoods in the city of Oujda, in the eastern region of Morocco, close to the Algerian border. Most of the inhabitants of these neighborhoods immigrated from the surrounding peasant and pastoral tribes. In-depth interviews were conducted with 133 illiterate housewives aged between fifteen and forty-nine and living in the suburbs of the city. Through these interviews, as well as through the observation of rituals related to reproduction and fertility, the aim was to understand women's attitudes and knowledge on issues such as family planning, sterility, childbearing, and child-rearing (Bourqia, 1992).

In listening to women I have studied and to the words they use to talk about their future and about children, I realized that women show a certain anxiety, especially those who do not have children. The word *zman* (time) is often used by women when speaking about property, life in general, problems, and the unforeseeable, to evoke the feeling of anxiety caused by uncertainty.

In Morocco, as in other countries, uncertainty is pervasive (Berque, 1974). It is a threat not only to women but also to the peasant's crop, livestock, and to individual destiny and progeny as well. Although this uncertainty is an inherent part of both the natural and the social world, its impact is stronger on women than on men, on the poor than on the rich, and on rural people than on the urban. The distribution of risk in society reflects that of power and status (Douglas, 1985). Indeed, the social groups at the lowest levels of the social hierarchy are most confronted with risk and uncertainty. Hazard and risk are seen as part of the unknown *(ghayb)*, and therefore a matter of God's will. Man has no grip over the course of events belonging to the future. "Everything is in the hands of God," women keep saying. From this perception stems an attitude which is expressed through the well-known Moroccan proverb "*Mnin yzid nsimmiwah Sa'id*" (When he is born, we'll call him Said). This means it is useless to name a baby before it is born, or that it is useless to try to foresee the future. This apparent fatalism expressed in men's and women's discourse does not, however, prevent women from developing strategies to face the future. They are constantly trying to deal with the risks that confront them and those that threaten other women. Divorce, repudiation, early death of the husband, the husband taking a second wife are all threats that press heavily on a woman's life.

Among women we have studied, marriage is a source of protection and security against shame and material needs. A woman who remains single becomes the target of gossip in the community, her behavior is watched and scrutinized by neighbors and the male members of her family. Moroccan dialect, in fact, has a pejorative term—*bayra*—to refer to a woman who cannot find a husband. The husband is expected to provide for the needs of his home, defend it, and work for his children. Poor women are not supposed to go out to work, and although many women do, they consider it as an act performed out of extreme necessity, and they do not feel any pride in doing so. The discourse of women and men on the family and on gender shows that the husband is the head of the family and is primarily responsible for it. This is further reinforced by the *Mudawwana* (Personal Status Code), which states that the husband should provide for all of his wife's material needs.

But marriage brings with it its own uncertainties. Women perceive themselves as being weak and vulnerable in marriage. Divorce, death of the husband, adultery, or polygyny are real as well as potential threats facing them, and constitute sources of risk and uncertainty. Most women say that a woman should not trust her husband, since he might have extra-marital relationships. Male adultery is tolerated by women, because they believe that man's nature and inability to control his sexual desires are different from woman's.

Divorce is negatively perceived not only because it is the result of a bad experience but also because of its negative social impact. In general, a woman does not seek divorce unless her marriage becomes extremely difficult to bear. According to a study carried out in 1987 in Rabat and Casablanca (Direction de la Statistique, 1989, 1990), the average age of women at the time of divorce is thirty, and most of the divorces happen during the three first years of marriage. Fifty percent of divorces happen to couples without children. Children are perceived as the most important tie binding the husband to his wife, and also as a means to keep the husband from leaving his wife. Since the authority to divorce is in the hands of the husband, a woman who wishes to divorce must resort to a form of divorce known as *khol'*.[3] The woman in effect 'buys' herself back from her husband by giving him material compensation, and he is in a position to negotiate a higher payment in exchange for his consent to divorce.

Polygyny is another indicator of the privilege of the Moroccan husband. Allowed by religion and by law, polygyny continues to be a threat to married women. In our survey in the city of Oujda, we asked about the reasons behind polygyny. The overwhelming reason was seen to be related to reproduction; indeed 75 percent of women answered that a man has to marry a second wife when the first one is old or sterile.[4]

Although polygyny is on the decline for economic and cultural reasons,[5] many men continue to repeat that shari'a law gives them the right to marry four wives. Among the women we interviewed, 15 percent were in a polygynous situation at given periods of their lives. Paradoxically, the relationship between the wives within the same household can be one of complicity and rivalry at the same time. Complicity between the wives is necessary to face the authority of the husband, and they cooperate in organizing the activities in the household and the sexual relationship with their husband according to what they call the *nuba* (literally: taking turns). In the domain of reproduction, however, rivalries appear, as each wife tries to have more children than the others and thus attempts to gain the favors of the husband. Because children are their only capital, sterility makes women especially vulnerable.

Another source of uncertainty comes from the fact that a lot of women do not have access to durable goods such as land, houses, or livestock, even though shari'a law has replaced customary law since independence.[6] In general, women do not inherit as much land as a man does, although they participate in the production process, and they do not own the animals or buy and sell them, although they have access to the milk of animals or their wool, and are involved in raising poultry, turkeys, or rabbits. Similarly, in urban areas, most women do not own property: within the family, the house and other real estate are owned by the husband.

The system of inheritance thus constitutes another source of uncertainty for women. The laws regulating inheritance are in favor of the man, who always inherits more than the woman. The Personal Status Code endows the woman with the right to inherit only half the share of her brother. In practice, however, a lot of women do not even claim this right, and leave their share of inheritance to their brothers or husbands. Except for some educated and professional women in the cities, the majority of women leave the management of property to their husbands or brothers.

Faced with a situation of potential insecurity, women have developed strategies to negotiate a better position despite socio-cultural constraints. For example, because they have less access to durable goods, women invest in gold and jewelry. These are valued both as ornament and as a capital that can be used in the future in case of extreme necessity. However, the most important investment and capital for women is to have children.

CHILDREN: A STRATEGY OF INVESTMENT

When I asked women about the ideal number of children, the majority said four or five. Having children gives the woman a role within the family, and her reproductive function strengthens her social status and defines her existence as a woman. Socially and psychologically, this function constitutes for the woman a source of equilibrium and dignity.

Moreover, the reproductive function of the woman is also a strategy to face uncertainty. There is a rationale behind this attitude. A woman perceives her children as a capital or as an investment which can be used at different phases of her life cycle, especially when she ages. Responses to the question "Why does a woman want to have a lot of children?" varied, but they shared the sense that children are an insurance against risk and a source of prestige for parents. One of the most frequent answers was that "women have children for *zman*," meaning women have children to face up to uncertainty. Having children is perceived by the woman as the best way to keep the husband, as expressed in the Moroccan saying, "Children break the wings of the husband."

Women are quite explicit about the importance of children for security in old age. Motherhood represents an opportunity to become a mother-in-law and to gain power in the household, and having children is like accumulating capital that could be converted into material income in the future. As was pointed out by a woman commenting on the fact she had six children, "Having no education and no savings for retirement, my children are my savings." Women often refer to education in their answers because they are aware that it could promote their status and improve their social condition.[7] Most of them say that being deprived of education makes them feel inferior to educated women who earn money and who can afford to adopt family planning.

Moreover, women distinguish children who are good (*durya salha* or *duryat lahlal*) from those who are bad (*durya fasda*). Good children are those who satisfy their parents, especially their mothers, by being obedient and caring for them, and who give, through respect and financial support, a return on the capital that their mother invested in them. Such expectations are supported by religious beliefs that emphasize the respect owed to parents, as in the *hadith* that states "Heaven is under the feet of mothers," and the belief that when a mother dies during childbirth she goes directly to heaven.

The reproductive function of the mother is thus sacred, and obliges children to show constant respect. This sacredness is symbolized in Moroccan culture by the breast-feeding of the child. Like any other gift, breast milk implies a reciprocity that binds the children to the mother. Another symbol of the vital line between mothers and children is the liver. In Moroccan culture, children are symbolized by the liver, which is considered central to human anatomy. Any harm done to the children is consequently done to the mother's liver, and suffering inflicted upon a mother through separation from her children is commonly expressed in the language as "the burning of the liver." A mother invests a lot of sentiment in her children in order to ensure that they provide her the affection and protection she will need when she ages.

Children owe a debt to their parents and live with the feeling that they are not able to repay it totally. When parents provide their children with education, these must return their debt by providing for the needs of their parents when they become old. Women explicitly use the language of religion to try to keep their children's loyalty and care. The notion of *sakht* (curse) and *rda* (benediction) are used by mothers as a punishment or a reward for the behavior of their children, and these notions are strengthened by the belief that the benediction of a mother is equivalent to that of God.

THE VALUE OF THE CHILD

Asked if they prefer to have female or male children, most women answered that they do not have any preference because children are a gift from God whether male or female. However, birth rituals, common beliefs, and the discourse of women about their children show that culture and society give some preference to the male child. Rituals of birth emphasize the difference between a girl and a boy: the birth of a boy is always announced with strident vocal sounds that accompany every happy event, while the birth of a girl is announced with silence. Women who visit a mother who has just given birth show more joy if the newborn is a boy *('azri)*.

This preference, however, changes with the life cycle, as expressed in a popular saying about God's blessing to children. It is believed that when a girl is born she has one *hasana* (blessing or bonus given by God to a good Muslim), whereas a male child is born with one hundred hasanas. As a girl grows up, she gains more hasanas until she has one hundred, whereas a boy gradually loses his hasanas until he is left with only one. This acknowledges that a boy comes to this world with an advantage which he loses over his lifetime, while a girl is born with a disadvantage, but gains the benediction of God because she gives birth to children.

Although women say that there is no difference between having a girl or a boy, male children represent a real investment to them. Female children have less value because they are always "given away" in the matrimonial exchange and lost to their families, while boys are always expected to take over the role of custodian and protector of the family. Male children raise a woman's status and give her more power in her everyday life as well as in negotiations with her husband. The laws regulating inheritance reinforce this attitude.[8] In the case of the death of the husband, a woman who has only girls is threatened by the fact that the most important part of the inheritance can be claimed in accordance with the law by her husband's family.

THE AMBIVALENCE OF WOMEN AND THE CONTRADICTIONS OF SOCIETY

While children are clearly valued for the security they represent, it is also true that women are aware that there are advantages to having fewer children. This ambivalence, which reflects the contradictions of a society in transition, is found in the domain of reproductive decision-making. The majority of women are not opposed to family planning—most of them have tried contraceptive methods—and are conscious of the link between large numbers of children and poverty. Having a great number of children is referred to pejoratively as having *bez* (brats) or *jrad* (locusts).

But although women are generally aware of all the advantages of reducing the number of their children, this strategy is a risky one, especially for those who belong to low social categories. Small families are advertised as ideal by family planning programs and by the media, but for a woman who is not educated, and who has no source of income, adopting this ideal represents a risk. The equivalence of children and education is expressed by a woman commenting on the fact that she had seven children: "I have no education," meaning that she invested in her children instead.

At the same time, however, children are becoming costly. Education, health, and nutrition absorb a large part of a family's income, and there are problems related to the exclusion of the majority of children from the educational system and to increasing unemployment. Women have come to realize that by reducing the number of children, they reduce costs automatically. But this comes at a price. Children still represent for an illiterate woman, for a housewife, and for the one who has no source of income, a social capital to face the future.

Underlying the language used by mothers when talking about their children is a kind of rationality built around the vocabulary of political economy. Children are considered as *ras al-mal* (capital) that might bring in *rbah* (profit) or *khsara* (loss). The first type of profit is material. All the effort women make to have children should be rewarded by the children when they grow up, thus repaying their debt toward their mothers. The second type of profit is the one gained with God. Women gain *ajr* (benefit) from God by having children. This is why even when mothers are disappointed by children who do not recognize their debt, they compensate by gaining the blessing of God.

One may compare women's attitude toward fertility to what is known as the Pascalian wager.[9] Women choose to have a minimum of four or five children so that some of these children will take care of them in their old age. If the children do not, these women will have lost very little. If on the other hand they choose not to have any children, they cannot benefit from the potential reward children would have brought them.

CONCLUSION

The continuing success of fertility reduction policies in Morocco depends in large part on the extent to which socioeconomic conditions improve; where they do not, women will continue to face the dilemma of choosing between the advantage of the lower cost of smaller families and the potential of a strategy of a large family, which makes them deal with uncertainty. If the population policy is not adequately carried out—in the sense of being imbedded in global development policy—it might appear to yield positive results by decreasing the evolution of the rate of fertility in the short term, while in the long term it might create a reverse process of involution and traditionalization of society. In other words, development can be a source of frustration and may not always satisfy all the needs of the different groups in society, which results in a return to traditions.

REFERENCES

Arnold, F. and J. Fawcett. 1975. *The value of children: A cross-national study.* Honolulu: East West Center.

Berque, J. 1974. Maghreb: Histoire et société. Gembloux: Duculot.

Bourqia, R. 1992. The woman's body: Strategy of illness and fertility in Morocco. In I. Sirageldin and R. Davis, eds., *Towards more efficacy in women's health and child survival strategies: Combining knowledge for practical solutions.* Baltimore: Johns Hopkins University.

———. 1994. *Femmes et fécundité.* Casablanca: Editions Afrique Orient.

Cain, M. 1984. *Women's status and fertility in developing countries: Son preference and economic security.* World Bank Staff Working Paper, no. 682. Population and Development Series, no. 7. Washington, D.C.: World Bank.

Caldwell, J. C. 1977. The economic rationality of high fertility: An investigation illustrated with Nigeria survey data. *Population Studies.* 31/1:5–27.

———. 1983. Direct economic costs and benefits of children. In R. Bulatao and R. Lee, eds., *Determinants of fertility in developing countries: A summary of knowledge.* Washington, D.C.: National Academy Press.

DHS. 1989. *Enquête nationale sur la planification familiale, la fécondité et la santé au Maroc (ENPS) 1987.* Rabat: Ministry of Public Health.

Direction de la Statistique. 1989. *Les mariages et les divorces: wilaya de Rabat.* Rabat: Direction de la Statistique, Centre d'Etudes et de Recherches Démographiques (CERED).

———. 1990. *Les mariages et les divorces: wilaya de Casablanca.* Casablanca: Direction de la Statistique, CERED.

———. 1992. *Niveaux de vie des menages: 1990–1991, premiers résultats.* Vol. 1, Rapport de Synthèse. Rabat: Direction de la Statistique.

Direction de la Statistique and CERED. 1992. *Fécondité, infécondité et nouvelles tendences démographiques au Maroc.* Rabat: Ministry of Planning, Direction de la Statistique.

Douglas, M. 1985. *Risk and acceptability according to social sciences.* New York: Russel Sage Foundation.

Lacoste-Dujardin, C. 1987. Fécondité et contraception au Maghreb. *The Maghreb Review.* 12/5–6:130–35.

LeVine, A. R. and S. C. Scrimshaw. 1983. Effects of culture on fertility: Anthropological contributions. In R. Bulatao and R. Lee, eds., *Determinants of fertility in developing countries: A summary of knowledge.* Washington, D.C.: National Academy Press.

Lorimer, F. 1954. *Culture and human fertility: A study of the relation of cultural conditions to fertility in non-industrial and transitional societies.* Zurich: UNESCO.

Nag, M., N. F. B. White, and R. C. Peet. 1978. An anthropological approach to the study of the economic value of children in Java and Nepal. *Current Anthropology.* 19/2:293–306.

Russo, F. 1968. Blaise Pascal. In *Encyclopedia Universalis.* Paris: Editions Encyclopedia Universalis.

Schultz, T. W., ed. 1973. *Economics of the family: Marriage, children and human capital.* Chicago: The University of Chicago Press.

NOTES

1 Since 1966, the Moroccan government has adopted a birth control policy, and in 1971 the Association Marocaine de la Planification Familiale was founded. In 1976, the program of family planning came to be supervised by the Ministry of Public Health and integrated within a broader health program.

2 The lowest rate of fertility is found in cities where the percentage of literacy is high, as in Rabat (3.45) and Casablanca (4.01). By contrast, in towns located in a rural environment and lacking in economic resources, like Chefchaouen, Ouarzazate, or Errachidia (7.96, 7.96, and 7.16, respectively), the rate is higher.

3 Husbands are usually reluctant to divorce because of the financial consequences they have to face when initiating divorce.

4 Twelve percent said that there is no particular reason that would push a man to remarry, 5 percent evoked the disobedience of the first wife as a major reason, 2 percent blamed it on Satan, 1 percent said that laziness of the first wife is the cause, and 5 percent said that money entices a man to have a second wife.

5 Husbands find it more and more difficult to provide for the material needs of more than one wife. This decline is probably due as well to the new image of the ideal monogamous couple spread by films and television.

6 In some Berber regions of Morocco during the pre-colonial and colonial periods before 1956, women were not allowed to inherit land so that land property could be kept for the family and within the village or the tribe.

7 The literacy level of women is far lower than that of men. The rate of literacy is 76.5 percent among urban men, 45.3 percent among rural men; and 51.4 percent among urban women, 12.3 percent among rural women (Direction de la Statistique, 1992).

8 A girl inherits only half the share of the boy according to Islamic law, as well as to the Moroccan Personal Status Code. Moreover, after the death of their father, female children who have no brothers share inheritance with uncles and grandparents from the father's side.

9 This argument of Pascal, derived from his book *Les pensées,* is that we believe in the existence of God not because there is logic behind it, but because it is to our interest to believe. The faith implies that if God exists, the believer wins; if not, there is nothing to lose by believing (Russo, 1968).

7

Women's Autonomy and Gender Roles in Egyptian Families

Laila Nawar, Cynthia B. Lloyd, Barbara Ibrahim

The international dialogue over what constitutes appropriate population policy hinges on concepts whose universal applicability across cultures and social settings have not been closely examined. These concepts of 'choice,' 'rights,' and 'individual autonomy' are especially problematic when they are employed according to purely Western understandings. Yet it is important to analyze their relevance for understanding the behavior of women and men around the world and for evaluating the way in which country-specific policies interact with individual and family realities.

This paper attempts to refine an understanding of personal autonomy as it applies to the lives of women—particularly married women—in contemporary Egypt. In doing so, we consider the cultural dimensions of gender relations as they were traditionally understood and as they are currently being modified by the social and economic realities of everyday life. The paper draws on recent data to link this profile of women's autonomy to some of the assumptions underlying population programs in Egypt.

Population policy in Egypt, in its pursuit of lower levels of population growth and fertility, has been primarily targeted at women as clients through the national family planning program. Women have been looked to as agents of change and leaders of the demographic transition, despite the fact that, within the traditional Egyptian family, men are expected to have most of the decision-making authority and women are assumed to have relatively little personal autonomy. To be effective, population policy must be based on a realistic view of family dynamics and women's role within the family. Are Egyptian policy makers, most of whom are men, expecting too much of women, given current patterns? Do they assume changes in women's ability to influence husbands and/or act autonomously that a conventional view of the Egyptian family fails to reflect?

It is clear from a number of studies and observations that the Egyptian family is indeed changing in response to a variety of influences, both external and indigenous. At the same time that education, economic transformation, and modern communication bring new ideas into the smallest village, a trend toward religious conservatism sends contradictory messages rejecting change and calling for a return to more traditional social arrangements. In the midst of these counter-pressures, women and men continue to pursue their daily lives, making whatever adaptations they see as desirable or necessary to meet their basic needs and fulfill their aspirations.

While facts about women's fertility and their practice of family planning abound, until very recently much less attention had been paid in demographic and economic surveys to the actual extent of women's personal autonomy. Outside of small-scale ethnographic studies, little was known about the roles of men and women within the home in terms of decision-making and domestic responsibilities, including child-rearing (Hoodfar, 1988; Singerman and Hoodfar, forthcoming). Fortunately, two recent surveys—the 1991 Characteristics of House-holds and the Role of Egyptian Women in the Family (ROWIF) (CAPMAS, 1991) and the 1988 Demographic and Health Survey (DHS, 1988)—have devoted considerable attention to these issues, and these data provide the basis for an assessment of women's autonomy and gender roles within the family in contemporary Egypt.[1]

The paper begins with some background on Egyptian women's marriage patterns and household living arrangements, followed by a discussion of the concept of autonomy and its various dimensions. Subsequent sections explore several aspects of women's autonomy, starting with early familial influences on the development of autonomy and proceeding to more contemporary assessments of women's gender awareness and views on autonomy, their role in family decision-making, and more overt manifestations of autonomous behavior (in particular, participation in the formal labor force). The discussion of autonomy concludes with an overall assessment of Egyptian women's level of autonomy as expressed in an autonomy index. The final portion of the paper looks at gender roles within the family in relation to women's autonomy and includes a discussion of possible implications of differing levels of autonomy for the fertility preferences and behavior of Egyptian women.

Throughout this paper, we focus on currently married women, for both practical and strategic reasons. Firstly, as will be seen below, the great majority of Egyptian women are currently married. Secondly, the strong social and religious sanctions against non-marital cohabitation mean that unmarried couples who live together are not a significant category, as they would be in some European, African, or Western settings. Thirdly, Egyptian family planning programs are addressed exclusively to married women. Finally, it is difficult to formulate and assess questions about (relative) autonomy and gender roles if a man is not present in the home.

THE SETTING: MARRIAGE PATTERNS AND HOUSEHOLD LIVING ARRANGEMENTS

According to the 1992 Demographic and Health Survey, women can expect to spend 71 percent of their reproductive years (ages fifteen to forty-nine) married.[2] There was virtually no change in the prevalence of marriage among women of reproductive age since 1980.[3] During the peak childbearing years, between the ages of twenty-five and thirty-four, 90 percent of Egyptian women are currently married (DHS, 1993). A continuing rise in the age at marriage is reflected in a slight increase in the proportion of a woman's reproductive years spent single (from 19 to 22 percent). Probably because of declines in mortality and delays in the initiation of marriage, there has been a small increase in the percentage of ever-married women who are still in their first marriage at the end of their reproductive years (from 73 to 77 percent). The most notable change in marriage patterns is a decline in the proportion of women remarrying: of women aged forty to forty-nine whose first marriage ended due to divorce or widowhood, the proportion who remarry declined from 48 to 38 percent between 1980 and 1988.[4]

The data presented in Table 1 show that, among all households that include married women, the nuclear family represents the dominant feature among Egyptian household types (84 percent).[5] The enlarged nuclear family type and the extended family type comprise the remaining 16 percent of all households.[6] The enlarged nuclear household is an adaptation of the nuclear type, whereas the extended family household is more complex in structure, often encompassing several families. Only 4 percent of households that included married women are identified as female-headed (not shown in the table), with the majority of nuclear-type households containing two generations and the majority of other household types containing three genera-

Table 1
Household type by selected characteristics[a]

| Selected household characteristics | Household type | | | Total |
	Nuclear[b]	Enlarged nuclear[c]	Extended[d]	
Average no. of residents	4.9	7.0	8.2	5.4
Distribution by residence (percentage)				
Urban	87	7	6	100
Rural	76	12	12	100
Number of generations (percentage)				
1	11	2	0	9
2	89	27	14	78
3+	–	71	86	13
Education among married women in households (percentage)				
Illiterate	61	65	80	63
Primary+[e]	30	28	12	27
Average SLI[f]	3.7	3.0	2.6	3.5
Percentage distribution	84	8	8	100
Number of households	1,240	126	118	1,484

Source: CAPMAS, 1991
[a]Only households that include married women
[b]Consists of husband, wife, and unmarried children; married couples with no children; or a single parent with unmarried children
[c]Is an extension of the nuclear family by including any immediate dependents (parents or unmarried brothers or sisters) related to the head of household
[d]Contains any kin resident other than immediate dependents within the nuclear family
[e]Attained primary education level or higher
[f]Standard of Living Index: quality of flooring (wood, tiles, marble, waxed plastic=1), kitchen inside house (yes=1), toilet facilities (modern=2, traditional with or without tank=1, other=0), drinking-water tap inside home (yes=1), hot-water heater (yes=1), car or video player (yes=2), color television (yes=1)

tions. Even in rural areas, over three-fourths of these households are nuclear. This reflects the tendency in contemporary Egypt for couples, urban or rural, to live apart from other family members.

As might be expected, nuclear-type households show the highest standard of living on average and extended family households show the lowest (see Table 1).[7] This is likely to reflect a preference for the greater privacy allowed by nuclear living arrangements that become more attainable as incomes rise. It is also interesting to note that a higher percentage of married women in extended-family households are illiterate (80 percent, as against 61 percent in nuclear households). Furthermore, 70 percent of nuclear households contain young children under the age of twelve, whereas only 48 percent of extended-family households do. This pattern suggests that most young couples achieve residential independence at marriage. The presence of an older generation in the household may come at a later point in the family-building process, possibly when a member of the older generation joins the household because of the death or departure of a spouse.

Two pieces of evidence suggest that the proportion of Egyptian households with extended families is continuing to decrease over time. Younger women are less likely than older women to have been raised in extended-family households (12 versus 19 percent). Furthermore, households of the extended type represent 22 percent of households of origin but only 17 percent of current households of residence.[8] The dominance and increasing prevalence of the nuclear household justifies our primary focus on the conjugal relationship in studying various aspects of women's autonomy.

THE CONCEPT OF AUTONOMY

The concept of personal autonomy is multifaceted, encompassing elements of individual temperament, past experience, and social conditioning. Autonomy is likewise displayed in a variety of contexts, ranging from decision-making within the family to personal independence of judgment and action. In recognition of this complexity, our study looks at a number of components of autonomy that appear to have relevance in the lives of Egyptian women. The following working definition of autonomy guided this study: personal autonomy is the ability to think and act independently of others to achieve one's goals or intentions.

Expressions of autonomy go beyond simple traits of personality or personal preference. Autonomy is conditioned by the fact that all human behavior is embedded in economic and institutional systems, social norms and influence, and personal interconnections. Therefore, the extent to which any individual achieves personal autonomy is highly relative to his or her social context. In all societies, gender is an important dimension of social differentiation but many other factors such as age, income, ethnicity, and religion can be factors as well. Indeed, the importance of gender as an independent determinant of levels of autonomy will also be conditioned by the relative importance of these other factors.

Given systematic differences between men and women in the division of social responsibilities, access to resources, and distribution of economic rewards, sexual, marital, and kin relationships have typically had more centrality to women's lives than to men's. As a result, the factors that need to be considered in assessing women's autonomy are not the same as those that might be used to assess variations among men in their autonomy. Various dimensions of their scope for independent action within marriage become important to measuring their autonomy. For example, Dyson and Moore (1983), in their analysis of female autonomy in India, included measures of women's ability to negotiate sexual relationships, to own property in their own right, and to associate freely with their own family after marriage to assess women's ability to manipulate their own personal environment. Doan and Bisharat (1990), in their study of female autonomy and children's nutritional status in Jordan, saw women's structural position within the household as a good indicator of their relative autonomy.

When looking at autonomy in terms of gender, a further complication arises in that the very definitions of appropriate gender behavior proscribe or encourage autonomy (Unger and Crawford, 1992). For example, in the psychology literature, theories about women's development often highlight the centrality of interpersonal connections in women's lives, contrasting the concept of affiliation with the concept of autonomy (Berlin and Johnson, 1989). Furthermore, in nearly all cultures, women are socialized to express lower levels of autonomy than men, even when their actual behavior suggests otherwise.

To add a further level of complexity, cultures differ in the extent to which autonomy is valued and sought as a social 'good.' Contemporary Western societies may equate autonomy with power, independence, and privacy, all of which are highly valued. Non-Western

societies, including Egypt, often place higher value on social interdependence and the support and status achieved from belonging to a
group. Even in these settings, however, there is tacit recognition that
the ability to carry out one's intentions is desirable, though it may be
expressed in terms of 'influence' as opposed to 'autonomy.'

THE EXTENT OF WOMEN'S AUTONOMY

For all of the above considerations, it is important to give close
attention to the particular social and cultural context in which women's
personal autonomy is expressed. In this study, we take advantage of
two recent surveys to look at several factors that may serve as
proximate indicators of autonomy. To do so, we have broken down the
concept of autonomy into several parts. These include items relating
to early life experiences that may later shape a woman's sense of
controlling outcomes, those having to do with independence of
opinion and gender awareness, items reflecting ability to act independently, and those relating to negotiated decision-making within the
family. One aspect of the ability to act independently—namely,
whether or not a woman works outside the home—is given special
consideration. In interpreting our findings, note must be taken of the
fact that the survey data consist of self-reports of women interviewed
by strangers in a society not accustomed to voicing individual opinions. Other studies in Egypt suggest that survey respondents tend to
report agreement with the cultural norms of their society, even when
those norms are at odds with actual behavior. For example, a woman
may tell an interviewer that it is a husband's right to stop his wife from
working, and later in the survey she will report that she actually works
outside the home despite her husband's strong objections (Tessler *et
al.*, 1985). This awareness makes us cautious about drawing firm
conclusions regarding behavior from opinion questions. At the same
time, it strengthens our conviction that when women do state views
that deviate from the norm, these in fact represent important information about diversity among women and changing attitudes in present-
day Egypt.

Early familial influences on autonomy
One important dimension of autonomy is personal mastery or efficacy, the sense of being able to control the outcome of events in one's

everyday life. Research findings suggest that mastery is acquired early in life as a result of childhood and teenage experience. Our data allow us to examine two areas of experience for young girls: school-leaving and the selection of a marriage partner.

A large proportion of Egyptian women are illiterate and never attended school. For those women who did start school, however, but were obliged to drop out, "family objections" are the most frequently mentioned reason for doing so (30 percent). Another 20 percent left school in order to get married and 20 percent left because of the "difficulty" of school (CAPMAS, 1991). If reasons for dropping out are compared by age, however, it is apparent that "family objections" are less important now than in the past. While 44 percent of women over age forty left school due to family pressures, that proportion is only 16 percent for women under thirty. For this younger age group, marriage and the difficulty of school are more frequently mentioned as reasons that led them to end their formal education. To the extent that family objections appear to be declining from earlier high levels, one might conjecture that girls are gaining more say in the decision to continue or leave school. However, leaving school in order to marry is gaining in importance as girls remain in school longer.

Indeed, marriage is the first nearly universal life event for which we have information about women's autonomy, and this concerns the choice of spouse and whether or not the spouse is a relative. Traditionally in Egypt, contact between unmarried men and women is restricted, and family members initiate marriage arrangements on behalf of both partners. In practice, the girl's involvement in choosing her spouse can range from a forced match to one in which she selects a man unknown to other members of the family. These are extremes, however, and most Egyptian marriages involve some pre-selection of suitable partners by family members, with the girl's consent in the final choice.

Table 2 shows that a majority of currently married Egyptian women were not primarily responsible for selecting the man they married. Regardless of education level, age at marriage, or household type, most Egyptian women form marriages based on a choice made by relatives rather than making an independent decision of their own. However, both the age at which a woman marries and her education level affect the likelihood that she will have a stronger voice in the decision. For women who married below the age of sixteen (which in

Egypt is the legal minimum age of marriage for girls), the likelihood is roughly one in ten that the woman chose her husband. For women who married over the age of twenty-five, on the other hand, the likelihood reaches 40 percent. Those women most likely to have chosen their husbands have ten or more years of schooling (46 percent). This is consistent with the fact that these women had more opportunity for contact with young men beyond the family network and also had achieved higher status from their higher education.

Marriage to a relative (often a first cousin) is both reasonably common (29 percent of currently married Egyptian women are

Table 2
Marriage arrangements of Egyptian women by selected characteristics

Variable	Marriage arranged by self (percentage)	Married to relative (percentage)	Sample size	
			n[a]	%
Current age				
<30	32	31	459	29.1
30–39	26	27	498	31.5
40–49	18	28	325	20.6
50+	10	28	297	18.8
Age at marriage				
<16	11	35	335	21.1
16–19	18	33	591	37.3
20–24	31	25	460	29.0
25–29	40	15	162	10.2
30+	31	17	36	0.2
Household type				
Nuclear	25	25	1,078	72.7
Enlarged nuclear	31	30	120	8.1
Extended	18	40	284	19.2
Education years				
None	16	33	1,005	63.6
<6[b]	22	26	137	8.7
6–9	28	27	155	9.8
10+	46	15	282	17.9
Type of marriage				
Relation	19	n/a	452	28.6
Non-relation	25	n/a	1,127	71.4
Total	23	29	1,579	100.0

Source: CAPMAS, 1991
[a]The sample size for individual categories is sometimes less than the total because of missing values on a particular variable. In the case of household type, the sample size is the number of households rather than the number of women
[b]Includes some women with informal education

married to relatives) and traditionally desirable in Egypt.[9] There is some evidence from our data that women exercise less personal autonomy in selecting a husband when they are married to a relative, but the differences are not substantial. While 25 percent of women in non-relation marriages had the primary say in choosing a marriage partner, 19 percent of women in relational marriages had the primary say. Furthermore, women married at the youngest age are much more likely to be married to a relative (35 percent) than women married in their late twenties (17 percent).

These findings suggest possibly contradictory trends. On the one hand, family members appear to have less control than in the past over their daughters in terms of school dropout and selection of a marriage partner. At the same time, however, many women continue to marry within the family. This apparent conflict exemplifies the coexistence of traditional and modern practices observed at many levels of developing societies.

Women's views on autonomy and awareness of gender issues
Information on the extent to which women express autonomy in their personal opinions about the need to seek their husband's approval, the appropriate reasons for women's income-producing work, and their knowledge of women's rights provide a sense of the degree to which women are able to both think and act alone, independent of husbands or others. For each of these dimensions for which data were collected in the 1991 survey, we look at the association with important background variables such as age, education, household type, and socio-economic standing.

Married women were asked whether it is important for a woman to seek her husband's approval on every matter or decision. Since this kind of question should be answered in the affirmative according to customary norms in Egypt, it provides a good indicator of movement away from those normative expectations. Overall, only 10 percent said that it is not always important to seek the husband's approval (see Table 3). The relationship between this measure of autonomy and education, employment status, and standard of living is in the expected direction, but in all cases the overwhelming majority of women felt the need to seek their husbands' approval. For women who said approval is not always necessary, a further question was asked about the areas in which they could act without seeking their husband's approval. Again, only a small percentage of women gave positive

Table 3
Attitudes toward personal autonomy among married women
(percentage answering 'yes')

Variable	Woman should always seek husband's approval	I know about women's rights	Work is important for women's personal fulfillment[a]	Sample size n[b]	%
Current age					
<30	94	19	22	459	29.1
30–39	88	26	26	498	31.5
40–49	86	21	27	325	20.6
50+	91	18	21	297	18.8
Household type					
Nuclear	89	24	26	1,078	72.7
Enlarged nuclear	93	27	27	120	8.1
Extended	95	8	15	284	19.2
Education (years)					
None	94	8	16	1,005	63.6
<6[c]	90	23	29	137	8.7
6–9	83	41	38	155	9.8
10+	81	59	45	282	17.9
Standard of Living Index[d]					
Low	94	11	18	690	43.7
Medium	87	24	25	553	35.0
High	86	39	36	336	21.3
Total	90	21	24	1,579	100.0

Source: CAPMAS, 1991
[a]Percentage of women who gave at least one out of the following answers: to acquire
social status, to acquire self-confidence, to gain economic independence
[b]See note a in Table 2
[c]Includes some women with informal education   [d]See note f in Table 1

answers. In the area of visiting family or friends, urban residence had
a strong positive influence on women's sense of independence and
tended to neutralize the effects of education levels; that is, urban
women are relatively autonomous when it comes to visiting, even if
they are not well educated. In fact, illiterate urban women are more
likely than highly educated women overall to say they can go visiting
without seeking their husband's approval—48 percent compared with
41 percent (not shown in the table). By contrast, the proportion of rural
women in all education categories who say they can visit without
approval is negligible.

Even though only a small percentage of Egyptian women actually
participate in the work force, all women express opinions about the
reasons women should work outside the home (or at home for pay).
They tend to believe that the legitimate reasons for working outside

the home are connected to economic necessity and helping the family financially. And, in fact, a majority of women who are working for an income state that they do so out of economic necessity. Given this overall context, it is interesting to look at the proportion of women who believe that outside work is primarily an avenue to greater personal independence.

In the 1991 ROWIF survey, women were asked to choose one or two reasons for the importance or value of work for women from a list of seven possible answers. Twenty-four percent mentioned "to acquire social status," "to acquire self-confidence," or "to gain economic independence" as answers. The more typical answers included "financial need," "family's wish," "husband's wish," or "to raise the economic standard of the family." Nonetheless, education was highly associated with attitudes about the importance of work: only 16 percent of illiterate women mentioned reasons for work linked to autonomy, while 45 percent of those with a secondary-level education and above did so. As was the case for other aspects of autonomy, education is strongly associated with the expression of more personal rather than collective interests.

Table 3 also gives information about an aspect of autonomy related to gender awareness. Married women were asked whether they were "aware of women's rights within personal status and political laws." Only 21 percent answered "yes." As would be expected, knowledge of women's rights was associated with higher education levels and with increased socioeconomic status. This is one dimension of potential autonomy (at least of attitude or awareness) in which there is considerable variation among women in the sample.

Autonomous behavior

The preceding discussion focused on aspects of women's knowledge and opinions. We now turn to some areas in which personal autonomy may be expressed through actual behavior. These include data on whether and to what degree married women were able to act independently in matters of leisure, civic participation, and health-seeking behavior.

We expected to find variation, for example, in the types of women who participate in cultural, social, or political associations in Egypt. There is a long tradition of volunteerism in the country, with over ten thousand local and national associations: even rural women presumably have access to membership in their local community development

Table 4
Aspects of autonomous behavior (percentage answering 'yes'; n=1,579)

Variable	Education				Work Status	
	None	<6[a]	6–9	10+	No	Yes
Member of association	0	1	1	18	0	18
Care for personal appearance at home	33	58	63	84	42	65
Care for personal appearance outside	40	67	73	92	51	76
Watch weight	2	8	16	27	6	19
Do sports/walk	2	7	12	24	6	17
Care for proper nutrition	15	23	30	44	21	31
Take outings/picnics	9	23	35	53	16	41
Care for own health as much as for children and husband	44	45	41	50	46	42
Have regular medical check-up	8	16	17	17	11	14

Source: CAPMAS, 1991
[a]Includes some women with informal education

association. In fact, among this sample of women, participation in any type of association is extremely rare. Even among women with a high school education, those participating in an association constituted only 18 percent (see Table 4). Of all women reporting association membership, 96 percent have a secondary school degree or higher and 92 percent are urban residents. It appears that the efforts to involve rural women in community associations has had limited success, at least in the case of married women. We are unsure, however, whether this pattern reflects low autonomy or not, since an alternative interpretation is that these women find adequate support and community involvement through more informal social networks, a finding noted in several ethnographic studies in Egypt (Rugh, 1979). Civic participation may be one dimension of autonomy, with greater relevance in Western contexts.

The survey also contained questions relating to women's self-care and ability to go out of the house for leisure activities. In all cases, illiterate women were least likely to report that they took specific measures to care for themselves. This pattern probably reflects two factors: less knowledge about proper care (exercise and diet, for example) and less access to resources to spend on their own care. This presumption is borne out by the data on medical check-ups. Illiterate women are half as likely as those with some education below the secondary level to have regular medical check-ups, even though they are as likely to state that caring for their own health is as important as for other family members. Other data (not shown) indicate that women at the lowest socioeconomic level express stronger concern for taking care of their health than either middle- or upper-income women. This exception to the usual positive relationship between autonomy and income could have two possible explanations. One is that poorer women recognize their health as one of their few assets and are therefore expressing a need to preserve and care for it. The other is that women from better-off families have adopted a gender norm whereby women are expected to express personal self-sacrifice for the sake of other family members. This disjuncture between lower-status women's assertion of their health needs and their ability to address them is an area that requires more attention from Egyptian health policy planners.

Work and autonomy

It can be reasonably assumed that, if women are working in the labor force, they have indeed achieved a fair measure of personal autonomy within the Egyptian context. Even when the work itself requires little skill and is poorly paid, it allows women to leave the confines of the household and acquire some resources that they potentially control. Ethnographic research on Cairo communities suggests that when women work for wages their status is elevated within the family, resulting, for example, in privileged treatment and a greater say in financial matters (Hoodfar, 1988; Ibrahim, 1982). Thus an analysis of women's labor-force participation or work for cash may provide important information regarding patterns of personal autonomy.

Regardless of the definition of work used, however, we found that relatively few married women report themselves as currently working outside the home. Even the broadest measures of women's labor-force participation, which include questions about income-generating activity (in the 1991 ROWIF survey), or assistance with work to family members or non-members (in the 1988 DHS), show no more than 19 to 20 percent of currently married women of reproductive age working outside the home or otherwise generating income.[10] According to the ROWIF survey, during the peak childbearing years—under age thirty—only 12 percent of currently married women are working outside the home, again using the broadest definitions. That percentage more than doubles to 26 percent for women in their thirties, which is the period of the life cycle when they experience their peak child-

Table 5
Women working for wages or engaged in income-generating activities
(women aged 15+)

Variable	Percentage earning income	Sample size[a]
Current age		
<30	12	459
30–49	26	498
40–49	20	325
50+	8	297
Residence		
Urban	21	998
Rural	12	581
Education (years)		
None	8	1,005
<6[a]	6	137
6–9	6	155
10+	60	282
Household type		
Nuclear	20	1,078
Enlarged nuclear	14	120
Extended	12	284
Standard of Living Index[c]		
Low	13	690
Medium	20	553
High	22	336
Marriage arranged by		
Others	15	1,216
Self	26	363
Total	17	1,579

Source: CAPMAS, 1991
[a]See note a in Table 2
[b]Includes some women with informal education
[c]See note f in Table 1

rearing responsibilities. During the later reproductive years, outside or non-domestic work rates are lower again, probably reflecting both a life-cycle phenomenon and a trend of rising labor-force participation among younger women.

As the data in Table 5 make clear, work for wages is more an urban than a rural phenomenon and is primarily carried out by highly educated women with at least secondary schooling. The likelihood of working for wages is nearly twice as high for urban as for rural women.[11] Whereas the proportion of women working for wages is well below 10 percent for women with less than secondary schooling, it is 60 percent for those with secondary schooling or above.

The type of work captured by these surveys is mostly formal labor-force participation, which usually involves an employer/employee relationship and takes women outside their homes. Over 50 percent of the employed women in our sample, even in rural areas, are government employees. A majority of paid workers are in white-collar clerical jobs in both rural and urban areas. Among the very few women in the labor force in rural areas, less than 20 percent work in farming. A demanding six-day work week is typical, with rural working women often reporting working seven days a week. This situation suggests that the meaning of work for women and the implications of having a personal income may operate through a differential definition of the quality of work (that is, as drudgery or as a dignified activity) that is class- and residence-based.

Surely, the roughly 80 percent of Egyptian married women who do not work for wages are not idle. They are doing a variety of economically productive (although not personally remunerative) tasks around the house that either produce income indirectly through other members of the family, free other family members to earn an income, or save the family cash outlays by producing goods and services directly for home consumption.

This discussion of various dimensions of personal autonomy suggests two overall conclusions. One is that the range of autonomous opinion and behavior among Egyptian women is fairly narrow. A majority of women in all categories express low autonomy in absolute terms, and also in relation to what could be expected from women from many other parts of the world. At the same time and within the low overall levels of autonomy, we have uncovered significant variation in independent thinking and behavior among women within the sample. The higher levels of personal autonomy sometimes expressed by younger women, and by those with more education and exposure to the work force, clearly suggest the direction of probable future trends in Egypt.

Women's influence in family decision-making
Within contemporary Egyptian families, as has traditionally been the case, the majority of married women report that their husbands decide important family matters. However, husbands and wives are more likely to make joint decisions when wives are working for wages or are highly educated, reside in urban areas, and live in nuclear families (see Table 6). The possibility of making joint decisions suggests the ability

Table 6
Gender roles in decision-making (percentage)

Variable	Who makes decisions in important family matters[a]			Who has the say in determining family size		
	Wife	Husband	Both	Wife	Husband	Both
Current age						
< 30	2	72	25[b]	9	21	67
30–39	4	61	34	14	20	62
40–49	7	64	29	18	16	60
50+	10	60	30	18	19	58
Residence						
Urban	7	52	40	18	16	63
Rural	1	86	12	8	25	61
Household type						
Nuclear	6	60	33	15	19	63
Enlarged nuclear	4	71	25	18	23	55
Extended	3	77	19	9	21	64
Education (years)						
None	6	72	21	13	22	59
<6[c]	5	57	37	21	16	60
6–9	8	52	40	20	15	63
10+	2	47	51	12	12	75
Standard of Living Index[d]						
Low	3	80	16	11	23	59
Medium	7	54	39	17	16	63
High	7	49	42	17	15	65
Work status						
Working	5	51	43	15	15	67
Not working	5	67	27	14	20	61
Total	5	65	30	14	19	62

Source: CAPMAS, 1991
[a]For example, travel, buying, and selling
[b]Percentages may not add up to 100 because other possible answers with very low response rates were disregarded
[c]Includes some women with informal education
[d]See note f in Table 1

to influence desired outcomes through negotiation—by our definition, an important dimension of autonomy.

In cases where differences of opinion arise between husband and wife, the majority say they finally agree or choose to accept the husband's opinion. However, women earning an income, more educated women, and, to a lesser extent, women in nuclear-family households are much less willing to accept their husband's opinion in the case of disagreements and are more likely to try to convince husbands of their opinion or attempt to find a compromise between the two views (see Table 7). On the other hand, it is rare for wives to insist on their own opinion, at least in their reports to survey interviewers.

On the question of decisions about family size, a majority of married women (62 percent) say this is a joint decision (Table 6). In the remaining cases, the husband is most likely to have the final word among women who do not earn an income, among illiterate women, and in rural households.

A slightly differently worded set of questions used in the 1988 DHS suggests that wives may indeed make a somewhat greater contribution to household decision-making. Table 8 compares women

Table 7
Gender roles in decision-making (percentage)

	What do you do if you and your husband disagree?		
	Insist on or try to convince him of my views	Reconcile the two views or try to involve some relatives	Comply with husband's views
Current age			
<30	8	31	60[a]
30–39	15	33	51
40–49	9	34	56
50+	11	29	60
Residence			
Urban	15	38	47
Rural	6	21	73
Household			
Nuclear	12	33	54
Enlarged nuclear	10	33	57
Extended	10	25	66
Education (years)			
None	7	25	68
<6	15	34	50
6–9	15	45	40
10+	24	48	27
Standard of Living Index[b]			
Low	8	25	67
Medium	12	37	51
High	18	38	44
Income-earning status			
Earning income	21	39	39
No earnings	9	30	60
Total	12	32	56

Source: CAPMAS, 1991
[a]Percentages may not add up to 100 because other answers with low percentages were neglected
[b]See note f in Table 1

Table 8
Gender roles and family decision-making (percentage answering 'yes')

| Variable | In disagreements, wife should speak up | Wife respects husband more if he listens and accepts her opinion | Wife's view should carry same weight as husband's | Husbands should not have last word on | | | | | | | Sample size[a] |
				Visits to relatives	Household budget	Lending and borrowing	Having another child	Children's education	Children's marriage plans	Use of family planning	
Residence											
Urban	61	65	50	47	57	52	78	80	76	87	3,998
Rural	32	39	32	25	28	29	57	52	49	63	4,215
Education level											
None	31	38	30	25	31	30	58	54	51	65	4,100
Primary	50	55	43	36	44	42	70	70	65	79	2,614
Secondary	79	78	65	58	65	57	86	91	88	93	1,069
Higher	86	86	76	76	83	73	95	97	95	97	424
Standard of Living Index[b]											
Low	28	35	30	22	26	28	54	48	45	59	3,294
Medium	50	55	41	36	45	43	71	71	68	81	2,907
High	73	74	61	59	67	58	85	88	86	93	1,725
Income-earning status											
Earning income	70	72	62	60	72	61	83	87	84	89	984
No earnings	44	50	39	33	39	38	66	64	61	74	6,566
Total	46	51	41	36	42	40	68	66	62	75	8,214

Source: DHS, 1988

[a] Total sample sizes vary because of varying non-response rates under different categories

[b] See note f in Table 1

by income-earning status, education, standard of living, and residence with respect to various measures of personal autonomy encompassing husband/wife communication and household decision-making. Regardless of the indicator, a larger share of income-earning women, more educated women, women with a higher Standard of Living Index, and urban women express views consistent with greater independence in relation to their husbands, and greater personal freedom of movement. For example, 70 percent of women who earn an income say that "a wife should speak up if she disagrees with her husband," whereas only 44 percent of the women who have no earnings express this view.

The greatest expressions of personal independence, particularly among women who have no earnings, illiterate women, and rural women, come in relation to those aspects of family life having most to do with children and marriage. Women are clearly articulating more assertiveness in those areas traditionally defined as appropriate spheres of concern for women. For example, roughly two-thirds of non–income-earning women do not think that the husband should have the last word on having another child, or on children's education and marriage plans. Three-fourths express this same belief about decisions involving the use of family planning. Of course, this does not mean that women believe they should have full independence in these areas, just that their husbands' views should not hold ultimate sway. Women concede greater control to their husbands in areas such as the household budget and lending and borrowing.

What is most striking here in our view is the relatively high percentage of non–income-earning women who hold independent attitudes with respect to household decisions. The overwhelming majority of women in Egypt do not work in the formal sector, and thus it should not be surprising that this group of women is quite diverse and holds a range of views on the matters closest to their role responsibilities.

An index of autonomy

In developing an autonomy index, we selected one indicator representing each dimension of autonomy, as discussed above. These ranged from whether or not a woman's marriage was arranged by someone else, to expressed views about women working for pay, evidence of actions reflecting self-care, affirmative roles in family decision-making, and actual participation in the formal labor market.

The value of the index ranges from 0 to 5. Women with affirmative scores on 1) self-choice of spouse, 2) current participation in the labor force, 3) paid work as important to women's personal fulfillment, 4) looking after one's own health, and 5) insisting on one's own opinion or trying to convince or reconcile in cases of disagreement with the husband, would rate 5 on the autonomy index.

As can be seen from Table 9, the mean level of autonomy for all married women in the 1991 sample is 1.2 out of a maximum of 5—a very low score. However, we do see some variations in the expected direction with age, residence, standard of living, and education. The surprise is that, with the exception of education, variations among women in this index are so small. Education is the factor most strongly related to women's personal autonomy, with the index ranging from 0.9 for illiterate women to 2.4—the highest score of any variable—for those with at least a high school education.

Table 9
Mean autonomy level by background variables

Current age	
<30	1.4
30–49	1.4
40–49	1.1
50+	0.9
Residence	
Urban	1.3
Rural	1.1
Education (years)	
None	0.9
<6[a]	1.2
6–9	1.3
10+	2.3
Household type	
Nuclear	1.3
Enlarged nuclear	1.4
Extended	1.0
Standard of Living Index[b]	
Low	1.1
Medium	1.3
High	1.4
Total (mean)	1.2

Source: CAPMAS, 1991
[a]Includes some women with informal education
[b]See note f in Table 1

WOMEN'S AUTONOMY AND GENDER ROLES WITHIN THE FAMILY

We have previously defined autonomy as the ability to think and act independently of others to achieve one's intentions. Having assessed the autonomy of married women in Egypt both in terms of its scope and of its variation among women, we now ask whether and how this ability or lack thereof affects gender roles within the home, including fertility decision-making.

Child-rearing and domestic tasks

Roughly half of all married women report that both parents are responsible for raising the children, and 40 percent say it is primarily the mother's responsibility. There is very little difference in these responses across groups. When it comes to helping with children's studies, however, 67 percent of married women rely on teachers or others to help, reflecting the high proportion of illiterate women in our sample. The percentage of women, sometimes alone and sometimes with the help of the husband, who help children with studies increases dramatically with education. While 82 percent of illiterate women rely on others to help their children study, only 21 percent of women with a high school education do so. Forty-five percent of women who earn an income are involved in helping their child study, as against 15 percent of women who do not earn an income. Despite their longer work hours, the women in the former group are much less likely to delegate this responsibility to others.

When gender roles are strictly segregated, as in Egypt, it is interesting to examine how male roles adapt to changing role configurations for women. Some earlier research in working-class areas of Cairo suggested that men are resistant to taking over domestic responsibilities when their wives go outside the home to work, although younger men are more willing than those in older age groups (Ibrahim, 1980). The ROWIF survey data indicate that women with greater autonomy are more able to get their husbands to help with the housework. However, even among the most educated women, 59 percent of husbands do not help at all, as compared with 87 percent for the least educated women. While 14 percent of husbands help sometimes, a larger percent of husbands do so when their wives work for pay (33 percent), when they live in nuclear-family households (23 percent), or when they have better living conditions (roughly 25 percent). Husbands help most often with shopping, but this is in fact a variation on a traditional male responsibility, since it involves contact outside the home. Help is rarely provided in cleaning, cooking, and washing, although here husbands of income-earning wives do sometimes help out.

Contribution to family maintenance

Information on how married women who work outside the home spend their income and to what extent they get support from their husbands and other relatives provides further evidence of gender-role adaptations in families where women participate in the labor force. Almost all women (95 percent) who earn an income do so to support their families. More than three-fourths (although less in rural areas) feel free to spend that money without interference from their husbands. This can be explained by the traditional separation of spousal assets within Egyptian marriage (Naguib and Lloyd, 1994). Surprisingly, more than half the income-earning women in urban areas report that they are responsible for all household expenses (though only 16 percent in rural areas), and roughly one-fourth of these women meet their own personal needs exclusively with their earnings, while a small proportion (roughly 20 percent) of married women who work outside the home receive regular contributions from their husbands to meet their personal needs. Given the legal and customary responsibility of a husband to provide financially for his wife and children, the high degree of exclusive financial contribution from income-earning wives in cities signals a trend that deserves further study. Relatively few employed women were found to use their earnings to support relatives other than their immediate families (spouse and children).

Forty percent of income-earning women report that they would quit their jobs if their husband's salary doubled. These women seem to imply confidence that their and their children's needs would be taken care of without their own earnings if household resources were adequate, and they also give a clear indication that the only purpose of their work is economic necessity. However, the majority of women, particularly in rural areas, would not be willing to quit under these circumstances. These women appear to value their freedom to allocate income as they choose without a husband's interference and without becoming dependent on him entirely.

The ability of income-earning women to take some personal benefit for themselves from their earnings depends on a variety of factors: their economic circumstances, their child-care burden, and

Table 10

Allocation of women's earnings (percentage of currently married women working outside the home, aged 15–49)

	Most to family	At least half to self[a]	Sample size[b]
Current age			
<30	72	28	298
30–39	81	19	479
40–49	81	19	208
Residence			
Urban	76	24	738
Rural	86	14	246
Education level			
None	88	12	146
Primary	87	13	91
Secondary	79	21	486
Higher	70	30	262
Standard of Living Index[c]			
Low	90	10	153
Medium	79	21	273
High	75	25	516
Presence of children			
No children	55	45	94
Children aged <12 only	78	22	589
Children aged >12 only	74	26	75
Children aged <12 and >12	91	9	225
Total	79	21	984

Source: DHS, 1988

[a]Combination of two responses: "most to self" and "divide equally"

[b]Sample size varies by category due to non-response

[c]See note f in Table 1

their exposure to modern influences. Table 10 presents data from the 1988 DHS on the proportion of income-earning women who are able to spend at least half their earnings on themselves, according to a variety of background characteristics. The higher the standard of living of the household, the larger the proportion of women allocating an even share of their earnings to themselves. Even among the best-off group, however, only 25 percent of women fall into this category. The greatest variation can be seen when comparing women according to the presence of children of different ages. While 45 percent of women with no children spend at least half of their earnings on themselves, only 9 percent of women do so when they have children both under and over age 12 in the home. While only 12–13 percent of the least educated women spend at least half of their earnings on themselves, 30 percent of those women with more than a secondary-level education do so.

Reproductive intentions and fertility decision-making

Because of the division of household tasks and allocation of women's earned income, married women clearly shoulder a particularly heavy burden during their childbearing and child-rearing years. The implications of this division for differences between husbands and wives in fertility preferences are apparent in Table 11. While the data do not provide information on husband's fertility preferences directly, it is possible to compare the expressed fertility preferences and achieved fertility of married women according to how they handle disagreements with their husbands. When women report their husbands as the dominant decision-makers, expressed fertility preferences are somewhat higher at all ages, but the differences are small for women currently in their reproductive years.

On the other hand, actual achieved fertility levels are dramatically lower among women who insist on their own views. The fertility of women aged over forty-five who reported complying with husbands' views was 3.6 children higher than those who insisted on their own views or tried to convince their husband of their views. The fertility levels of women who work toward reconciliation were roughly halfway between the other two groups.

Implications of women's autonomy for future fertility behavior

Despite relatively low levels of autonomy overall, Egyptian women have shown a growing interest in controlling their fertility, as reflected in the most recent 1992 data from the DHS showing 47 percent of currently married women practicing contraception (DHS, 1993). As indicated earlier, this is the area of family decision-making in which women are most likely to play a role. In Table 12, we can see that fertility preferences are low, even among the least autonomous women, and when other relevant factors are adjusted for, no systematic variation is evident by autonomy level. However, among the youngest women, greater autonomy appears to be more likely to be expressed in terms of lower fertility preferences than among older women (for example, 1.9 children versus 2.7 children for women under age thirty). Thus, further improvements in women's education and economic conditions, as well as increased urbanization and women's labor-force participation—factors that support a more inde-

Table 11

Reproductive intentions and behavior by style of family decision-making

	Women who usually tend to		
	Insist on or try to convince husband of own views	Reconcile the two views or try to involve relatives	Comply with husband's views
	I. Mean desired number of children (by age)		
Age			
<30	2.3	2.2	2.4
30–39	2.3	2.5	2.5
40–49	2.2	2.2	2.4
50+	1.9	2.5	2.5
	II. Completed fertility (by age)		
Age			
45–54	3.1	4.8	6.7
55+	3.9	6.4	7.5

Source: CAPMAS, 1991

pendent role for women—are likely to contribute to some further declines in fertility preferences.

Despite relatively low expressed family-size desires, achieved fertility is high among women past the end of their childbearing years (see Table 12). While the gap between actual fertility and fertility preferences remains wide among all autonomy groups, more autonomous women who have completed their fertility appear to bear fewer children on average than women scoring lower on the autonomy scale, even after other relevant factors have been controlled for statistically. Thus we can posit that the future importance of growing autonomy for women, particularly in fertility decision-making, is likely to be expressed in terms of a reduction in the level of unwanted fertility, as actual fertility falls closer to desired levels.

With regard to longer-term implications, however, even currently married women with few of the characteristics associated with autonomy have aspirations for their daughters that imply dramatic changes in women's roles as they relate to work and fertility. Table 13 shows married women's aspirations for their daughters—specifically, whether they would approve of their daughters working for pay, at what age their daughters should marry, and how many children they should have. Eighty percent of women approve of the idea of their daughters earning an income, and the percentages remain high even among the least autonomous women, as measured by work status or

Table 12
Desired and completed fertility by autonomy level and age

	Autonomy level		
	Low	Medium	High
	Mean desired fertility (by age)		
Unadjusted			
<30	2.7	2.4	1.9
30–39	2.9	2.4	2.6
40–49	2.7	2.6	2.7
50+	3.1	2.9	—[a]
Adjusted[b]	2.8	2.6	2.8
	Mean completed fertility (by age)		
Unadjusted			
45–54	6.3	5.3	5.0[c]
50+	7.8	6.6	—[a]
Adjusted[d]	6.3	5.9	5.8

Source: CAPMAS, 1991
[a]No cases in cell
[b]Adjusted using multiple classification analysis with women's education, number of living children, and rural/urban residence as independent variables, and current age as a covariate
[c]Based on only one case
[d]Based on women aged 40+ and adjusted using multiple classification analysis for current age, education, and rural/urban residence, with age at first marriage as a covariate

education. For example, 79 percent of women who do not earn an income approve of the idea of their daughters working for pay. Fifty-four percent of all currently married women think that their daughters should have no more than two children, and the percentage remains surprisingly high even among the most traditional groups: for example, 44 percent of women with no education express a preference of no more than two children for their daughters.

On the other hand, the large majority of women (75 percent) expect their daughters to marry by the age of twenty. The preferences for daughters' marriage after the age of twenty show the largest variation by education, with only 11 percent of illiterate women thinking their daughters should marry after the age of twenty, compared with 80 percent of the most highly educated group. As marriage age has an important link with educational attainment and the selection of a spouse, it appears that the daughters of women who prefer early marriage may be less likely to realize their mothers' other aspirations for them, in terms of both fertility and work, because they will not be in a position to think and act independently.

Table 13
Aspirations for daughters (percentage of currently married women, age 15–49)

	Approve of daughters working	Suitable age of marriage >20	Daughter should have no more than two children
Current age			
<30	82	22	53
30–39	81	29	57
40–49	76	27	52
Residence			
Urban	86	42	66
Rural	76	10	43
Education level			
None	74	11	44
Primary	86	27	60
Secondary	88	57	71
Higher	90	80	72
Standard of Living Index[a]			
Low	73	7	39
Medium	85	27	60
High	87	57	70
Work status			
Working for cash	89	58	71
Not working[b]	79	22	52
Total	80	25	54

Source: DHS, 1988
[a]See note f in Table 1
[b]Excluding women assisting in family work

CONCLUSION

On the whole, Egyptian women are remarkably consistent in expressing dependence on their spouses with respect to family decision-making and extraordinarily committed to their families in terms of the amount of domestic responsibility they assume. Their overall levels of autonomy remain very low. However, beyond this general characterization lies a much more complex reality in which women within families do have a voice in particular decisions of most relevance to them, such as family planning and child-rearing.

Furthermore, they are able to gain stronger influence within the family and greater personal independence when they have more education, when they make a greater economic contribution to the family, and when they live in a more urban or modern environment. The waning of extended-family living arrangements is also supportive of these trends. Indeed, it appears that Egyptian women's scope for increased autonomy of thought and action is potentially quite broad. However, the realization of the potential for change depends heavily on parents and other relatives, who continue to make early critical decisions on their daughters' behalf in terms of schooling and choice of marriage partner. The data on parental aspirations for daughters are encouraging, but these aspirations have a greater chance of being turned into reality when daughters' marriages are delayed—much more likely if the daughter has an educated mother.

Levels of autonomy among married women are positively associated with age, education, urban residence, and more affluent living conditions. However, even among the least advantaged groups, many women express a concern for attending to their health and an assertive role in family decision-making within traditional domains. On the other hand, and even among the most advantaged groups, most women continue to seek their husbands' approval and show limited knowledge of gender issues or involvement in activities outside the family. Over time, women's scope for autonomy within marriage can be expected to grow as the economy continues to modernize and education for women continues to improve. Women's autonomy is linked to slightly lower family-size preferences, but more significantly to an increased ability to achieve their family-size goals. Indeed, these changes, among others, have most certainly played a role in the rapid increase in contraceptive prevalence in Egypt in recent years (DHS, 1993).

The implications of our findings for population policy planners are clear: investments in female education, employment, and programs to reduce underage marriage should receive high priority, alongside the current emphasis on family planning services. How the trends among Egyptian women toward greater autonomy will be integrated within the social system in the future depends on policy leadership and a host of social and cultural forces currently buffeting the traditional Egyptian family. But given the very high value that Egyptian women and men continue to place on family life, we can be sure that the institution of the family will be resourceful and flexible enough to accommodate the changes.

APPENDIX: THE ROWIF SURVEY DESIGN

The Central Agency for Public Mobilization and Statistics (CAPMAS) conducted the survey on Characteristics of Households and the Role of Egyptian Women in the Family (ROWIF) in 1991. The survey was undertaken as a case study in three selected areas, each reasonably representative of one of the three major human environments of Egypt: urban governorates, other urban areas, and rural areas. The study was based on a complete enumeration of all households (and their members) found in the three areas.

For the selection of the three areas, three indicators were used that were related to issues to be investigated and for which data were available on the level of village and *shiakha* (small administrative areas in rural and urban areas, respectively) from the latest available census data of 1986: household size, educational status of females, and occupational distribution of males. Three areas were selected for which the averages of these indicators were closest to the national averages for the three major environment types. The three selected areas were a shiakha in Alexandria (urban governorate) with 559 households, a shiakha in Sharqiya (other urban area) with 665 households, and a village in Beni Suef (rural Egypt) with 611 households. Thus the total sample size was 1,835 households.

Two questionnaires were used in the study. The first collected data on household members (socioeconomic and demographic characteristics), household type, structure, and size, and household living conditions. The second questionnaire was administered to all ever-married women found in the households surveyed. It collected detailed data on characteristics of these women, situation in the family, intrafamilial relationships, and current situation of and attitudes toward education and work. The number of ever-married women included in the sample was 1,992. The analysis in this paper was based on replies from 1,579 currently married women.

REFERENCES

Berlin, S. and C. G. Johnson. 1989. Women and autonomy: Using structural analysis of social behavior to find autonomy within connections. *Psychiatry.* 52:79–95.

CAPMAS. 1983. *Labor force sample survey report.* Cairo: Central Agency for Public Mobilization and Statistics.

CAPMAS. 1991. *The characteristics of the household and the role of Egyptian women in the family (ROWIF).* Survey results. Cairo: Central Agency for Public Mobilization and Statistics.

DHS. 1988. *Egypt demographic and health survey 1988.* Cairo: National Population Council.

DHS. 1993. *Egypt demographic and health survey, 1992.* Cairo: National Population Council.

Doan, R. M. and L. Bisharat. 1990. Female autonomy and child nutritional status: The extended family residential unit. Amman, Jordan. *Social Science and Medicine.* 31/7:783–89.

Dyson, T. and M. Moore. 1983. Kinship structure, female autonomy, and demographic behavior in India. *Population and Development Review.* 9/1:35–60.

FAO. 1993. Gender disaggregated data and statistics on human resources in the Middle East. Unpublished paper. Food and Agriculture Organization.

Hoodfar, H. 1988. Household budgeting and financial management in a lower-income Cairo neighborhood. In D. Dwyer and J. Bruce, eds., *A home divided: Women and income in the third world.* Stanford: Stanford University Press.

Ibrahim, B. 1980. Social change and the industrial experience: Women as production workers in urban Egypt. Ph.D. diss., Indiana University.

———. 1982. Family strategies: A perspective on women's entry to the labor force in Egypt. *International Journal of Sociology of the Family.* December.

Naguib, N. G. and C. B. Lloyd. 1994. *Gender inequalities and demographic behavior: The case of Egypt.* New York: The Population Council.

Rugh, A. 1979. Coping with poverty in a Cairo community. *Cairo Papers in Social Science.* 2/1.

Singerman, D. and H. Hoodfar. Forthcoming. *Development, social change and gender in Cairo: A view from the household.* Bloomington: Indiana University Press.

Tessler, M., M. Palmer, T. Farah, B. Ibrahim. 1985. *The evaluation and application of survey research in the Arab world.* Boulder and London: Westview Press.

United Nations. 1987. *Fertility behavior in the context of development.* New York: United Nations.

Unger, R. and M. Crawford. 1992. *Women and gender: A feminist psychology.* New York: McGraw-Hill.

NOTES

1 See the appendix for a description of the ROWIF survey design.
2 This is a synthetic cohort estimate based on the age-specific proportions married in each five-year age group between fifteen and forty-nine. The calculation is based on Table 9.1 in DHS, 1993.

3   The proportion of time spent married was estimated to be 72 percent of reproductive years in 1980 (United Nations, 1987).

4   These trends have been assessed by comparing the data in Tables 46 and 47 from United Nations (1987) with similar tabulations based on the 1988 Egyptian DHS standard recoded tape.

5   The nuclear household consists of husband, wife, and unmarried children; or married couples with no children; or a single parent with unmarried children.

6   The enlarged nuclear household includes, in addition to the nuclear family members, any immediate dependents (parents or unmarried brothers or sisters) related to the head of the household. The extended family household contains any kin resident other than immediate dependents within the nuclear family.

7   A Standard of Living Index was constructed for the present study on a comparable basis using data from the DHS and ROWIF household surveys. Each household was assessed with respect to the quality of flooring (wood, tiles, marble, waxed plastic=1), the presence of a kitchen inside the house (yes=1), type of toilet facilities (modern=2, traditional with or without tank=1, other=0), the presence of a drinking-water tap inside the home (yes =1), the presence of a hot-water heater (yes=1), the possession of a car or video player (yes=2), and the possession of a color television set (yes=1). The possible values of the index ranged from 0 to 8; the average value for all households in the 1991 ROWIF survey is 3.5.

8   Tabulations based on 1991 ROWIF Survey (not shown here).

9   Data from the 1991 ROWIF survey.

10   In order to compare the 1988 DHS and 1991 ROWIF surveys, we had to focus only on women aged fifteen to forty-nine, because these are the ages covered by both surveys. Thirty percent of the women in the ROWIF survey are over the age of fifty and 15 percent are over sixty, while the DHS encompasses only women aged fifteen to forty-nine.

11   Caution is needed here, however, because several studies have shown that women's work is more likely to be underreported in rural than in urban areas (FAO, 1993; CAPMAS, 1983).

8

Changing Hierarchies of Gender and Generation in the Arab World

Philippe Fargues

This paper explores the relationship between the changing order of the family and the demographic transition in the Arab world. It develops the following three points: 1. The specificity of an Arab model of the demographic transition, if any, is attributable to the existence, until recently, of a strong patriarchal order of the family and a strong neopatriarchal order of the society and the political system.[1] 2. The way in which the demographic transition developed in the Arab world (in particular the increasing levels of education) has key implications for the traditional order of societies: while the patriarchal order may be temporarily reinforced, in the long run the hierarchies that it represents are weakened, as women's educational levels tend to converge with men's and younger men come to overtake their elders. 3. The resistance of the old patriarchal order to these transformations is likely to create a context of social crisis, which can be manifested by political violence.

DEMOGRAPHIC TRANSITION AND PATRIARCHAL ORDER

Institutional relations between sexes and age groups in Arab societies of the past are commonly described as 'patriarchal,' a system characterized by the domination of men over women and older men over younger men. Most scholars also agree that modernity is now altering to a certain extent this double domination.

That Arab demographic patterns bear the mark of patriarchy is demonstrated by present fertility differentials and what they disclose about the factors leading to, or inhibiting, fertility decline. Like other social changes, fertility decline first appeared in limited sub-populations, usually an 'elite.' Then it gradually spread to the masses along with the diffusion of some of the values and patterns of behavior of this elite. Presently, the Arab world stands somewhere at the midpoint of this diffusion process. Variance in fertility levels both within and between nations is higher than ever. Total fertility rates in Arab

Figure 1
Fertility and wealth in the Arab world

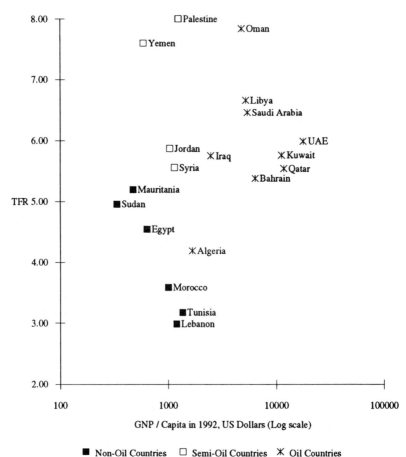

countries range from a relatively low 3.0 children per woman on average in Tunisia and Lebanon to a pretransitional 6.5 children among nationals of the Arabian peninsula and the Gulf (see updated estimates of national levels of fertility in Courbage and Khlat, 1993; Farid, 1993), and to a record 8 to 9 children in the occupied territories of Palestine.[2] The range of fertility levels within countries is even wider, as subgroups that have almost completed their fertility transition (with only 2 children per woman) coexist with other groups that have not yet begun the process of transition.

The characteristics of the subgroups with the lowest fertility levels are commonly referred to as 'factors' of fertility decline. As in other parts of the world, these factors are mainly related to the socioeconomic position of the family, and to the status of children and women both within the family and in the society as a whole. But countries of the Arab world differ from the rest of the world in that those factors that are relevant to explain differentials within national populations are irrelevant to explain differentials between national populations. In this paper, I argue that one of the reasons for this distinctiveness is that the strength of the patriarchal order varies from one Arab society to the other. In order to document this assertion, I examine two factors that are closely correlated with fertility patterns and sharply differentiated between societies as well as within any given society of the region: wealth and the education of women.

FERTILITY AND WEALTH

Research on the demographic transition in developing countries has shown that the economic welfare of households is a key factor of fertility decline. This is true of Arab countries as well, where the highest fertility levels are now found among the poorest categories of any given population, while the lowest levels are among middle- or upper-income classes. But if we examine the association of wealth and fertility between countries, the relationship is almost reversed (Figure 1): the highest levels of fertility are those of the richest countries of the Gulf and the Arabian peninsula, together with Jordan and Yemen,[3] while the lowest levels are those of middle income or relatively poor countries: Tunisia, Lebanon, Morocco, and, to a lesser extent, Egypt. This is partly due to differences in the mode of wealth accumulation and in the social and political allocation of wealth.

At first sight, Arab countries can be considered as polarized into two distinct macroeconomic patterns: on the one hand, those economies that are based on relatively diversified systems of production and on the other hand economies primarily based on oil revenues. To each pole corresponds a pattern of population reproduction. In the first set of economies, the costs of childbearing increase with modernity (as the cost of health and education rise in an increasingly monetarized economy), and it becomes necessary to improve the resources of the household by several means, in particular by mobilizing the labor of women. Thus, the classical factors of fertility decline—changing roles of children and women—are operating in a context of economic pressure. This type of fertility transition, which is moved by economic pressure, is accelerated when the state adopts a set of policies that improve women's status. Tunisia is an eloquent example of this situation.

In the second set of economies, the state is able to support households by shouldering the costs of children and by importing labor. In particular, importing female labor makes it possible to keep national women at home, while insuring that those modern services that usually require women (education, health, administrative services) are provided by immigrant women. Oil wealth thus prevents the usual factors of fertility transition from playing their role, and this was especially true during the oil boom of the 1970s and 1980s when other aspects of these societies were modernizing rapidly. This is in a way an 'oil-revenue-inhibited' fertility transition: by making it possible to raise many children and to maintain the woman inside the home, oil wealth has acted to provide a reprieve to the patriarchal order.

These two models of transition are in reality the two poles of a continuum. In varying degrees, each Arab country, whether oil exporter or not, has diverted a certain part of the Gulf wealth and drawn benefits, even very limited, from its revenue. Every Arab state has thus been able to distribute more than the country produces,[4] so that both models of demographic reproduction described above can coexist in a given population. Algeria and Egypt offer two convincing examples of this coexistence.

In Algeria, a very slow fertility decline was hardly perceptible until the mid-1980s, when the total fertility rate was still above 6 children per woman. This could have been partly attributable to the relative welfare provided by oil and gas exports.[5] An indication of the *rentier* nature of Algerian high fertility was given by the fall of fertility that followed, in 1985, the collapse of oil and gas incomes that had begun two years before: in four years, the TFR lost 1.5 points, falling from 6.24 in 1985 to 4.72 in 1989. This drop, associated with a rapid deterioration in the economic resources of the families, may have been reinforced by a reversal in the population policy of Algeria, which had been pro-natalist until 1982 and then became anti-natalist (on the relation between oil rent and fertility in Algeria, see Fargues, 1990).

In Egypt, a different story reveals a similar phenomenon. This country was among the first in the region to experience a decline in fertility, starting in the mid-1960s. The early birth control policy may have been partly the result of an early awareness on the part of President Nasser of the economic problems linked with rapid population growth. Between 1965 and 1972, the TFR declined from 6.5 to 5.0 children per woman. Between 1973 and 1985, however, the 'Open-Door Policy' *(infitah)* of President Sadat was associated with an increase in fertility from 5.0 to 6.5.[6] New wealth originating from outside poured into the country: mass emigration to Arab oil countries brought Egypt remittances amounting to more than US$ 5 billion a year, and the flow of American money, as a reward for the Camp David peace accords, made Egypt the leading recipient of US aid after Israel. At the household level, this entailed a substantial increase in the standard of living.[7] Events progressed as though increasing incomes allowed more children to be procreated while keeping women at home: according to the population censuses, activity rates for females aged fifteen and above remained very low, gaining only a slight increase, from 5.5 percent in 1976 to 10.5 percent in 1986 (for a reassessment of female activity rates, see Fergany, 1994). Wealth was giving a new impulse to the patriarchal order, which thus appeared to have been only superficially altered by Nasser's policy.

THE SOCIAL CONDITIONS OF AN INHIBITING EFFECT OF FEMALE EDUCATION ON FERTILITY

A great deal of evidence has been collected in developing countries that shows female education as a major factor of fertility reduction. Arab countries are no exception. Within each country the same pattern is observed among subgroups: TFR decreases regularly with the elevation of the average number of years spent at school. In Egypt for example, according to the last Demographic and Health Survey

(1992), illiterate women have a total of 5.0 children on average, while women with primary, secondary, and higher education have respectively 4.0, 3.0, and 2.9 children (DHS, 1993). Here again, however, as in the case of income differentials, female education is irrelevant to comparisons between countries: Jordanian or Syrian women, for example, are more fertile than Tunisian or Moroccan women despite their higher levels of education.[8]

Elsewhere, I have argued that the influence of a woman's education on fertility is affected by the likelihood that she will be involved in an economic activity outside the home (Fargues, 1989 and 1994a). In other words, both girls' enrollment at school and women's work in cities are indicators that females have a recognized place outside the world of kin. They also suggest an openness of men to non-patriarchal values: openness of the father in the former case, openness of the husband in the latter. They both contribute to the increased autonomy

Figure 2
Birth rate and education of women in the Gaza Strip, 1968–94

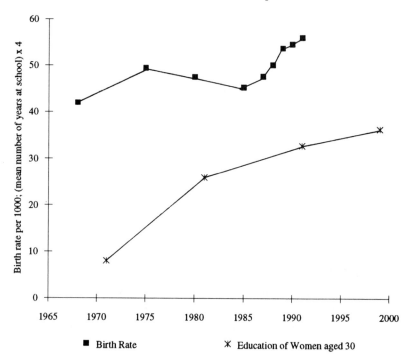

of women and act in synergy to modify their status within the family, in particular by providing alternatives to the roles of wife and mother assigned by the patriarchal order.

The case of Palestinian women in the Occupied Territories illustrates most eloquently that education is not sufficient in itself to produce new roles in the family. With crude birth rates (CBR) reaching 46.5 in the West Bank and 56.5 in Gaza in 1991, Palestinian women now have probably the highest fertility in the world, at least if national levels are considered. Paradoxically, they also have the highest levels of education in the Arab world,[9] with the possible exception of Lebanon: in 1991, women aged thirty—the mean age at childbearing—had on average attended school for nine years.[10] What is more, fertility and education have not evolved in opposite directions, but have both increased in parallel since the beginning of the Israeli occupation, in particular with the Intifada (see Figure 2). In Gaza for example, while in the late 1960s the overall CBR was 42.0 per thousand and women of childbearing age had attended school for two years on average, in the mid-1980s these figures had become 48.0 and 6.5, and in the early 1990s 56.5 and 9.0, respectively. This is contrary to expectations that a high rate of school attendance combined with a deep economic distress of this fully urban population would have led families to reduce the burden of numerous children.

Part of the explanation for the fact that education and economic distress do not produce the expected effect on fertility is to be found in the political conditions of belligerence, which have inhibited the effect of an increasing level of schooling. Indeed, data on employment indicators show that the education of girls does not produce the expected improvement in women's status: when they become adults, women find no job opportunity in territories where unemployment already forces one-third of active men to work in Israel.[11] Employed women thus represent only 5 percent of those in the active age groups (Abu Shukr, 1992). In addition, the costs of child-rearing at the level of the household are alleviated thanks to the assistance of numerous solidarity movements: international agencies such as UNRWA, NGOs, political organizations such as the PLO and Hamas, and a very active network of associations. At the level of the family, fertility is thus divorced from its costs. One should not, however, avoid a more strictly political explanation. Keeping fertility high, in spite of educational and economic conditions that would normally bring it down, was seen as the best weapon in the hands of the Palestinians, ensuring that they would soon represent a majority in the territory of the Palestine of the British Mandate.[12] Things happened exactly as if there existed a division of political labor between sexes: men were fighting while women were raising numerous children. How such a collective goal was translated into individual choices as private as the size of the family is a question that belongs to the domain of political psychology. It is enough here to take note of the way in which this hyperfertility fits perfectly with patriarchal values.[13]

HIERARCHIES OF KNOWLEDGE: TOWARD GREATER GENDER EQUITY AND GREATER GENERATIONAL INEQUALITIES

School education is not evenly distributed in the society. Rather, access to school varies with many factors. Some of these factors, such as socioeconomic status or place of residence, are commonly shared by the members of a given family, but others are not, in particular age and sex. Thus, school education introduces or strengthens differences, not only between sub-groups of the society, but within the family itself. Because boys and girls do not have equal access to schooling, and because school is for children and adolescents but not adults, the spread of education is in effect a powerful differentiating process (for a case study of Egypt, see Fargues, 1994b).

A consideration of the disparity in access to education between the sexes suggests that education at first contributes to greater differentiation between the sexes and later to homogenizing gender conditions. In all countries of the region, during the first part of this century, school was a privilege of the very few. This minority was almost exclusively limited to boys, with the exception of a few experiments designed for girls (mainly in Egypt and Lebanon), which were politically significant but statistically negligible. Since the majority of the population, whether male or female, was to remain illiterate, the distribution of knowledge in the society was relatively undifferentiated.

As school began to spread, it remained quite exclusively intended for boys, because patriarchal values made parents reluctant to send girls outside the family home. Inequality of access between the sexes started to increase, and thus a modern institution was contributing to a reinforcement of traditional inequalities. Even when girls began to have access to primary school, the duration of boys' schooling grew even faster. In terms

Figure 3
Average gap in education between men and women in selected Arab countries

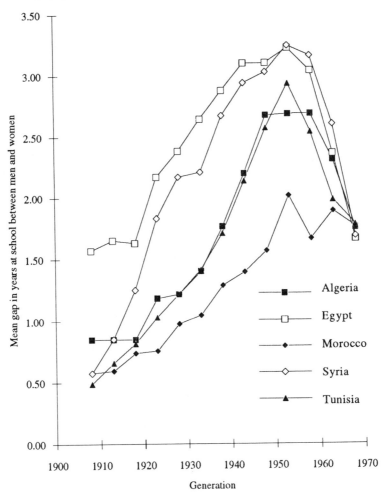

of average number of years spent at school, the maximum gender inequality was found throughout the region in those generations born between 1950 and 1960 (see Figure 3). These are the very generations that are now at the age of power, both within the family and in the political sphere. As a result, with regard to gender inequalities of knowledge, the patriarchal order is at this time stronger than ever.

Further increases in schooling are beginning to narrow the gender gap. Recent population censuses and surveys show that, in most parts of the region, the generations born in the 1970s, that is, those who are now reaching the age of demographic reproduction but will only tomorrow reach the age of political power, are no longer unequal with regard to primary school, and are rapidly catching up with regard to secondary school. It is enough to look at the well-balanced sex ratios of the populations that are presently enrolled in school to predict that the patriarchal system will soon be confronted by a serious challenge.

Along with this reduction of the gender gap, the rapid spread of school among young people has created another gap, one between generations. This generation effect of the diffusion of school education interacts with the particular type of demographic transition that has characterized Arab countries. The fact that the decline in fertility has lagged for a longer time than elsewhere behind the beginning of mortality decline has had two important consequences for family life. First, with the decline in mortality, the number of surviving siblings increased, and a new 'horizontal' competition, that is between brothers, took place. Arab populations are presently at the precise point in their history where the proportion aged twenty to twenty-nine—an age group of pressing economic needs and political claims—is the highest out of a total population aged twenty and over. In the coming decade, the recent fertility decline will diminish their relative weight.

The second consequence of the dramatic drop in mortality is a longer duration of the coexistence between generations. In a patriarchal system, a continuous increase in longevity means that fathers will hold power over their sons for a longer time than ever before, and the 'vertical' competition between sons and fathers will also sharpen. This holds true not only of the family but of the political system as well (see, for example, Richards and Waterbury, 1990). The context of this increased competition is strongly marked by the rapid spread of education. Only the young have access to school, and the result is that sons are more educated than fathers (see Figure 4), even though the latter remain in positions of power. A disparity thus appears between the power inherited from patriarchal rules, and the authority based on knowledge gained at school: the over-fifty generations have the monopoly of power, while younger generations have a quasi-monopoly on formal knowledge. Such a situation has great potential for cleavages leading to protest against the social order.

In the following section, the case of Egypt is used to illustrate the way in which such protest is related to change in the hierarchies of age and gender in the country.

Figure 4
Educational inequality between generations of men, Algeria and Egypt

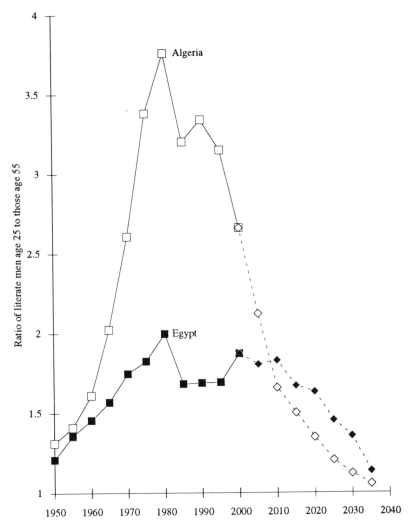

Note: Boys' attendance at school (primary level) is assumed to reach
100 percent in 2000

POLITICAL VIOLENCE AND THE DEMOGRAPHIC TRANSITION: THE
CASE OF EGYPT

Egypt, like other Arab countries, has since 1992 witnessed an increase
in political violence. Political violence is obviously a response to a

political situation, notably to strong imbalances that exist between political forces and democratic institutions. However, careful consideration of current events suggests that there exists a contrasted geography of violence. The location of violence in the country is not random, but rather clusters in selected places: Middle and Upper Egypt, Cairo suburbs, Suez city. The existence of a marked regional pattern of violence clearly shows that explanations at the national level, highlighting factors related to the global political situation, are not sufficient, and that one needs to consider local situations in which political violence takes root.

Elsewhere, I have presented the results of research addressing the possible links between political violence and demography in Egypt (Fargues, 1994a, 1994d). The study started from the notion that political violence is a response, among others, to collective frustration, that is, to gaps between expectations and realizations.[14] It investigated the relationships between political violence and potential demographic or socioeconomic cleavages, and looked at behavioral factors that can act as 'safety valves' inhibiting violent action. A number of variables were considered in each of these two categories. Here I summarize the major findings as they pertain to the argument presented here, namely that political tensions are to a certain extent related to demographic change.

Political violence was estimated by the number of violent episodes reported in the daily paper *Al-Ahram* between 1988 and 1993 under the rubric of terrorism. These included the actions of those usually labeled as terrorists, as well as their repression by the state. Based on the location of the incident, an indicator of violence was calculated for each governorate: the mean annual number of acts of violence per one million inhabitants. This rate of violence ranges from 0.4 (Kafr al-Shaykh governorate) to 11.7 (Asyut governorate). The explanatory variables, including possible safety valves, comprise thirty-three indicators at the governorate level that reflect demographic, social, and economic factors. These include population density, population growth, proportion of young adults, urban population, growth of cities, average family size, proportion of polynuclear families, immigration, emigration, international return migration, migrants' remittances, communal heterogeneity (proportion of Christians), infant mortality, fertility, marriage patterns, unemployment, underemployment, poverty, and average number of years spent at school by generation. Indicators were chosen according to three criteria: a clear position in the explanatory model, a good reliability, and a wide regional variance. We tested for correlations among them.[15]

Economic distress is usually pointed out as a major cause of political violence. However, the Egyptian data clearly show that economic imbalances between governorates do not explain the distribution of violence. Regional rates of acts of violence, be they carried out by individuals claiming their affiliation to extremist movements or by the state against these movements, show no significant statistical relation with phenomena such as unemployment, level of poverty, or the density of inhabited areas. The conclusion is that economic frustration does not directly entail violence. This is partly because emigration—positively correlated with violence in the poorest governorates—offers an alternative to violent mobilization; it is also because other factors, independent of economic distress, have a stronger effect.

In fact, the most significant geographical correlations that we observed were:

1. That violence is positively correlated with heterogeneity of the population, in terms of both religious composition and regional origin: violence is the highest in governorates where either the proportion of non-Muslims or the proportion of the urban population born outside the governorate is high. The explanation here may be that heterogeneity has a greater potential for conflict and that a high rate of internal migration weakens traditional mechanisms of social control, in particular control by the family and the neighborhood, thus leaving room for violent acts.

2. Political violence is higher in those areas with a high proportion of polynuclear families (see Figure 5). The relation is positive at the national level (the correlation coefficient r is high at 0.50) and becomes particularly strong when only the governorates of Upper Egypt are taken into consideration. One can argue that the coexistence of several nuclei in the same household reveals the strength of patriarchal order, implying a rigid hierarchy of generations. It is likely to sharpen both the horizontal competition between peers and the vertical competition between age groups.

3. The level of schooling and its pace of increase are positively correlated with violence (see Figure 6). This suggests that rapid increases in schooling can sharpen vertical competition by differen-

Figure 5
Family structure and political violence in Egypt

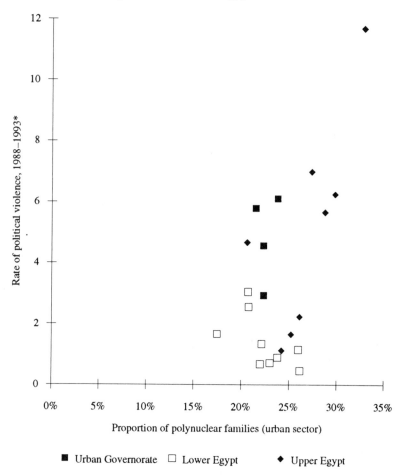

Urban Governorate ☐ Lower Egypt ◆ Upper Egypt

*Computed as the mean number of incidents of protest or state violence per one million inhabitants and one year, by governorate

tiating the youth from the elders and raising their level of expectations, as well as their subsequent frustration. The combination of correlations (2) and (3) means that political violence appears to be greater where hierarchies inherited from the patriarchal order are still active, but challenged by forces of change.

4. Political violence showed a strong positive correlation with the total fertility rate and the infant mortality rate (r=0.66) as well. This is

Figure 6
Level of education of young men and political violence in Egypt

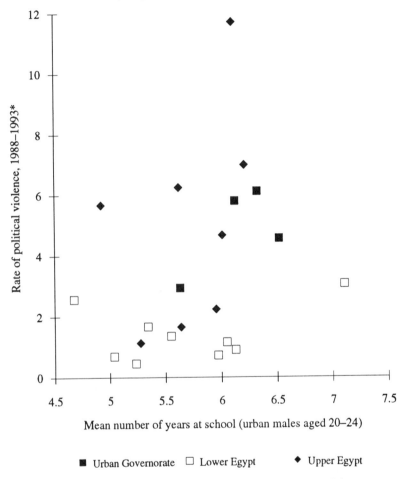

Mean number of years at school (urban males aged 20–24)

■ Urban Governorate   □ Lower Egypt   ◆ Upper Egypt

*Computed as the mean number of incidents of protest or state violence per one million inhabitants and one year, by governorate

a correlation for which one cannot find an easy explanation, especially given the fact that it does not seem to be merely a reflection of economic factors. Just as we could not find a statistical relation between poverty and violence, there is no relation between poverty and infant mortality at the governorate level (r=0). In other words, infant mortality does not vary so much with the income of the family as with its mode of organization, in particular with the status of the woman and her autonomy.[16]

Thus the explanation is not the expected one, that is, that economic distress entails both a poorer health status of children and a higher degree of frustration, leading in turn to violent protest. Rather, a possible explanation for the association between infant mortality and violence could be that it is a function of the status of women: in communities where women's options are limited, one finds both a worse health status of children and a higher degree of overall frustration, which in turn is linked with violence.

What the Egyptian case shows is that the relation between demographic change and political violence is not, as one may have expected, simply mediated by economic pressures. Rather it is mediated by changes in the order of the family: the demographic transition is indirectly related to a crisis of society, which can lead to political violence. Education seems to play a key role by accelerating the demographic transition process and by deepening the frustrations of young educated people still deprived of power by patriarchal rules.

However, it is important to note that such discrepancies may be a temporary phenomenon. If we project the horizontal and vertical imbalances described above into the future, it becomes clear that they will become attenuated. Indeed, when the young generations (in which almost all boys and girls receive an education) become adults, the sharp sex and age differentials according to education will have all but disappeared. It is also likely that the confrontations that have characterized previous generations will have faded away.

CONCLUSION

Population and the political domain are commonly associated in the notion of 'population policies,' referring to the means through which policy makers try to influence population trends, and in particular patterns of family formation. This chapter briefly attempted to reverse the perspective and show how changes in the family can have an effect on political processes. Demographic transitions have affected family patterns both quantitatively and qualitatively. In terms of numbers, a long period of mortality decline without any change in fertility has produced the largest group of young adults relative to elders, and the longest period of coexistence between these two groups. The potential of competition between individuals in the same young age groups has increased, while the dominance of older generations over younger ones has become protracted. Economic circumstances prevailing in the region during the 1970s and 1980s, in particular flows of wealth originating from those countries that are either oil exporters or able to divert a substantial part of oil rent, have strengthened these character-istics by making a faster fall of mortality possible, while keeping fertility at pretransitional levels. The patriarchal order, based upon the domination of men over women and of older groups over younger, was maintained. It is only recently that rapid declines in fertility have reversed the trend, notably in countries deprived of oil revenue. This decline is closely correlated with the spread of schooling, in particular among girls. School education not only results in lower fertility but introduces qualitative changes in the families. Because women tend, in the long run, to become almost as educated as men, and the youth to be much more educated than their elders, the roots of the patriarchal order are challenged and the potential frustration is growing. At a time when values, social structures, and political systems are hotly debated in Muslim societies, such a process of transformation is likely to exacerbate tensions. Insofar as they deal with matters such as the position of women and the education of young people, current population policies are thus indirectly playing a role in the political change itself.

REFERENCES

Abu Shukr, A. 1992. *al-Bitala fi-l-aradi al-filastiniya al-muhtalla, 1968–1991.* Amman/Nablus: Economic and Social Commission for Western Asia.

El-Beblawi, H. and G. Luciani. 1987. *The Rentier State.* London: Croom Helm.

Caldwell, J. 1986. Routes to low mortality in poor countries. *Population and Development Review.* 12/2:171–220.

CBS. 1993. *Statistical Yearbook of Israel 1992.* Jerusalem: Central Bureau of Statistics.

Courbage, Y. and M. Khlat. 1993. Population structure and growth in the Arab world: Recent trends. Paper presented at the Arab Population Conference, Amman, April 1993.

DHS. 1988. *Egypt demographic and health survey, 1988.* Cairo: National Population Council.

———. 1993. *Egypt demographic and health survey, 1992.* Cairo: National Population Council.

Fargues, P. 1989. The decline of Arab fertility. *Population English Selection.* 1:147–75.

———. 1990. Algérie, Maroc, Tunisie: vers la famille restreinte? *Population et Sociétés.* 248.

———. 1994a. Demographic explosion or social upheaval. In G. Salamé, ed., *Democracy without democrats.* London: Tauris.

———. 1994b. La diffusion de l'instruction scolaire d'après les recensements égyptiens. *Revue Egypte/Monde Arabe.* 18–19:115–34.

———. 1994c. Démographie de guerre, démographie de paix. In G. Salamé, ed., *Proche-Orient, les exigences de la paix.* Paris: Complexe.

———. 1994d. Violence politique et démographie en Egypte. In *Le phénomène de la violence politique: perspectives comparatistes et paradigme égyptien.* Cairo: Centre d'Etudes et de Documentation Economiques et Juridiques.

Farid, S. 1993. Family planning, health, and the family well-being in the Arab world. Paper presented at the Arab Population Conference, Amman, April 1993.

Fergany, N. 1994. On the age pattern of the participation of women in economic activity in Egypt. Cairo: *Al-Mishkat Research Notes.* 4.

Gurr, T. R. 1970. *Why men rebel.* Princeton: Princeton University Press.

Hausman, L. J., A. D. Karasik, et al. 1993. *Securing peace in the Middle East: Project on economic transition.* Cambridge: Harvard University Press.

Heiberg, M. and G. Ovensen, eds. 1993. *Palestinian society in Gaza, West Bank and Arab Jerusalem: A survey of living conditions.* FAFO report 151, Oslo.

Al-Laithy, H. and H. Kheir Al-Din. 1993. Evaluation de la pauvreté en Egypte en fonction des données sur les ménages. *Revue Egypte/Monde Arabe.* 12–13:109–144.

Lama, Y. and M. Ferraro. 1989. *General survey of health services in the occupied territories.* Jerusalem: Ministry of Foreign Affairs, Government of Italy.

Richards, A. and J. Waterbury. 1990. *A political economy of the Middle East: State, class and economic development.* Oxford: Westview Press.

Salman, H. K. 1993. *Palestinian women and economic and social development in the West Bank and Gaza Strip.* New York: UNCTAD/DSD/SEU/Misc. 4.

Sharabi, H. 1988. *Neopatriarchy: A theory of distorted change in Arab Society.* Oxford and New York: Oxford University Press.

Waterbury, J. 1994. Democracy without democrats? The potential for political liberalization in the Middle East. In G. Salamé, ed., *Democracy without democrats.* London: Tauris.

World Bank. 1993. Human resources and social policy. *Developing the occupied territories: An investment in peace,* vol. 6. Washington, D.C.: The World Bank.

NOTES

1   The hypothesis of 'neopatriarchy' is borrowed from Hisham Sharabi. It asserts that the authoritarianism of Arab political regimes has cultural roots in traditional patterns of gender relations and authority within the family, which are themselves reinforced by the powerful means of modern states (Sharabi, 1988).

2   Palestinian fertility in the Occupied Territories is not precisely known: births are recorded but the total population is merely updated from a (probably understated) figure obtained at the 1967 census. As a result, there are various estimates of total fertility rates. A Government of Italy study gives a TFR of 7.2 in Gaza and 6.5 in the West Bank (Lama and Ferraro, 1989). A World Bank report indicates that births may be under-registered in the same proportion as the population (World Bank, 1993), thus giving unbiased estimates of crude birth rates (56 and 46 per thousand in 1992 in Gaza and the West Bank respectively, which correspond approximately to TFR of between 8 and 10 children). A recent demographic survey provides (with what level of reliability?) an age-pyramid of the population which would indicate a lower fertility: 7.6 in Gaza and 5.7 in the West Bank (Heiberg and Ovensen, 1993). My own estimates (9 in Gaza and 8 in the West Bank) are based on Israeli data (Fargues, 1994c).

3   Jordan, the Occupied Territories of Palestine, and Yemen are referred to as 'semi-oil' countries in Figure 1, in the sense that their economy is supported in large part by the oil revenue of the Gulf states.

4   Several scholars have characterized Arab economies as 'distributive.' They have pointed out that in Arab countries by and large, the share of the state's budget that comes from direct taxation is relatively low. This 'low fiscality' means that the functioning of the state is relatively independent of household assets, and consequently, that the correspondence between individual's duties and rights toward the state is somewhat loose (see, among others, Waterbury, 1994; El-Beblawi and Luciani, 1987).

5   Oil and gas together represent more than 90 percent of total exports in Algeria.

6   These figures are higher than those of the Demographic and Health Surveys of 1988 and 1992, which found a steady decline in fertility during the 1970s and 1980s. But the 1988 DHS reveals a potential bias in the samples, and a resulting under-estimate of fertility. Indeed, applying age-specific fertility rates found in the DHS to the actual female age distributions based on census data leads to absolute numbers of births that are largely below those registered in vital statistics records. Since vital statistics are not susceptible to over-registration, this clearly indicates an underestimation of fertility levels by the DHS.

7   Household surveys have documented an increasing average level of income among Egyptian families from 1974–75 to 1981–82, along with

an impoverishment of the poorest, followed by a stagnation (if not a decrease) of household welfare after the mid-1980s (see Al-Laithy and Kheir Al-Din, 1993).

8 One can object that, before comparing countries, years of schooling should be weighted by the quality of teaching, or by other factors related to the process, education itself, such as the extent to which school provides a context for the free mixing of the sexes.

9 However, according to the World Bank, the quality of school education in the West Bank and the Gaza Strip seems to remain below regional norms (World Bank, 1993).

10 Calculated by the author, from CBS, 1993.

11 According to Abd al-Fattah Abu Shukr, the unemployment rate in the Occupied Territories was 27.2 percent in 1990 and climbed to 42.7 percent in June 1991, as a result of return migration following the Gulf war, and 40 percent of active men living in the Occupied Territories work in Israel (Abu Shukr, 1992). Hausman, Karasik, *et al.* (1993) give the figure of 110,000 Palestinians employed in Israel, representing 31 percent of the male active population in the West Bank and 39 percent in the Gaza Strip. These authors note that the magnitude of Palestinian employment in Israel has been lowered by the Intifada.

12 The media, particularly in Israel, has written much about the "Palestinian Demographic Bomb."

13 Hind Kattan Salman presents evidence that the Israeli occupation has worked to maintain a traditional status for a majority of women (Salman, 1993).

14 This is the central thesis of a classic book on political violence (Gurr, 1970).

15 As this was a complex set of variables, only the major clusters relevant to the purpose of this chapter can be summarized here.

16 Many scholars have shown that infant mortality is linked more closely to the status of women than to purely economic factors (Caldwell, 1986). In fact, the strong linear correlation that we found between infant mortality rate (IMR) and political violence is independent of economic indicators, including poverty. We thus argue here that a high IMR can be used as a good proxy for a low status of women.

9

Target-Setting in Family Planning Programs: Controversies and Challenges

Karima Khalil, Cynthia Myntti

National family planning programs in developing countries arose out of global and national concerns that rapid population growth would have a detrimental effect on socioeconomic development. Programs defined the central problem as high fertility and they sought to control women's fertility in particular. Thus, reduced fertility became the basis for judging the success or failure of programs. Broader reproductive health concerns were not part of the early family planning agenda.

Public and private efforts to address the problem of global population growth began as early as the 1950s and built on the efforts of pioneers such as Margaret Sanger and Marie Stopes, who had advocated birth control earlier. But it was not until the World Population Conference held in Bucharest in 1974 that the first intergovernmental meeting on population espoused a distinct philosophy and drew up a global plan of action to address population problems. While the meeting is best remembered for the 'anti-family planning' stand taken by many countries and the statement "development is the best contraceptive," it did set forth specific guidelines for the development of national population policies, goals, and programs.

National family planning programs were established and grew in sophistication in the 1970s and 1980s. Program managers used the guidelines set forth in the Bucharest documents and, with the encouragement of donors, moved from general statements about what they hoped to achieve to explicitly-worded policies and measurable goals. Countries in Asia led the way by strongly endorsing state efforts to control population growth. The Third Asian and Pacific Population Conference, held in Colombo, Sri Lanka, in 1982, produced the following recommendation:

> Countries are urged to review and modify existing targets and goals in the implementation of population and development programs for reducing birth and death rates so as to attain low levels as early as possible and to attain a replacement level of fertility by the year 2000 (United Nations, 1982:28; United Nations, 1989:3–4).

The Fourth Asian and Pacific Population Conference, held in Bali, Indonesia, in 1992, reaffirmed this commitment. However, recognizing that several countries in the region have lagged behind in their demographic performance, the meeting recommended attaining replacement level fertility by the year 2010, or sooner (United Nations, 1993:4).

DEFINITIONS

Both qualitative and quantitative targets have figured in national development plans. A qualitative target, which will not be discussed further in this paper, is a general goal such as the improved status of women, or "health for all by the year 2000." A quantitative target is "a numerical goal directly pertaining to any one or more of the basic demographic variables that a national or subnational group sets up for itself to achieve, often according to some designated time plan" (United Nations, 1989:4).

Quantitative targets to track population dynamics have typically measured fertility, mortality, marriage, morbidity, and migration. These are usually phrased as a desired reduction in certain rates, including rate of natural increase, crude birth rate, total fertility rate, net reproduction rate, crude death rate, infant mortality rate, maternal mortality ratio, and the incidence or prevalence of certain diseases. Used in this sense, a quantitative demographic target is a macro-level indicator of population change; it reflects desired outcomes or impact. A number of output measures are also used as targets. These include prevalence and incidence measures, such as contraceptive prevalence (current users of contraception) or new acceptors (of any method).

Most governments have tied their demographic targets to the time frame of periodic national development plans. Tunisia, for example, since the Fourth Plan for Social and Economic Development (1973–76), has regularly stated its desire to achieve the fertility target of a gross reproduction rate of 1.15 per woman by the year 2001. Egypt and Tunisia are two Arab countries which have clearly defined total fertility rate and contraceptive prevalence rate targets for the 1990s (see Tables 1 and 2).

Today, however, when one hears the term 'target,' one thinks of a different, more micro-level measure, such as the number of IUD acceptors a certain family planning worker must recruit in a given year. Indeed, as funding increased for programs designed to control

Table 1
Total fertility rate objectives for the nineties: Egypt and Tunisia

	Egypt	Tunisia
1992/93	4.0	3.45[a]
1993/94	3.9	
1994/95	3.8	
1995/96	3.7	2.98[b]
1996/97	3.5	
2001	2.9	2.05

Sources: Egyptian National Population Council, 1992; Tunisian National Family and Human Resources Council, 1991; Zaghloul, 1993
[a]1991   [b]1996

Table 2
Contraceptive prevalence rate objectives for the nineties: Egypt and Tunisia

	Egypt	Tunisia
1992	47.8	53.84
1993	49.1	54.86
1994	50.6	55.92
1995	52.0	56.98
1996	53.5	59.12
1997	55.0	60.19
2001	64.4	63.07

Sources: Egyptian National Population Council, 1992; Tunisian National Family and Human Resources Council, 1991; Zaghloul, 1993

population growth, their quantitative goals became more specific and sophisticated, and soon, in some countries, provider- and/or contraceptive-specific quotas were in place at the local level. Under this system, aggregate targets are passed mechanically from senior officials down to peripheral family planning workers, who must deliver predetermined numbers of contraceptives (often enumerated by method) within a specified period of time. These quotas have raised controversy due to the potential for abuse of client rights and needs.

To understand how this change in the definition and use of targets came about, we must examine the role of professional demographers in refining the methods of measurement, of donors in encouraging measures for evaluating program achievements, and of local bureaucratic culture in defining both the basis for assessing performance and the nature of citizens' rights. Targets as quotas have been most problematic in China, India, Bangladesh, Indonesia, and other countries in Asia. The Arab world has not yet experienced a major push toward quotas, although there is evidence that the Egyptian family planning program uses them. We will return to the Egyptian case below.

THE VARYING USES OF TARGETS

Demographers eagerly developed the quantitative measures of family planning program performance (Bogue, 1972, 1993; Bongaarts, 1984, 1986; Fong, 1982). When a particular country set macro-level demographic goals, more specific indices could then be worked out. Mathematical models could show, for example, the number of additional couples needed to practice family planning in order to achieve a specified reduction in the birth rate. This was in turn broken down by contraceptive method, making certain assumptions about method effectiveness and the age structure of the population. Computer software packages such as Target were developed to assist the calculations and their graphic presentation. Policy makers could learn in an instant how many births would be averted through their family planning efforts. Further refinements continue by adding costs, demand conditions, and use effectiveness into the calculations (Moreland, 1993). Even at this specific level, targets were originally intended to be used as a tool to aid top- to intermediate-level managers in estimating supplies, budgeting, and hiring staff. Donors, many of whom were contributing contraceptive supplies as well as funds to national family planning programs, also needed numbers for planning purposes.

Yet, as with any hard or soft technology, the social and political context determined how targets were ultimately used. Donors certainly played a role in what happened. Target-setting for forward logistical planning was part of modern management taught in training programs for family planning managers. But donors—bilateral donors in particular—were also under pressure to show to their tax-paying constituencies that their development assistance in population was having a measurable impact. Demographers continued to refine their measurement tools to assist donors and program managers in the task of program evaluation. Program 'success' became equated with reduced population growth, reduced fertility and birth rates, and increased contraceptive use. The role of targets changed accordingly, from logistical planning to evaluating performance at all levels of the system.

The international preoccupation with controlling population growth in developing countries and the continuing dependence of many national programs on external funding provided the context in which targets were used. The poorest countries with the highest growth rates received most attention from the donor community. Pressures to meet targets were transferred down through the system to the community-based family planning worker, who was also then made to show numerical results.

Bangladesh offers a clear example of how these pressures worked (United Nations, 1989:77). The fertility target set by the central government and donors was converted to a number (contraceptive prevalence), which was divided among districts and subdivisions to set local quotas for family planning 'acceptors.' In addition, long-term fertility targets were converted to those for five-year periods, which were in turn divided into annual and even monthly quotas to be met by family planning workers. In an article on ethics and family planning, Warwick explains:

> The threats to free choice, welfare, justice and even the physical survival of users mount when field workers who do not meet quotas are threatened with dismissal from their jobs or with having their salaries withheld. In Bangladesh family planning field workers, village midwives, and members of the public have received a fee for each person they motivated or referred for

sterilization. Until 1985, field workers could also be penalized for shortfalls on sterilization quotas (1990:27).

A number of evaluators of the program in Bangladesh have argued that the targets were merely too ambitious, and therefore the gap between planned and actual results was wide and performance judged as negative. Others have suggested that the process of target-setting in such a centralized way is itself highly problematic; national targets are divided mechanically into district quotas, and thus do not take into account variations from one district to the next, and one month to the next.

Donald Bogue, a demographer who was involved early on in establishing the techniques for target-setting, said recently that targets were always meant to be set through a consultative process—between donors and recipient governments, and between central administrations and workers at the periphery—so as to insure realistic goals and to respect regional diversity (Bogue, 1993). This clearly did not happen in countries where top-down programs precluded any consultation with lowest-level workers about fair and realistic goals. If anything, targets made already unwieldy governmental bureaucracies more oppressive and inevitably less responsive to the needs of their people.

The experiences of the family planning program in India during the Emergency Period (June 1975–January 1977), when extremely heavy-handed tactics were used to meet sterilization quotas, put these issues into dramatic relief. Concerned with rapid population growth, the government of Indira Gandhi set ambitious sterilization targets. Widespread abuse was reported; fraudulent reports were filed and even elderly men were hunted down by armed 'multidisciplinary' sterilization teams with quotas to meet (Larsen, 1987:22; Maloney, 1986:2). Although the abuses led to the downfall of Mrs. Gandhi's government, targets continue to be used in the program (Bang, 1988; Jain, 1989). In a thorough analysis of the systemic problems of the family planning program in one state of north India, Misra and colleagues (1982:340–41) describe the unidirectional decision-making behind target-setting there:

Neither the formal program documents nor our individual discussions with program officials reveal that information about target feasibility was ever requested from lower levels within the program . . . . the existence of highly unrealistic targets has led to more frustration and disillusionment than it has contributed toward inspiring the family planning staff to accomplish maximum goals.

Critics have argued further that targets in the Emergency Period and today encourage workers to inflate their performance figures (Townsend and Khan, 1993:4). Targets also violate the norms of ethical medical practice (*Economic and Political Weekly*, 1986).

Short-term and method-specific quotas given to local providers also raise troubling ethical dilemmas and affect the quality of care offered. Workers who are required to meet certain contraceptive quotas in a year or month, and who are penalized when they fail to do so, cannot be expected to offer unbiased information, a choice of methods, or the most clinically appropriate care.

Coercion represents the most extreme means for meeting quotas. However, more subtle examples can be found in other countries where information and choice are compromised in order to meet quotas. Indonesia is a case in point. In 1989, for example, President Suharto was given an award by the United Nations for creating a political climate supportive of the national family planning program, and facilitating a dramatic decline in fertility there. That program is often referred to as the world's most successful. One strategy employed has been the encouragement of what are referred to as 'secure' methods, namely the IUD, Norplant, and sterilization. Workers are assessed on how many new recruits to these methods they get, irrespective of whether the method is desired or appropriate. In one-day campaigns ('safaris'), which have been a long-standing feature of the program and essential for reaching quotas of 'secure' methods in a given locale, hundreds of new 'acceptors' are gathered for mass services. Although the government family planning program no longer officially uses safaris, they continue unofficially under the sponsorship of other institutions. Likewise, targets have been officially discontinued in Indonesia (National Family Planning Coordinating Board, 1993). It remains to be seen whether the new approach termed 'demand fulfillment' means anything different in practice.

Ironically, quotas may undermine program goals. Indonesian target-mindedness has had a striking effect on the population of women whom the program was meant to serve. Women to whom the 'secure' methods have been directed feel that the family planning workers are not interested in what is best for them as individuals, that they give biased information, and prescribe methods that might actually harm them. So where possible they avoid family planning workers or, if they have the means, they go to private services where they perceive the care to be of a better quality (Sciortino, 1992:22).

Medical associations, women's health advocates, and human rights groups have labeled targets as a central problem in population control policies and family planning services. Targets as contraceptive or provider-specific quotas have been criticized because they ignore the right of women and men to voluntary fertility regulation, take no account of the user's needs or intentions, and compromise the quality of care by limiting choice, information, and even clinical appropriateness (Bruce, 1990).

TARGET-SETTING IN THE EGYPTIAN PROGRAM

The government of Egypt has had a nationally supported family planning program since 1965, making it the first country in the Arab world to identify population growth as a problem and to promote the use of contraceptives as a means of fertility reduction. The reduction of fertility and slowing of population growth remain the overall aims of the program.

Using fertility reduction as the standard of evaluation, Egypt's program has been reasonably successful. The most optimistic estimates suggest that between 1980 and 1988 the total fertility rate fell from 5.2 births per woman to 4.4 (the 1992 Demographic and Health Survey shows a further drop to 3.9). And between 1980 and 1991, contraceptive prevalence rose from 24 to 47 percent. The 1992 DHS found that a full 66 percent of all currently married women of reproductive age did not want another child. A further 16 percent wanted to wait at least two years before the birth of the next child. This suggests that, with appropriate effort, the program could reach many more women wanting family planning services.

Although many different governmental and non-governmental organizations are currently active in family planning in Egypt, the Ministry of Population and Family Welfare (until November 1993 called the National Population Council) is the primary architect of national population policy, and the Ministry of Health is the country's main provider of family planning services. Since 1987, the United States Agency for International Development has funded a large Systems Development Project (SDP), a family planning program within the Ministry of Health. The project is currently operating in three thousand rural Ministry of Health clinics and two hundred hospital outpatient departments, and represents perhaps the most innovative governmental approach to family planning in Egypt. More will be said about SDP efforts below.

Both the Ministry of Population and the Ministry of Health employ targets for planning and evaluation purposes. The following discussion highlights the different uses of such numerical goals, and problems associated with their use.

The Ministry of Population sets national, regional, and local targets. Targets (outcomes and outputs) and quotas, as we have defined them, are used. For example, as shown in Tables 1 and 2, Egypt aims to have a total fertility rate of 2.9 and a contraceptive prevalence rate of 64.4 by the year 2001.

The Ministry of Population has specified these goals in annual increments during the 1990s. Each year the national-level demographic targets are broken down into achievements expected by smaller and smaller administrative units, such as governorates, *aqsam*, and *marakiz*. At these lower administrative units, the main measure of achievement has been the output measure 'couple years of protection' (CYP). This is calculated by counting the number of contraceptives distributed, then applying a conversion factor to allow comparability among methods. To evaluate family planning program performance, the ministry compares CYP achieved with that targeted for a particular locale.

The ministry also compares another output measure, the governorate-level count of new 'acceptors,' against the goal it has set for that governorate. For example, 629,205 women were recruited as new family planning users in Cairo in 1992. This number represented 87.6 percent of what the ministry had hoped to achieve in Cairo for that year.

The Systems Development Project (SDP) of the Ministry of Health uses a different system of setting its goals, and clinic-level staff provide data for the calculations. Every clinic or unit director is responsible for setting the unit's prospective quota by calculating contraceptive prevalence for the current year from the numerator (CYP based on contraceptives actually distributed by the clinic) and the denominator (estimated married women of reproductive age in the health unit's service area); desired contraceptive prevalence for the following year is then defined as this year's contraceptive prevalence multiplied by 1.7. This multiple assumes a reduction in the crude birth rate by one per thousand per year, and is applied similarly across all SDP units. The multiple of 1.7 implies a 70 percent annual increase in contraceptive prevalence.

Although this method of quota-setting is based on realistic numerators and denominators (actual numbers of contraceptives distributed and women counted in the service area), the very ambitious increases required for the following year are centrally determined. This is a problem. In addition, the method-mix is generally assumed to stay the same from year to year, but managers may adjust the CYP figures if a shift to one method becomes apparent.

CONCERNS ABOUT TARGETS IN THE EGYPTIAN PROGRAM

After discussing the Egyptian family planning program with providers, policy makers, and donors in Egypt, as well as reviewing the scarce literature on Egypt's experience with target-setting, we have a number of concerns. Firstly, the process by which targets and quotas are constructed and assigned to different administrative areas is sometimes confusing and arbitrary, resulting in often unrealistic goals. Zaghloul and Fouttouh (1993), for example, have shown that 'averaged' goals are applied across governorates, without any regard for obviously different populations, such as urban and rural women, who have different contraceptive practice. Top-down target-setting cannot reflect the diversity of local conditions. To redress this problem, a new Ministry of Population project, the Institutional Development Subproject, aims to improve the way targets are set. Governorate-level staff are being trained in the methodology of setting numerical goals. This activity merits further attention, although it may simply improve the mechanics of calculation rather than address the more basic problems of target-setting.

Secondly, and perhaps more fundamentally, the reaching of quotas and targets has become a common—sometimes the sole—means of evaluating the performance of family planning workers, clinic managers, and district- and governorate-level administrators. The rationale for work becomes meeting the quota, rather than serving clients well or promoting health and welfare.

And indeed, the numbers used are not necessarily hard, valid, or objective measures of performance. The measure most often used in

Egypt, the 'couple years of protection' (CYP), a variant of contraceptive prevalence, is problematic (Zaghloul and Fouttouh, 1993; Jain and Bruce, 1993). It is merely a measure of contraceptives distributed, and does not measure use or effectiveness. Many contraceptives counted in the calculations of CYP may actually have been discarded, removed, or never used at all. A recent study on IUDs in Bangladesh states that such calculations led to an over-estimation of use by 40 percent (Kamal *et al.*, 1992).

Adding financial incentives into the equation further complicates the situation, particularly when workers have to meet quotas and certain methods are rewarded more than others. In Egypt, incentives are routinely used to supplement the very low salaries of government-employed family planning providers. Incentives are calculated as a proportion of the cost of the contraceptive method. So, for example, incentives for offering IUDs are greater to the provider than those for contraceptive pills. Incentives of this kind strongly limit the possibility of informed choice for women seeking contraception, and may lead to the prescription of methods that are not appropriate.

So the conflict is between the quantity of contraceptives distributed and the quality of care received. The preoccupation with numbers—numbers of contraceptives distributed and the number of new acceptors of certain methods—affects the kind of information communicated between provider and client, the real choice of method given, and possibly even its clinical appropriateness. This quantitative orientation must be understood in the Egyptian context, where a wide educational and class gap between most providers and their clients exists, as is the case in many countries. Many Egyptian health and family planning providers have so little trust in the knowledge and abilities of their clients that their respect for the clients' right to informed choice is minimal (Sayed *et al.*, 1992). To such providers, quotas may seem a reasonable management tool.

There are some signs of change, however. The Ministry of Health's Systems Development Project (SDP) has not discarded incentives or quotas but is working to make them less prone to abuse and more supportive of quality improvements. The project plans to make incentives uniform across all methods, for example. They also plan to add selected qualitative indicators to the assessment of performance in the project's clinics across the country. Clients will be asked, for example, about the services they have received, the duration of waiting time, the politeness of the provider, information provided, cleanliness of the unit, and cost of the method. Whether the new attention to clients' perspectives will make a difference remains to be seen, particularly in face of the continuing use of incentives and quotas.

The family planning program in Egypt is at a crossroads. National policy makers, together with Egypt's main population donors, should reexamine the dichotomy between quantity and quality. In particular, Egypt's ministries of population and health should learn from other countries' negative experiences in the use of quotas, and consider alternative, more client-sensitive methods for monitoring program performance.

THE GLOBAL ISSUES

Two pressing questions emerge from the debate about targets that merit serious attention by the population community. Firstly, are the population control objectives that guided family planning program efforts from the 1970s still valid? To what extent should 'success' be measured in terms of reduced population growth? Secondly, recognizing that targets as quotas have led to abuse, what are the other options for motivating staff and assessing performance at the local level? What should be the objective of family planning programs in the 1990s and beyond?

A spectrum of opinions exists, ranging from the traditional or orthodox approach, which aims to reduce the population growth rate by spreading the use of contraceptives, to one espoused by women's health and rights advocates, which states that the only valid intervention is that which holistically addresses individual women's and men's reproductive health needs.

The definition of program 'success' will obviously depend on which approach is taken and which goals are targeted. We agree with Berer (1991) that unlimited population growth is a problem for sustainable development. But it is time to move away from the limits of the traditional approach to one that places health needs and rights at the center of the debate. Others have argued similarly for a comprehensive approach to reproductive health services (Jain, 1992; WHO, 1991).

Meeting reproductive health needs and respecting individual rights are basic program requirements, and, in our view, the only ethical approach. Much new epidemiological evidence underlines the need for comprehensive reproductive health care. Studies such as that by Zurayk, Khattab, and Younis (this volume), suggest that women bear an extraordinary burden of reproductive illness, and family planning programs can no longer be ethical or credible if they ignore these broader health issues.

We hypothesize that a broad reproductive health approach may actually increase the efficacy of family planning programs in reaching their goal of reduced population growth. Standard approaches are inefficient. As Jain (1992) has argued, recruiting a small number of new contraceptive users each year and taking better care of them (along with existing users) may have a greater demographic impact than concentrating efforts on recruiting more and more acceptors. There is further evidence that unsatisfactory services frighten away would-be clients: women will avoid providers whom they consider uninterested in their well-being. It has also been hypothesized that contraceptive use effectiveness might actually increase if women were given the opportunity to ask questions and have them answered. In countries like Egypt, discontinuation and failure rates remain high, and point to the need for new approaches. Propaganda and 'motivation' represent a unidirectional flow of information from the program to the client; they tend to increase suspicion and concerns rather than minimize them.

If a program were to espouse the health and rights approach advocated here, how would performance be measured? Contraceptive- and provider-specific quotas have no place in a program that begins by considering the needs of individual women and men. And macro-level demographic measures are at once too narrow in their exclusive attention to fertility, and too general because they consider general population statistics rather than individual data to be of use to program managers.

At a recent workshop among donors sponsored by the World Bank (1992), it was argued that attention to the quality of care in family planning programs leads to increased contraceptive prevalence and, ultimately, more effective programs. Care of high quality responds to reproductive health needs and respects individual rights. One way to improve quality is to reward individuals and systems offering that kind of care. It might therefore be possible to develop locally appropriate indicators of quality at all levels of the program, and then to assess performance against them.

Process measures should be considered, and could be used in conjunction with or substituted for the conventional quantitative output measures solely relied upon by most programs. Such process measures (the average amount of time spent with the client, hygienic conditions, provider knowledge, etc.) would be relatively easy to measure, difficult to falsify, and have no detrimental side effects on program performance.

Quality measured by client satisfaction is, in theory, another good place to begin. However, assessing satisfaction in practice is notoriously difficult, particularly in societies where consumer awareness is non-existent, expectations for respectful treatment are low, deference to professionals is the norm, and the social gap between providers and clients is wide. Despite these general problems, focus group discussions with clients and providers have been successful in the evaluation of the quality of care in Egypt (Sayed *et al.*, 1992). Client exit questionnaires have also been used in Egypt for the same purpose (CAPMAS, 1992).

For family planning programs wishing to switch gear and be more responsive to the reproductive needs of women and men, numerical goals and methods of evaluation remain important. However, methods of evaluation never stand alone and are part of a system that may or may not be conducive to offering care of high quality. We believe that the 'culture' of family planning and health service organizations must change to be more oriented to service. So long as family planning workers look at clients as mere numbers rather than as persons who should be treated respectfully and empathetically, there is the risk that any system of performance measurement—CYP, unmet need, demand fulfillment, and even qualitative indicators—will be subverted to a potentially abusive end.

While recognizing the necessity of transforming family planning organizational 'culture' to one where the quality of care is valued, one promising approach to assessment is being developed and improved by Jain (1992; Jain and Bruce, 1993). Recognizing that the quality of care needs to be analyzed from a systems perspective, Jain has recommended a series of diagnostic and problem-solving studies for assessing the entire system, from clients' knowledge, logistical support to providers, and managers' attitudes. These diagnostic studies assist problem-solving, rather than assessment per se, but lay the foundation for analyzing the gap between the expected quality of care and the reality of what has been given and received.

Jain has further recommended a client-based indicator of performance, the HARI Index ('Helping Individuals Achieve their Reproductive Intentions'). Unlike contraceptive prevalence, which assumes that all women are equally in need of contraception, HARI divides the population of users into three groups: 'spacers,' who want to delay their next pregnancy; 'limiters,' who want to stop childbearing altogether; and those wishing to become pregnant. The program is assessed on how well it is helping the spacers, limiters, and those desiring a pregnancy achieve their intentions. HARI incorporates the experience of couples over time; it follows people, not methods. It does not penalize the program for those who discontinue because they want to get pregnant, or for those who switch methods, if the first one they choose is unsatisfactory.

The HARI index is calculated by subtracting from 100 the percentage of women who have unplanned (for spacers) or unwanted (for limiters) pregnancies during a specified period (such as twelve or twenty-four months) following the initiation of the method in the program. The index would be 100 if the program is successful in helping clients achieve their intentions to space, limit, or become pregnant. It would be zero if the program is a complete failure. The data required are information on reproductive intentions collected from the client upon initiating the method and periodic follow-up surveys to compare actual experience with intentions. Thus the data needed to calculate the index are collected prospectively, and can be incorporated into DHS surveys, for example.

The HARI index offers a new way to think about assessing program performance by focusing the measurement on each individual woman's needs. This idea is revolutionary, and merits further attention.

ACKNOWLEDGMENTS

We thank Sjaak Bavelaar, Judith Bruce, Med Bouzidi, Oona Campbell, John Cleland, Hassan el-Gebaly, Olfat Haroun, Bert Hirschhorn, Valerie Hull, Barbara Ibrahim, Anrudh Jain, Laila Nawar, Carla Makhlouf Obermeyer, Max Rodenbeck, Hussein Abdul-Aziz El Sayed, Amani Selim, and Saad Zaghloul Amin for their help during the research and writing of this paper. We have not always taken their full advice, but have learned from them all.

REFERENCES

Arango, H. 1989. The MEXFAM community doctors project: An innovative service delivery strategy. *International Family Planning Perspectives.* 15/3:96–105.

Bang, R. 1988. An Indian perspective. *People.* 15/4:2.

Berer, M. 1991. More than just saying 'no': What would a feminist population policy be like? *Conscience.* 12/5:1–5.

Bogue, D. 1972. The magnitude of the population communication task during the remainder of this century. Unpublished paper.

————. 1993. Personal communication.

Bongaarts, J. 1984. A simple method for estimating the contraceptive prevalence required to reach a fertility target. *Studies in Family Planning.* 14/4:184–90.

————. 1986. Contraceptive use and annual acceptors required for fertility transition: Results of a projection model. *Studies in Family Planning.* 17/5:209–216.

Bokhreis, M. 1991. *Population policy and family planning: Strategy for the nineties.* Tunis: The Tunisian National Family and Human Resources Council.

Bruce, J. 1990. Fundamental elements of the quality of care: A simple framework. *Studies in Family Planning.* 21/2: 61–91.

CAPMAS. 1992. Assessment of family planning service delivery in Egypt. *Population Policy Occasional Paper* no. 2. Cairo: Central Agency for Public Mobilization and Statistics.

DHS. 1988. *Egypt demographic and health survey, 1988.* Cairo: National Population Council.

————. 1993. *Egypt demographic and health survey, 1992.* Cairo: National Population Council.

Economic and Political Weekly. 1986. Family planning: dangers of chasing targets. Editorial. 714–15.

Fong, C. O. 1982. A model for analysis of the Malaysian family planning program. *European Journal of Operational Research.* 11:133–44.

Jain, A. 1989. Revising the role and responsibility of the family welfare program in India. *Economic and Political Weekly.* 2729–37.

————, ed. 1992. *Managing quality of care in population programs.* West Hartford, Conn.: Kumarian Press.

Jain, A. and J. Bruce. 1993. *Implications of reproductive health for objectives and efficacy of family planning programs.* New York: The Population Council, Programs Division Working Papers, no. 8.

Kamal, G. M., S. Rahman, T. Nasrin. 1992. *IUD annual evaluation 1990.* Dhaka: Associates for Community and Population Research.

Larsen, T. 1987. Of policies and actions. *People.* 14/2:22–23.

Liberi, D., H. Destler, J. Smith, J. Stover. 1990. *Family planning: Preparing for the twenty-first century.* Washington, D.C.: Office of Population, Family Planning Services Division.

Maloney, C. 1986. India's population—What is being done? *Universities Field Staff International Reports.* 28:1–9.

Misra, B., A. Sharaf, R. Simmons, G. Simmons. 1982. *Organization for change: A systems analysis of family planning in rural India.* Ann Arbor: The University of Michigan Center for South and Southeast Asian Studies.

Moreland, S. 1992. Optimal targeting of family planning: A new method. Research monograph no. 22. Cairo: Cairo Demographic Center.

National Family Planning Coordinating Board (Indonesia) and The Population Council. 1993. *Final report of the operations research workshop on the development of the principles of quality of care in family planning programs in developing countries.* Jakarta: Badan Koordinasi Keluarga Berencana Nasional.

National Population Council (Egypt). 1992. *The population component in the five-year plan: 1992–1997.* Cairo: National Population Council.

Sayed, H. A. A., F. El-Zanaty, N. Guhl. 1992. Quality of family planning services in Egypt (pilot study). Cairo: Cairo Demographic Center.

Sciortino, R. 1992. Fertility and family planning policies in Indonesia. Unpublished report for the Working Group on Indonesian Women's Studies, Leiden.

Townsend, J. and M. E. Khan. 1993. Target-setting in family planning programs: Problems and potential alternatives. Paper presented at the Annual Meeting of the Indian Association for Population Studies, Annamalai University, Chitambran, Tamil Nadu, India, December 16–19.

United Nations. 1982. *Report of the third Asian and Pacific population conference.* Bangkok: United Nations, Economic and Social Commission for Asia and the Pacific.

United Nations. 1989. *Review of recent national demographic target-setting.* New York: United Nations, Department of International Economic and Social Affairs.

United Nations. 1993. *Population and research leads: Overview of population targets and goals for the ESCAP region.* Bangkok: United Nations, Economic and Social Commission for Asia and the Pacific.

Warwick, D. 1990. The ethics of population control. In G. Roberts, ed., *Population policy: contemporary issues.* New York: Praeger.

World Bank. 1992. Effective family planning programs. Unpublished report of a workshop in London, February 1992. World Bank Population, Health, and Nutrition Division.

WHO. 1991. *Creating common ground: Women's perspectives on the selection and introduction of fertility regulation.* Geneva: World Health Organization.

Zaghloul, S. and M. Fouttouh. 1993. Estimation of fertility and of the target population for family planning activities in Egypt 1991–2001. In Arabic. Cairo: The Population Council.

10

Broadening Contraceptive Choice: Lessons from Egypt
Ezzeldin O. Hassan, Mahmoud F. Fathalla

Broadening contraceptive choice is an important element of a quality health care service and a successful family planning program. It is not, however, without problems. This paper draws on the Egyptian experience to derive lessons concerning successes and problems in the introduction of new methods to broaden contraceptive choice.

Contraceptives are needed by people in varied social circumstances, who have different needs and perspectives. They live in skyscrapers, in rural areas, and in urban slums. They include women and men. They come from all socioeconomic strata. Most are healthy. Some have health problems, or have adopted an unhealthy life style. They include young people trying to postpone a first pregnancy, mothers spacing childbirths, and women putting an end to their childbearing career. They hold widely different cultural values and religious beliefs, and they are served or underserved by different health care systems. Meeting the vastly expanding demand for contraceptives is a major concern for all who worry about human welfare at the national and international levels.

The scientific community once hoped to come up with an ideal contraceptive that would serve the needs of everyone, everywhere, at all times. Researchers in the field now realize that this dream cannot come true. Instead, a wide range of contraceptives must be tailored to distinct human needs: for people, circumstances, and phases of life that are different (Fathalla, 1990). Broadening contraceptive choice is the key to ensuring the quality of family planning services. When people do not get contraceptives that meet their needs, a number of scenarios are possible: they may not use contraception; they may discontinue contraception after trying a method not suitable for them; the method may prove ineffective, and an unwanted pregnancy may result; or they may be exposed to unnecessary health hazards. It is not sufficiently realized that the hazards of contraception are not generally inherent in the method, but are the result of a mismatch between the method and the user.

It could be argued that broad contraceptive choice is not necessary for expanding contraceptive prevalence, since the demographic transition in developed countries was achieved without any modern contraceptives. This argument holds the view that contraceptive use is a subjective matter: people who want to use a contraceptive will use one, however unattractive or inconvenient it may be, and those who do not want to use a contraceptive will not. It is true that there will always be a 'yes' group of highly motivated couples and a 'no' group who are ideologically opposed to the concept of contraceptive use. There is, however, a group in between for whom the availability of attractive and convenient methods can make the difference between using and not using contraceptives. The size of this group remains relatively large when the demand for contraceptive use is still fragile (Fathalla, 1989).

The early experience of family planning programs in developing countries indicates that the addition of a new method attracts a new layer of users (Freedman and Berelson, 1976). A more recent study based on data from several developing countries found that the addition of one method in a given country will, on average, increase the contraceptive prevalence rate by 12 percentage points (Jain, 1989). More recent experience with new methods also supports this evidence. In a study of Norplant introduction in Indonesia involving 8,681 subjects, 46.7 percent of the acceptors were previously not using any contraceptive method (Affandi, 1987). In general, it is noted that the greater the number of methods available, the higher the country's overall contraceptive prevalence rate will be (Ross *et al.*, 1989).

The availability of a broad choice of methods makes it possible for clients who are dissatisfied with one method to switch to another, more acceptable method rather than discontinuing contraceptive use altogether. This was demonstrated in the Matlab project in Bangladesh, where method-specific continuation rates were low but overall contraceptive continuation and prevalence rates were high, in part because other method choices were made available (Phillips *et al.*, 1988). A study of contraceptive continuation in Indonesia (Pariani *et al.*, 1991) also found that women who were given the method they requested were much more likely to continue using the method after one year (91 percent continuation rate) than women who had been denied their original choice (28 percent continuation rate).

Broadening the range of methods available also has important safety implications. While methods of contraception are subject to rigorous testing before they are approved for general use, they are not necessarily safe for every user. In this connection, it should also be noted that effectiveness is part of the equation for safety. A method that has no side effects but has a relatively high failure rate will subject the woman to the health risks of unwanted pregnancy, which can be substantial.

In sum, limiting the choice of contraceptives will result in more people using methods that are not optimal for their particular circumstances (Fathalla, 1991). Making a wide range of methods available, on the other hand, will help to ensure that methods and users are better matched to improve user safety.

DIVERSITY IN THE PREVALENCE OF SPECIFIC CONTRACEPTIVE
METHODS

A brief review of the worldwide prevalence of contraceptive methods shows that there is no uniform mix of contraceptive methods. There are variations from region to region, and from country to country, which are the result of the availability and promotion of certain methods, rather than the result of cultural differences. In the Middle East and North Africa (Table 1), Turkey has the highest prevalence of use of contraceptive methods (63 percent), followed by Lebanon, Tunisia, and Egypt (53 percent, 50 percent, and 47 percent respectively). IUDs and oral contraceptive pills are the two most widely used methods in this region (Ross *et al.*, 1993).

Population-based studies carried out in Egypt over the past decade indicate an ongoing trend of increased IUD use, an increase in overall

Table 1

Percentage of couples of reproductive age using contraceptives

	Year of survey	Prevalence	Sterilization	IUD	Pill
Algeria	1986	36	1	2	27
Egypt	1992	47	1	28	13
Iraq	1974	14	1	1	8
Jordan	1990	35	6	15	5
Lebanon	1971	53	1	1	14
Morocco	1992	42	3	3	28
Syria	1978	20	1	1	12
Tunisia	1988	50	12	17	9
Turkey	1992	63	2	14	6
Yemen AR	1991–92	10	1	1	3

Source: Ross *et al.,* 1993

contraceptive prevalence, an increase in the use of modern methods, and a switch from use of the oral contraceptive pill to IUD use (Figures 1 and 2; Ross *et al.*, 1993). Results of the 1992 Egyptian Demographic and Health Survey showed that women's knowledge about the different contraceptive methods available to them in Egypt was quite high, whereas their previous and current contraceptive practice, by comparison, was very low (Table 2). The same survey also demonstrated marked changes in contraceptive prevalence, mainly related to patterns of marriage and fertility. For women aged 15–44, the total fertility rate decreased from 5.2 in 1980 to 3.9 in 1992 (a 25 percent decline). Contraceptive prevalence almost doubled during the same period, increasing from 24 to 47 percent during the same period. Changes have also taken place in the family planning program itself: in its focus and contraceptive method mix and in its emphasis on training providers to help overcome barriers to use. The desired number of children, however, was found to be much less than the total fertility rate, indicating the potential for an unmet need by couples who would limit their fertility if contraceptive methods appropriate to their needs were available.

INTRODUCTION OF CONTRACEPTIVE METHODS IN EGYPT: THE PILL AND THE PROBLEM OF NON-COMPLIANCE

The National Family Planning Program was initiated in Egypt in 1966, and family planning services were provided along with other basic health services at a negligible cost to a large segment of the

Figure 1
Current use of contraception in Egypt by method

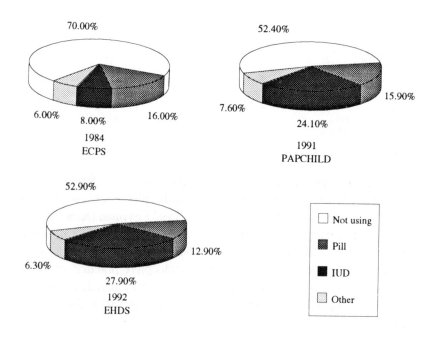

Figure 2
Trends in contraceptive prevalence by method over time in Egypt

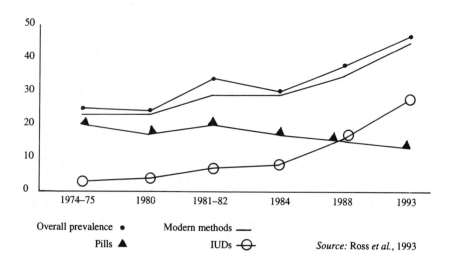

Table 2

Knowledge and use of methods among currently married women in Egypt (percentage)

	Knows method	Ever used	Currently using
Pill	99.3	44.0	12.9
IUD	98.7	39.7	27.9
Injection	81.1	2.9	0.5
Vaginal methods	36.8	3.6	0.4
Condom	53.7	7.5	2.0
Female sterilization	70.0	1.1	1.1
Male sterilization	12.5	0.0	0.0
Safe period	31.2	3.4	0.7
Withdrawal	27.6	2.6	0.7
Prolonged breastfeeding	71.8	4.9	0.9
Other traditional methods	2.4	0.4	0.1
Any method	99.5	64.6	47.1
Any modern method	99.4	62.9	44.8

Source: DHS, 1992

population. The program has evolved over the years from focusing predominantly on the pill to offering a broader contraceptive choice to its clients.

During the first decade of the program, emphasis was placed on pill distribution and use. However, distribution of pill cycles to prospective clients did not ensure that proper directions were given in order to maximize compliance. Discrepancies between service statistics for distribution levels of pill cycles and their actual use rates were repeatedly documented in population-based surveys. Today in Egypt, the pill is less frequently used than in the 1980s (see Figure 1). The recent Demographic and Health Survey (DHS, 1993) shows a further decrease in pill use to only 27.4 percent of all contraceptive users, down from 69 percent of users in 1980 (CAPMAS, 1980).

In the past, guidelines for pill distribution were limited to the exclusion of breast-feeding women and those over thirty-five years of age. Little attention was given to counseling and educating users. This may have greatly contributed to the existing problem of poor compliance and the fact that women in Egypt, as in many other countries, misuse the method, either because they have not been properly counseled, or because they have misconceptions about its harmful side effects. Information on patterns of use from the 1988 and 1992 DHS studies shows that more than half of the pill users at the time of either survey did not use it properly: they did not know the proper time interval between the end of one cycle and the start of a new one, they forgot to take pills or took them inconsistently, or they stopped taking them altogether when the pills ran out. On the other hand, some improvement has taken place in the last few years regarding the knowledge of users in the case of a missed pill: in 1988, DHS results showed that only 28.2 percent of the users knew that they should take two pills following a missed one, compared to two-thirds of current pill users interviewed in the 1992 DHS.

Other studies of pill use based on qualitative research methods have shed light on the issue of poor compliance. While the theoretical failure rate of combined oral contraceptive pills is estimated at only 1 percent, the actual failure rate in Egypt was found to be as high as 8 percent (Fateem, 1986; DHS, 1993). Some of the most frequent problems included using the pill 'on demand,' that is, only at the time of sexual intercourse; starting the new cycle incorrectly by waiting until menses stops; discarding the iron supplement pills that are to be taken during menstruation; interrupting the intake of the pill to reduce the chances of side effects; missing the pill and misinterpreting the resulting breakthrough bleeding as the onset of menstruation—with the consequence that pill use is discontinued at several incorrect intervals; and "taking a rest" after a period of continued use, without switching to another method (Loza and Potter, 1990).[1] Poor counseling is evidenced by the fact that in a survey carried out in 1985, more than half the women in both urban and rural areas perceived the pill as being unsafe (Table 3) and a substantial number considered pill use to be as risky as going through a pregnancy (Grubb *et al.*, 1987).

Proper use of the oral contraceptive pill was found to be directly related to the woman's education. With the prevalence of illiteracy among Egyptian women, providing information and counseling to prospective pill users is most crucial for proper use and higher

Table 3
Perception of pill safety among women (percentage)

Residence	Pill has substantial health risks			Compared with pregnancy, pill use is			
	Yes	No	Don't know	More risky	Equally risky	Less risky	Don't know
Urban	57	36	7	2	27	61	10
Rural	52	42	4	3	21	70	6

Source: Grubb *et al.*, 1987

continuation rates. However, counseling has for long been the weakest aspect of family planning services in Egypt, as it requires staff time, training, and careful follow-up. The shift toward greater emphasis on the quality of care will—in the long run—help address this problem and fill in the current service gaps, especially the deficient counseling of oral contraceptive users.

A key factor in the provision of oral contraceptives in Egypt is the potential role of the pharmacist, given the fact that in Egypt, as in other countries, contraceptive pills are sold in pharmacies at very low cost. From 1981 to 1987, an extensive effort was made by the Egyptian Fertility Care Society to train this 'hidden provider.' Technical bimonthly bulletins were issued in simple Arabic and mailed to six thousand pharmacists and pharmacy employees to provide them with up-to-date information on contraceptive methods, especially those sold through pharmacies. These bulletins provided information on the proper criteria and contraindications for each method, and their recommended use and storage systems. Pre- and post-tests showed that this activity had a measurable impact on improving the knowledge, attitudes, and practices of pharmacists toward contraceptive methods, especially that of pharmacy workers, who undertake most of the sales in pharmacies.[2] Such efforts, however, were not sufficient to halt the decline in the use of the pill.

THE SUCCESS OF THE IUD

Introduction of intrauterine contraceptive devices into the Egyptian National Family Planning Program took place in the early 1970s, first with the Lippes Loop, then with the various types of copper-bearing IUDs. A careful strategy was designed to maximize the IUD's chances of success. Initially, only trained specialists in obstetrics and gynecology were allowed to insert IUDs; nurses were also trained in client counseling and in aseptic and sterilization procedures; and insertions were carried out only at hospitals and health units.[3] Investment in the training of providers served to prepare them not only for proper service provision, but also to strengthen their capabilities in the management of side effects and the provision of good counseling. Later on, the base of trained specialists was expanded to include other providers, including general practitioners working at health units and hospitals. Training programs adhered strictly to aseptic techniques and emphasized the importance of good counseling, and the drawbacks of unnecessary removal and reinsertion of the IUD. The fact that the IUD is now the most prevalent method used in Egypt is attributable to the gradual and careful introduction of IUDs in different service settings.

While the introduction of the Cu T380A IUD in the program means that women could in theory be protected from pregnancy for ten years, actual patterns of IUD use suggest that women mainly use the IUD for short durations, and especially during lactation, for an average of eighteen months. Research on the reasons for the short duration of IUD use has shown that even women who appear satisfied with the method request removal after two to three years of use, either to "take a rest," or to have a new IUD inserted. The majority of IUD users are not aware of the type of IUD that they are using and are not advised of the extended eight-year period of use. This suggests that there is a gap between the distribution and use of IUDs,[4] and that improved education and information are necessary.

BARRIER METHODS: DO THEY WORK?

Barrier methods, especially condoms and diaphragms, have been available in Egypt since the 1950s. The success or failure of these methods is user-dependent and is determined by the consistency of use and adherence to instructions. After the introduction of more effective modern methods of contraception in Egypt, the use of barrier methods continued to decline and they are now the least frequently used methods. The overall acceptability of barrier methods has been known to be rather low among Egyptian couples, showing fourteen-month continuation rates of 48 percent (Population and Family Planning Board, 1981). The reason is not the fact that diaphragms involve vaginal administration, as many Egyptian women are used to regular and thorough genital cleaning. Rather, the poor acceptability was reported to be due to complaints of burning sensation, skin irritation, and rash, husband's dislike of the methods, the complicated mode of administration, and the high failure rate (7 percent discontinued use because of an unplanned pregnancy). Mass media and educational programs promoting these methods are handicapped by their relative lower efficacy, the need for male cooperation, the lack of back-up abortion services, and the long history of association of the condom with extramarital relations and sexually transmitted diseases.

INJECTABLES: A SET-BACK

Depoprovera (DMPA) was registered in Egypt in the early 1980s as a treatment for endometrial cancer, in other words not specifically as a contraceptive method. Along with Noristerat (NET-EN), it was tested by individual researchers in clinical trials of limited scope that catered to the research agenda of different international agencies involved in their subsequent worldwide introduction. Data from these studies were handled and analyzed abroad, and the ensuing reports were poorly disseminated to Egyptian medical professionals, policy makers, and the public. Within a short period of time from their local testing, injectable contraceptives became available and were distributed through a social marketing program. They were provided in health units as part of the family planning services and without reference to the required guidelines on screening of users, counseling requirements, and the management of side effects.

The absence of an introduction plan and of clear guidelines on their use, as well as the poor knowledge on the part of both service provider and policy planners of the existing international literature on these injectable methods, resulted in great controversy over their safety. The debate in the United States and the position of the United States Food and Drug Administration at the time added to the confusion. There was much adverse publicity in the national press and concern among the public, especially regarding the possible carcinogenic effect of injectables. As a drastic measure to end this problem, a ministerial decree was issued, prohibiting the use of all injectable contraceptives and their sale through pharmacies.

Increased awareness about these problems coincided with the undertaking of a large-scale multicentric comparative clinical trial of DMPA and NET-EN involving 3,200 women living in eight Egyptian governorates. The trial was sponsored by the World Health Organization as a pre-introductory trial coordinated by the Egyptian Fertility Care Society in collaboration with eight Egyptian university hospitals. Data from this study were locally analyzed and later served to inform policy makers, Ministry of Health officials, and the public about the efficacy, side effects, and acceptability of injectable contraceptives in Egypt. The study report assisted in the formulation of guidelines on the use of hormonal injectable contraceptives and in their gradual introduction into the services. Their administration was restricted at first to family planning units run by obstetricians/gynecologists; this was later modified to allow trained general practitioners to prescribe them in family planning service units, and a recent decree now allows their sale by prescription in pharmacies.

VOLUNTARY SURGICAL CONTRACEPTION AND ABORTION: MISSING METHODS

The family planning policy of Egypt does not recognize surgical sterilization or abortion as methods of fertility control. Religious and cultural factors have contributed to this firm policy stance (although it is not interpreted uniformly in all Islamic countries). Official guidelines clearly restrict their use to medically-indicated cases, and abortion is even criminalized in the legal code except if performed for medical indications that threaten the woman's life.[5]

It is necessary to acknowledge the fact that induced abortion is a reflection of an unmet need, which may be addressed by proper education and information and by adequate services that provide a variety of suitable contraceptive methods. Consideration should still be given to the need for provision of abortion services as a back-up to family planning services in cases of contraceptive failure.[6]

NORPLANT: THE INTRODUCTORY TRIAL

Norplant (subdermal contraceptive implant) is a highly effective long-acting method. It does not affect lactation and its contraceptive effect is readily reversible after removal. For these reasons, Norplant can be a positive addition to the Egyptian Family Planning Program method mix, since it satisfies the needs of women who want to space their pregnancies for long periods of time, or wish to terminate their fertility without resorting to surgical sterilization. It is not, however, without potential drawbacks. Experience with Norplant in Egypt started in the early 1980s, with the Rockefeller/Population Council– supported study of Norplant, which was carried out at four university centers. Results of that study suggested the need to address both the clinical and the social aspects of this method, and concerns were heightened by the delay in the approval of Norplant by the United States Food and Drug Administration, which led to suspicions that Egyptian women were being used as experimental bodies for contraceptives not approved in the West. Research carried out at that time also highlighted the critical need to provide proper counseling, to inform users about the potential side effects, and, most importantly, to insure that the implants would be removed on demand (Morsy, 1993).

Following these developments, a study of Norplant in Egypt was initiated by the Egyptian Fertility Care Society in 1988. The project began with clinical trials in five teaching hospitals and was followed by a study of acceptability, which aimed to measure women's satisfaction with Norplant services. It inquired about whether women had easy access to removal services, whether they intended to use Norplant in the future, and whether they would recommend it to others. It also addressed women's perceptions and perspectives, the social and cultural determinants of method acceptability among users, and attitudes of service providers. Both qualitative and quantitative research methods were used. A longitudinal cohort study of Norplant was later initiated to detect unexpected side effects, especially those occurring after a long period of time. The study concluded with a profile of the appropriate candidate to use this method in Egypt (Hassan *et al.*, 1992).

The lessons learned from the poor and unplanned introduction of long-acting injectable contraceptives helped define more careful plans for the introduction of Norplant in Egypt. The large-scale program of clinical training and research on Norplant was carefully designed and implemented. It included a multicentric clinical trial of the method; a program of training for service providers in counseling, insertion, and removal; and guidelines for the management of side effects.

Policy makers were involved in the implementation of all components of the pre-introductory trials, and the Egyptian Fertility Care Society provided them with periodic interim reports that were reviewed by the technical advisory committees of the Ministry of Health and the Supreme Organization for Pharmaceuticals. Information on Norplant as a contraceptive method, its efficacy, and its acceptability were continuously disseminated to both the medical professionals and the public. Information based on results of local research was made available through scientific conferences and a low-key media campaign. At an intermediate stage of research implementation, the results of the clinical trial and the review of acceptability studies were encouraging enough to policy makers to warrant the approval by the technical committee of the expanded use of Norplant and its local registration. The number of women included in the Norplant clinical trial was 1,536, of whom 82.1 percent were followed up after three years. Over 66 percent of the users continued to use Norplant for three years. Of those who stopped using Norplant, 1.6 percent discontinued due to an unplanned pregnancy, 11.39 percent due to menstrual problems, 8.21 percent due to other medical problems, and 8.41 percent due to personal problems (of whom 3.3 percent discontinued because they desired pregnancy). Only twenty-one women complained of post-insertion complications (infection or expulsion of one or more capsules), and thirty-six women developed an unexpected adverse reaction. Method acceptability was highest among previous users of hormonal methods, those who knew another Norplant user, and women whose husbands were supportive of its use.

Guidelines were carefully developed, specifying the criteria for choice of the suitable user, the management of side effects, the adjustment of the recommended use duration in cases of obesity or excessive weight gain, and the recommended schedule for patient follow-up. In addition, a plan is now being developed for introducing Norplant outside the research setting at the different levels of service delivery, starting with a phased introduction from higher to lower service settings. The plan includes the training of service providers; the insurance of requirements for quality of care, including ready access to removal services and removal on demand (earlier reports had emphasized that difficult access to removal services was a factor behind poor acceptability); setting up a National Norplant Registry to be able to contact users for periodic follow-up and removal; careful planning of the logistics and distribution procedures; and estimation of the cost to be paid by users for receiving Norplant services.

With these developments, the Egyptian National Family Planning Program has moved from emphasizing distribution of contraceptive commodities to introducing new methods dependent on pre-introductory research to guarantee the accuracy of information about potential users and their perceptions.

CONCLUSION: CONSIDERATIONS IN BROADENING CONTRACEPTIVE CHOICE

Broad contraceptive choice does not mean that everyone should be offered every method of contraception. Firstly, cost must be considered. Programs can offer people only the methods they can afford to provide and/or people can afford to buy, while insuring sustainability of supplies. Secondly, the delivery system must be capable of administering contraceptive methods and providing adequate follow-up as needed according to proper standards of quality care. Clients should not be offered methods which cannot be adequately supported by the health delivery system. They should be counseled and offered a choice among the methods that are affordable and can be properly administered by the service. Their decision will be based on their own judgment, which is determined by their perceptions about methods of contraception and their convenience (coitally-related, oral daily, or long-acting). Family planning programs need to undertake trials before introducing new contraceptives in their services. Only through this research can they decide whether such methods will be acceptable and feasible (WHO, 1991). This research should, to the extent possible, involve women—the potential users—in the decision-making process.

The current range of contraceptive hardware is adequate to carry us through this century, if complemented with the necessary and appropriate software. The agenda for the twenty-first century must provide people with more and better options. Science, in a collaborative partnership with women and women's groups, can respond to the unmet need.

REFERENCES

Affandi, B. 1987. Clinical, pharmacological and epidemiological studies on a levonorgestrel implant contraceptive. Unpublished Ph.D. dissertation. Jakarta: University of Indonesia.

Brook S. J. and C. Smith. 1991. Do combined oral contraceptive users know how to take their pill correctly? *British Journal of Family Planning.* 17/1:18–20.

CAPMAS. 1980. *Egyptian fertility survey: Report number one.* Cairo: Central Agency for Public Mobilization and Statistics.

DHS. 1988. *Egypt demographic and health survey, 1988.* Cairo: National Population Council.

———. 1993. *Egypt demographic and health survey, 1992.* Cairo: National Population Council.

Fateem, E. 1986. Consumer panel—A longitudinal study in urban Egypt of the contraceptive market. Reports on the first and second wave. Cairo: Family of the Future Association.

Fathalla, M. F. 1989. New contraceptive methods and reproductive health. In S. J. Segal and S. M. Rogers, eds., *Demographic and programmatic consequences of contraceptive innovations.* New York and London: Plenum Press.

———. 1990. Tailoring contraceptives to human needs. *People.* 17:3–5.

———. 1991. Contraceptive technology and safety. *Population Sciences.* 10:7–26.

Freedman, R. and B. Berelson. 1976. The record of family planning programs. *Studies in Family Planning.* 7:1–39.

Grubb, G. *et al.* 1987. Women's perceptions of the safety of the pill: A survey in eight developing countries. *Journal of Biosocial Science.* 19/3:313–22.

Hassan, E. O., L. Kafafi, M. El-Husseini, K. Hardee-Cleaveland, L. Potter. 1992. The acceptability of Norplant in Egypt. *Advances in Contraception.* 8/4:331–48.

Jain, A. K. 1989. Fertility reduction and the quality of family planning services. *Studies in Family Planning.* 20:1–16.

Loza, S. and L. Potter. 1990. Qualitative study of oral contraceptive pill use in Egypt: Interviews with OC users and providers. Final Report to USAID and the National Population Council, Cairo.

Morsy, S. A. 1993. Bodies of choice: Norplant experimental trials on Egyptian Women. In B. Mintzes, A. Hardon, J. Hanhart, eds., *Norplant: Under her skin.* Delft: Eburon.

Pariani, S., D. M. Heer, M. D. Van Arsdol, Jr. 1991. Does choice make a difference in contraceptive use? Evidence from East Java. *Studies in Family Planning.* 22:384–90.

Phillips, J. F., R. Simmons, M. A. Koenig, J. Chakrabarty. 1988. Determinants of reproductive change in a traditional society: Evidence from Matlab, Bangladesh. *Studies in Family Planning.* 19/6(1):313–34.

Population and Family Planning Board. 1981. *Summary of the final report of the barrier methods study.* PO 2. Cairo, June.

Ross, J. A., W. P. Mauldin, V. C. Miller. 1993. *Family planning and population: A compendium of international statistics.* New York: The Population Council.

Ross, J. A., M. Rich, J. P. Molzan. 1989. *Management strategies for family planning programs.* New York: Center for Population and Family Health, School of Public Health, Columbia University.

United Nations. 1989. Levels and trends of contraceptive use as assessed in 1988. *Population Studies.* No. 110 (ST/ESA/SER.A/110). New York: Department of International Economic and Social Affairs, United Nations.

WHO. 1991. *Creating common grounds: Report of a meeting between women's health advocates and scientists.* WHO/HRP/ITT/91.Geneva: World Health Organization.

NOTES

1   It should be emphasized, however, that this problem is not unique to Egypt or even to developing countries. A study carried out in the United Kingdom revealed similar findings, with 17 percent of women not knowing they should leave a seven-day pill-free interval between packets (Brook and Smith, 1991).

2   Long-term funding and maintenance of training of pharmacists are still lacking as part of the training activities provided by the National Family Planning Program.

3   Since Egypt has a vast number of evenly-distributed health service outlets and a sufficient number of physicians in almost all parts of the country, physicians were the major providers of this service, which was performed at health facilities, rather than mobile units.

4   Research has now been initiated by the Egyptian Fertility Care Society with the assistance of The Population Council to explain this gap. The research specifically addresses the patterns of IUD use and the problem of frequent removal from both the service provider and user points of view.

5   Efforts have been made by the non-governmental sector to promote voluntary surgical contraception and to highlight the hazards of unsafe abortion.

6   See the proceedings of the Conference on Medical Management of Effects of Contraceptive Failure, hosted by the Cairo Family Planning Association, April 3–4, 1984.

11

Rethinking Family Planning Policy in Light of Reproductive Health Research

Huda Zurayk, Nabil Younis, Hind Khattab

Around the middle of this century, concern with levels of reproduction in countries of the developing world began to intensify. The high rate of growth experienced in these countries as a result of declining mortality and persistently high fertility was considered a problem that formed an obstacle to development and threatened the balance of the world's population. Population policy in developing countries came to be equated with fertility reduction, and family planning policy was seen as the only viable short-term mechanism for addressing the inflated rate of growth (Jain and Bruce, 1993).

Over the decades that followed, huge material, technical, and human resources were mobilized to address these issues. Policy makers, both at the international level and in developing countries, began to assess how reproductive needs—particularly those of women—were constructed, and how solutions were defined. The policies that resulted aimed at establishing national family planning programs and recruiting an increasing number of contraceptive acceptors (Jain and Bruce, 1993). Policies with this limited scope persist today in many developing countries.

New approaches have since developed as a reaction against such narrow definitions of population policy (see Dixon-Mueller, 1993; Kabeer, 1992), attempting to view reproduction in its larger social context, and to give due attention to the health dimension of reproduction, particularly as it affects children and women. This broader perspective considers population policy as a part of a country's overall development policy (Jain and Bruce, 1993) and views the conditions of women's lives as directly relevant to fertility policies. Moreover, health consequences of reproduction for women and children have become central concerns of population policy. Thus, the scope of population policy now includes societal (rate of growth) as well as individual (health and well-being) manifestations of reproduction.

Recently, feminists and health advocates have strongly supported this wider view of population policy (Berer, 1993; Dixon-Mueller, 1993; Eschen and Whittaker, 1993; Hartmann, 1987; Jain and Bruce, 1993; Kabeer, 1992; Koblinsky, Timyan, and Gay, 1993; Ravindran, 1993). These new voices emphasize that while population policy cannot ignore societal changes influencing fertility, it must address the individual needs of women by widening its strategy to include reproductive health services. These services, they argue, should assist couples in meeting their reproductive goals, while taking into account the related health needs of children, and particularly of the women who bear them. Thus, combining provision of services with structural interventions can help fulfill both the societal goals of a reduced rate of growth and individual goals of desired and healthy reproduction.

The new emphasis on reproductive health has created an impetus to rethink family planning policy. There are indications, in fact, that those who were originally strong supporters of limited family planning policy are now beginning to incorporate the concepts of health and reproductive health into their discourse. We find, however, that such changes remain generally cursory, while in substance policy makers remain firmly wedded to the traditional concerns of family planning programs, which focus attention on number of acceptors, prevalence of use, and the unmet need for contraception.

On a more positive note, feminists and health advocates have adopted reproductive rights as women's entitlement and are working both conceptually and operationally to broaden the scope of family planning policy to incorporate these concerns (Dixon-Mueller, 1993). Their priorities include the need to address abortion, maternal health, and the treatment of sexually transmitted diseases and other reproductive tract infections within an expanded family planning framework (Berer, 1993; Dixon-Mueller and Germain, 1992; Elias, Leonard, and Thompson, 1993; Jain and Bruce, 1993; Kabeer, 1992; Ravindran, 1993). Some even argue convincingly that family planning programs could be substituted by reproductive health programs, which would work toward empowering women along with providing quality medical, counseling, and health education services aimed at healthy reproduction (Dixon-Mueller, 1993).

Although not yet tested at the programmatic level, these attempts to rethink family planning (both the 'cautious' and the 'truly committed') have the potential to transform policy and better serve the interests of women, families, and communities in developing countries. Now efforts are needed to support the discussion of principles with real evidence about women's reproductive health. This chapter is based on a field study that was undertaken in two villages in the Giza governorate of Egypt to investigate the level of reproductive morbidity among women in this community. By revealing the heavy disease burden that women bear in silence (Khattab, 1992; Younis *et al.*, 1993), and by showing its connection with their use of contraception, this paper argues that family planning policy cannot ignore the health dimension. To do so imperils both the effectiveness of family planning programs and the health and well-being of women. Based on the results of the study, the paper provides guidance about how to rethink family planning policy in light of the realities of women in developing societies.

THE GIZA MORBIDITY STUDY

The Giza morbidity study was conceived as part of a larger research program established in 1988 by The Population Council Office for West Asia and North Africa in Cairo to look at links between women and children's health within the context of the family and the community (The Population Council, 1990). Little was known at the time about women's health at the community level. Still, it was believed that women experiencing high levels of fertility—particularly in poor communities of the Middle East—were also suffering from reproductive health problems similar to those found in other regions such as Bangladesh (Wasserheit *et al.*, 1989) and India (Bang *et al.*, 1989).

The Giza morbidity study was undertaken in two villages in rural Giza in Egypt in 1989–90. One of the main objectives of the study was to determine the prevalence of gynecological and related morbidity conditions (see Table 1) through a medical examination of women in the community. A second objective was to test the ability of a carefully developed interview-questionnaire on symptoms of these conditions to reflect the results of the medical examination, thus serving as an instrument for community diagnosis and screening. The study was undertaken by an interdisciplinary research team including medical scientists (two obstetrician–gynecologists and a microbiologist) and social scientists (an anthropologist and a biostatistician–demographer).

A random sample of households was selected based on geographical mapping of the two villages. Households were visited sequentially in selected blocks, and ever-married, non-pregnant women were invited to join the study following the division of the sample into age quotas determined to make the age distribution similar to that of the last population census for these two villages (CAPMAS, 1986). The size of the sample was determined at five hundred on the basis of prevalence of morbidity conditions in this low socioeconomic community, and taking into consideration the cost of laboratory testing. At the beginning of the field work, some women refused to participate,

Table 1
Measurement of gynecological and related morbidity

	Interview questionnaire	Clinical exam	Laboratory test
Gynecological morbidity			
Reproductive tract infections			
Lower			
Vaginitis	x		x
Cervicitis	x	x	
Upper (pelvic inflammatory disease)	x	x	
Cervical ectopy		x	
Suspicious cervical cell changes			x
Genital prolapse	x	x	
Menstrual problems	x		
Problems with intercourse	x		
Infertility	x		
Related morbidity			
Urinary tract infection	x		x
Anemia			x
Obesity		x	
High blood pressure		x	
Syphilis			x

mainly because they feared the medical examination, or because they were older women past the age of reproduction. As the study progressed, however, the field team achieved a very good rapport with the community (particularly the women). Consequently, many women changed their minds and asked to join the study. The final percentage of women who refused to participate amounted to only 8.6 percent, with no differentiating characteristics compared to the women who joined the study.

A total sample of 509 women was achieved and each woman was interviewed in two visits. During the first visit, characteristics of the household and the woman, as well as information on contraceptive practice, were collected. Then a second interview was scheduled, during which information on symptoms of gynecological and related morbidity conditions was collected; following this the field worker accompanied the woman to the health center for a gynecological examination. The examination was undertaken at each of the two health centers by the female physician in charge of the medical services for the past seven to eight years, who had received intensive training by the study physicians. After completing the examination, which included general, abdominal, speculum, and bimanual examination, laboratory specimens were taken by a specially trained laboratory technician, and on the same day transported to the laboratory in Cairo. As the data collection proceeded, the interview-questionnaire responses and the data from the medical examination were coded and integrated into woman-based records for data analysis.

A description of the sample indicates that in this community, women and their husbands were mostly uneducated, with illiteracy reaching 82 percent for women and 69 percent for the husbands. The ages of the women were distributed evenly in the categories of less than twenty-five, twenty-five to thirty-four, and thirty-five and older, with a maximum age of sixty years. Most of the women married at a very young age. About 8 percent were not currently married (widowed or divorced), and about 7 percent had husbands who were working abroad at the time of the study. The number of deliveries ranged from none to thirteen, with 45 percent of the women being grand-multiparae (five or more deliveries). About 52 percent of the women had had a pregnancy which had ended within the preceding two years.

EVIDENCE FROM REPRODUCTIVE HEALTH RESEARCH: CONTRACEPTIVE PRACTICE AND DISEASE BURDEN

We begin our exploration of the information provided by the Giza Morbidity Study by looking at contraceptive use in this community. We next examine the medical data at hand collected for the prevalence of gynecological and related morbidity conditions. By combining those data on patterns of family planning with those related to health, we can show the pattern of interaction of contraceptive use with health conditions and on the basis of this evidence call for a reconsideration of family planning policy. Because attempts to reconsider family planning programs have focused mainly on a health service approach, a second relevant set of evidence to consider is how often women reporting symptoms of a health condition consulted the health system, and to evaluate the system's impact on their health.

It is important to note that the analysis of data from the Giza study is based on the entire sample of 509 ever-married women whose ages range between fourteen and sixty years. Some of these women (8 percent) are not currently married, since they are widowed or divorced; some of these women (7 percent) have husbands who are working abroad; and a few of the married women, specifically older women with disabled husbands, are not sexually active. Nevertheless, all these women were considered in our analysis because the health consequences of their reproductive patterns are often felt even more strongly beyond the reproductive years. Although our experience in the field suggests that women in these three categories are wary of addressing gynecological concerns because of the impression they fear it would give of their current sexual behavior, we feel that counseling and health education could allay these fears. We note that this dilemma is even more difficult for single women (mostly adolescents), whom we could not include in our study. We believe these realities to be relevant to most settings in the Middle East region.

The contraceptive use patterns of women in this community (Table 2) were very close to the national pattern for Egypt at the time of the study, with 39 percent of ever-married women and 42 percent of currently married women using contraception. This is not unexpected, since the two villages studied are close to Cairo and have had their family planning services upgraded through a special national project. When we consider only the currently married women whose husbands are living with them, the rate of current use rises to 45 percent. As was observed for a national sample in Egypt (PAPCHILD, 1993), women in our sample are primarily using the IUD and the pill, with almost a third of currently married women of twenty-five to forty-four years old using the IUD (Table 3).

The scope of the study of disease conditions covered in the Giza morbidity study (see Table 1) was defined according to a conceptual framework that was developed by the team of researchers as the most appropriate for representing reproductive morbidity at the community level (Zurayk *et al.*, 1993a). By inviting women from the community to undergo a gynecological examination at the village health center, the Giza study results allow us to determine the prevalence of these conditions in the community.

Table 4 presents the prevalence of gynecological and related morbidity conditions and reveals a heavy disease burden borne by women in this community. Half the women suffer from reproductive tract infections, most of them vaginitis. Over one-fifth of the women have cervical ectopy and 11 percent have cervical cell changes that could indicate a premalignant situation. The majority of women have genital prolapse, with close to a third suffering from serious prolapse. Moreover, a majority of the women suffer from anemia, a substantial prevalence of obesity is demonstrated, hypertension is present in just under one-fifth of the women, and urinary tract infection is present in 14 percent. An analysis of risk factors associated with these conditions (Younis *et al.*, 1993) showed the contribution of various social conditions and medical factors to their prevalence in the community.

Table 2

Use of contraception (percentage) by marital status, Giza morbidity study and Egypt maternal and child health survey (1991)

	Giza morbidity study		Egypt maternal and child health survey (1991)
	Ever married n=509	Currently married n=469	Currently married n=8,406
Never users	40	38	35
Past users	21	20	17
Current users	39	42	48
Oral pills	13	14	16
IUD	22	24	24
Other	4	4	8

Table 3

Use of contraception by age group (currently married), Giza morbidity study (percentage)

	Age		
	14–24 n=171	25–44 n=273	45+ n=25
Never users	55	25	48
Past users	12	24	36
Current users	33	51	16
Oral pills	13	15	8
IUD	18	30	4
Other	2	6	4

Table 4

Prevalence of gynecological and related morbidity conditions

	Percentage n=502[a]
Reproductive tract infections[b,c]	51
Vaginitis[b]	44
Bacterial vaginosis	22
Trichomonas	18
Candida	11
Cervicitis[c]	10
Pelvic inflammatory disease[c]	2
Cervical ectopy[c]	22
Suspicious cervical cell changes[b]	11
Genital prolapse[c]	56
Posterior or anterior vaginal	27
Posterior and anterior vaginal	21
Vaginal and uterine	8
Urinary tract infection[b]	14
Syphilis[b]	1
Anemia (Hg<12 gm/dl)[b]	63
10–11.9 gm/dl	46
<10 gm/dl	17
High blood pressure (diastolic >90)[c]	18
90–99 mm Hg	12
100+ mm Hg	6
Obesity (weight/height^2 >25)[c]	43
25–29.9 kg/m^2	23
30+ kg/m^2	20

[a]Every condition has a few missing women, so the average number of women over all conditions is shown
[b]Laboratory test   [c]Clinical exam

These figures are alarming in and of themselves, and they become even more serious when we consider the multiplicity and the severity of occurrence of disease conditions. Table 5 indicates that only 15 percent of women are free of gynecological and closely related conditions, while half the women suffer from two or more of these conditions. Table 6 examines the severity of morbidity with age. We find that reproductive tract infections maintain their high level through the reproductive life cycle and beyond. Cervical ectopy occurs in close to a fourth of women during the reproductive years and drops to a negligible proportion after women reach age forty-four. On the other hand, the prevalence of suspicious cervical cell changes rises with age and reaches a level of over a fifth of women beyond age forty-four. We note that serious prolapse (posterior and anterior vaginal with or without uterine prolapse) occurs in almost a third of women, with the prevalence of this severe condition being particularly high in the age group of twenty-five to forty-four years (38 percent). Urinary tract infection is prevalent among a fourth of women forty-five years of age or older. Anemia in severe form is present in 17 percent of the sample and in one-fifth of women under twenty-five years of age. The decline of prevalence with age unique to anemia is due to biological considerations, as well as to the possible improvement of the social conditions of women in this community with age (Younis *et al.*, 1993). The prevalence and the severe manifestation of both obesity and high blood pressure increase with age, with prevalence reaching a majority of women at age forty-five years and over for both conditions.

Table 5

Prevalence of one or more morbidity conditions (reproductive tract infections, cervical ectopy, suspicious cervical cell changes, genital prolapse, urinary tract infection, syphilis)

Number of conditions	Number of women	Percentage
None	76	15
One	185	36
Two	163	32
Three or more	85	17
Total	509	100

Table 6

Prevalence of gynecological and related morbidity conditions in different age groups (percentage)[a]

Morbidity condition	Age group			Total	P-value[b]
	14–24 n=171	25–44 n=287	45+ n=44	n=502	
Reproductive tract infections	50	53	42	51	.38
Vaginitis only	44	40	36	41	
Cervicitis only	2	7	–	5	
Combination of vaginitis, cervicitis, PID	4	6	5	5	
Cervical ectopy	25	22	3	22	.01
Suspicious cervical cell changes	8	11	22	11	.03
Prolapse	34	68	63	56	.00
Posterior or anterior vaginal	21	30	35	27	
Posterior + anterior vaginal	8	28	21	21	
Vaginal + uterine	5	10	7	8	
Urinary tract infection	12	13	25	14	.08
Anemia (Hg<12 gm/dl)	69	61	49	63	.03
10–11.9 gm/dl	48	46	37	46	
<10 gm/dl	21	15	12	17	
Obesity (weight/height^2 >25)	27	50	61	43	.00
25–29 kg/m^2	20	25	25	23	
30+ kg/m^2	7	25	36	20	
High blood pressure (diastolic >90)	7	19	55	18	.00
90–99 mm Hg	6	13	32	12	
100+ mm Hg	1	6	23	6	

[a]Every condition has a few missing women, so the average number of women over all conditions is shown
[b]Tests for association between age and prevalence

THE LINK BETWEEN DISEASE BURDEN AND CONTRACEPTIVE USE

While establishing a causal association is beyond the limits of the Giza Morbidity Study, it is important to examine the connection of contraceptive use with the health conditions of women. Our findings call into question the assumption that clients of family planning programs come from a healthy population (see also Elias, Leonard, and Thompson, 1993).

We begin by reviewing the disease conditions known to represent a medical risk that are linked to the IUD or the pill. Reproductive tract infections can be aggravated by the presence of an IUD. Lower tract infections have the potential to be carried to the upper tract, using the thread of the IUD as a route, with serious health and fertility consequences to an affected woman. The IUD in a woman with cervical ectopy can lead to increased discharge, causing discomfort to the woman, and can further irritate the surface of the cervix, aggravating the ectopy. It can intensify cervical cell changes when these changes are already present. It can also lead to increased menstrual bleeding, the increase being larger for women with anemia, which aggravates the condition. The IUD can make genital prolapse, particularly in its serious form, more uncomfortable. Moreover, because prolapse results in congestion of the genital organs, the menstrual bleeding usually associated with the IUD would be even greater in the presence of prolapse. The danger that an infection in the urinary tract may spread to the reproductive tract is increased in the presence of an IUD, which lowers the resistance of the genital organs.

The pill is contraindicated for women with high blood pressure, and for some older more obese women, for the risk these conditions contribute to cardiovascular disease. Through hormonal mechanisms, the pill might aggravate the condition of cervical ectopy and of suspicious cervical cell changes when these changes are already present.

Table 7 examines the prevalence of disease conditions among the 113 IUD users, the sixty-seven pill users, and the 329 remaining women, most of whom were not using contraception at the time of the study. Considering IUD users first, we note a high prevalence of reproductive tract infections, of prolapse and of anemia, with a third suffering from serious prolapse and a fifth suffering from severe anemia. We also find among IUD users some cases of cervical ectopy, suspicious cervical cell changes and urinary tract infection. These results are certainly a cause for worry, and they become even more worrisome when we consider the multiple occurrence of disease conditions among IUD users. Table 8 shows that 70 percent of IUD users have two or more conditions that carry medical risk for IUD use.

An important result to note from Table 7 is that IUD users are at increased risk of reproductive tract infections. In a multiple regression analysis of risk factors for reproductive tract infections, a significant contribution to prevalence was associated with several factors, including occurrence of uterovaginal prolapse, having a husband living at home (indicating regular sexual intercourse), and current IUD use (Younis *et al.*, 1993). An examination of the relation of duration of last episode of IUD use to type of infection (Table 9) shows that the

Table 7
Prevalence of gynecological and related morbidity conditions among women using different contraceptives[a]

Morbidity condition	IUD n=113		Pill n=67		Other/none n=329		P-value[b]
	n	%	n	%	n	%	
Reproductive tract infections	68	60	28	42	157	48	.02
Cervical ectopy	20	18	17	25	71	22	.44
Suspicious cervical cell changes	8	7	9	13	36	11	.34
Genital prolapse	72	64	41	61	173	52	.09
Posterior or anterior vaginal	36	32	21	31	83	25	
Posterior + anterior vaginal	31	28	15	22	60	18	
Vaginal + uterine	5	4	5	8	30	9	
Urinary tract infection	18	16	8	12	45	14	.74
Anemia (Hg<12 gm/dl)	75	66	41	61	197	60	.52
10–11.9 gms/dl	51	45	31	46	147	45	
<10 gms/dl	24	21	10	15	50	15	
Obesity (weight/height^2 >25)	48	42	34	51	133	40	.34
25–29 kg/m^2	26	23	21	31	70	21	
30+ kg/m^2	22	19	13	20	63	19	
High blood pressure (diastolic >90)	18	16	12	18	62	19	.86
90–99 mm Hg	15	13	8	12	40	12	
100+ mm Hg	3	3	4	6	22	7	

[a]Numbers and percentages do not always add up due to the presence of multiple conditions
[b]Tests for association between type of contraceptive use and prevalence

Table 8
IUD users with multiple conditions (reproductive tract infections, serious genital prolapse, cervical ectopy, suspicious cervical cell changes, anemia, urinary tract infection)

Number of conditions	Number of women	Percentage
None	4	3
One	30	27
Two	47	42
Three or more	27	24
Four	5	4
Total	113	100

infection remains mostly in the lower tract even at higher durations of use. It must be noted, nevertheless, that some women, particularly those complaining of symptoms of infection, might have had their

Table 9
IUD users with reproductive tract infections: duration of use by type of infection

Duration (years)	Type of infection					Total
	Vaginitis	Cervicitis	Vaginitis + cervicitis	Cervicitis + PID	Vaginitis + cervicitis + PID	
<1	17	1	5	2	2	27
1	13	–	1	–	–	14
2	6	–	1	1	–	8
3	10	1	–	–	–	11
4+	5	2	–	–	–	7
Total	51	4	7	3	2	67[a]

[a]Information was missing for one woman

IUDs removed, thus dampening the observed relation of IUD use to type of infection. The spectrum of infection for the twenty-seven women whose last episode of use is less than one year is worth considering. The existence of multiple infections for nine of the twenty-seven women, and the involvement of the upper tract for four of them, suggests that some infection could have been present at the time of insertion, or could have been introduced at insertion.

We consider next the sixty-seven pill users (Table 7) and select the twelve suffering from hypertension. Table 10 gives detailed information on the occurrence of other contraindicated conditions for pill use. We find that seven of the twelve women are thirty-five years of age or

Table 10
Individual pill users with hypertension[a]

Diastolic BP	Obesity	Age
90	No	20–24
90	No	25–34
90	Mild	20–24
90	Mild	20–24
90	Mild	35–44
90	Severe	35–44
90	Severe	35–44
90	Severe	35–44
100	No	25–34
100	Mild	45+
100	Severe	35–44
100	Severe	35–44

[a]All but one woman had obtained pills at a pharmacy

older, and five are both older and severely obese. Although these numbers are relatively small, they do indicate dangerous cases of an accumulation of risk factors among women using the pill. Moreover, Table 7 shows that one-fourth of pill users have cervical ectopy and 13 percent have suspicious cervical cell changes.

CONTACT WITH THE HEALTH SYSTEM

The high disease burden among women in the study community and its overlap with contraceptive use raise some key questions concerning the contact of women with the health system in its role both as a source of contraceptives and for the treatment of reproductive health problems. Each of the two villages in the Giza study is served by a health center provided by the Ministry of Health and run by a female physician, one of whom has been practicing in the village for seven years, the other for twelve. Both physicians are general practitioners, but they also cover gynecological complaints and family planning.

We examine first the source from which women are obtaining the contraceptives currently used. Table 11 shows that the main source for the IUD is a health facility, including government health center and hospital, and that in addition the private physician plays a substantial role in the provision of IUDs to this community. For the pill, on the other hand, the pharmacy is shown to be the major source. These results are consistent with those observed for Egypt (PAPCHILD, 1993), where the source for the IUD is a health facility for 60 percent of users and the private physician for 40 percent, and where the major supplier (87 percent) of the pill is the pharmacy. For women with one or more disease conditions, the same general pattern in relation to source of IUD is observed (Table 11). Women with anemia seem to use the health facility more often as a source of contraceptives, probably reflecting a socioeconomic constraint. Thus both the health facility and the private physician appear to be equally implicated in the observed disease prevalence among IUD users. For the pill, only one of the women with hypertension obtained her supply from a health facility, while the remaining eleven used the pharmacy as a source.

We examine next the extent and result of utilization by women of the health care system for gynecological and related conditions. Women were asked during the home interview about those symptoms of disease conditions with a clear symptomatology (see Table 1);

Table 11

Percentage distribution of IUD users and pill users by source of contraceptives

	Pharmacy	Health facility	Private physician
All IUD users (n=113)	–	57	43
IUD users[a] with			
Reproductive tract infections (n=68)	–	57	43
Genital prolapse (n=72)	–	51	49
Anemia (n=75)	–	65	35
Urinary tract infection (n=18)	–	67	33
All pill users (n=67)	85	15	0
Pill users with high blood pressure (n=12)	92	8	–

[a]Numbers add up to more than 113 because of the presence of multiple conditions

those who responded positively were asked whether they consulted a physician for the symptom. The women who did consult were then asked whether the physician gave a treatment, whether they followed the treatment, whether that made them feel better and whether they consulted someone other than the physician for the symptom.

We begin by considering the level of reporting by women of symptoms of relevant conditions (Table 12). For reproductive tract infections, in an attempt to capture what women consider an abnormal discharge, we asked each woman whether she experienced a vaginal discharge which was "different from her nature." All women reporting any discharge were also asked to describe the discharge in terms of color, odor, consistency, and itching that accompanied it. We note that most women (77 percent) reported currently experiencing discharge, but that only 13 percent of women reported a discharge that was different from their "usual nature." On the basis of reported characteristics of the discharge, we find that 64 percent of women could be considered to have a suspicious discharge. This indicates that, in addition to other constraints on use, women may not perceive certain symptoms as dangerous or abnormal, considering them part of their reproductive reality (Zurayk *et al.*, 1993b). Symptoms of two other disease conditions were included on the interview-questionnaire (genital prolapse and UTI), and we find that a third of the women reported that they were currently suffering from heaviness below and/ or protrusion of reproductive organs, and 59 percent of women reported at least one of the seven symptoms included for urinary tract infection.

Table 12
Prevalence of symptoms of disease as reported in the interview (n=509)

Condition	Number	Percentage
Reproductive tract infections		
Discharge		
Present	392	77
Suspicious medically[a]	324	64
Suspicious to woman[b]	68	13
Genital prolapse		
Heaviness below or feeling of protrusion of organs	158	31
Urinary tract infection		
At least one symptom[c]	302	59

[a]Based on color, consistency, odor, and itching
[b]Described as "not her nature"
[c]Burning outside, burning inside, frequent urination, night urination, interrupted flow, stress incontinence, urgency

Table 13 presents data linking complaint of symptoms with utilization of the health care system.[1] It indicates that around a third of women reporting symptoms for each of the three conditions under consideration have consulted a physician for the symptom. The main point to note from Table 13 is that no significant difference exists in the prevalence of disease conditions among those who consulted and those who did not consult a physician. Table 14 shows that physicians generally prescribe a treatment during these consultations, that a majority of women report following the treatment, and that some report feeling better afterwards. We are not able to judge with the data at hand the medical value of the treatment, the information that was

Table 13
Consultation of physician by women reporting symptoms of disease conditions

	Reporting symptoms for		
	Reproductive tract infections n=68	Genital prolapse n=158	Urinary tract infection n=302
Percentage consulting physician	32	30	26
Disease prevalence (percentages) among			
Women consulting	41	70	14
Women not consulting	57	64	14
Women reporting symptoms	51	66	14

Table 14

Consultation, treatment, and outcome for women reporting symptoms
(numbers)

	For symptoms of		
	Reproductive tract infections	Genital prolapse	Unrinary tract infection
Consulted a physician	22	47	80
Treatment was prescribed	20	38[a]	79
Treatment was undertaken	17	33	76
Feel better	15	24	63
Definitely	6	10	23
Somewhat	9	14	40
Went for other advice	–	2	6
Did not consult a physician	46	111	222
Consulted other than physician	5	8	10
Total	68	158	302

[a]Treatments prescribed included a recommendation for an operation, drugs for pain, or pelvic decongestion

given to the woman about it, or the degree to which the woman followed the treatment appropriately. The fact that the prevalence of disease remains the same among those who consulted a physician and those who did not indicates problems in the process of seeking health care and receiving appropriate treatment.

ELEMENTS FOR RETHINKING FAMILY PLANNING POLICY

Although the information in this paper comes from a limited geographical area representing two villages in rural Egypt, it does provide forceful evidence for the need to reconsider thoughtfully family planning policy. The fact that the area under consideration is close to the capital city of Cairo suggests in fact that the problems we uncovered may be even graver in more isolated or disadvantaged areas. Evidence from studies in Bangladesh (Wasserheit *et al.*, 1989) and India (Bang *et al.*, 1989; Ravindran, 1993), as well as in reviews for developing countries (Belsey and Royston, 1987; Muir and Belsey, 1980), suggest that such problems are widespread in developing countries. Since the Giza study was undertaken by an interdisciplinary research team of social and medical scientists, it allows us to include the social context of these findings in the framework necessary for a rethinking process. In this section, we make use of these findings to suggest what needs to be taken into account in rethinking family planning policy in developing countries, with special reference to Egypt and the Arab world.

THE HEALTH SITUATION OF WOMEN

The Giza morbidity study's revelation of the heavy disease burden women bear in silence strongly supports the need to expand family planning policy's scope to include women's reproductive health. Although feminists and health advocates have argued forcefully for such expansion, little evidence of the magnitude of the health problem has been uncovered to support their claims. Our findings emphasize the urgency of the health dimension, and suggest ways to include it in the process of redesigning programs.

1. The range of concern with reproductive morbidity conditions: Demands for the expansion of family planning policy to deal with the health problems of women have been based mainly on an overriding concern with sexually transmitted diseases. Some arguments, however, have focused more generally on reproductive tract infections (Dixon-Mueller and Germain, 1992; Elias, Leonard, and Thompson, 1993; Jain and Bruce, 1993; Wasserheit and Holmes, 1992). The latter focus results from a realization that the prevalence of reproductive tract infections is growing in the developing world, and that these infections have dangerous health sequelae for women and their families. Reproductive tract infections are associated with infertility, cervical cancer, adverse outcomes of pregnancy, and HIV transmission. These infections also have socioeconomic costs related to their treatment and to their impact on functioning and status (Wasserheit and Holmes, 1992).

Our reproductive health research has shown that women in the Giza community are suffering from a spectrum of disease conditions, not limited to reproductive tract infections, and that many of these conditions are contraindicated for the method of contraception being used. It is clear that disease conditions that are contraindicated for methods of contraception should be of concern to a family planning policy. For many communities in Egypt and the Arab world, our findings suggest that it is necessary to consider a wide spectrum of conditions,[2] including reproductive tract infections, serious prolapse, anemia, urinary tract infection, obesity, and hypertension. The pattern of prevalence of these conditions will not be uniform in all communities, making it necessary to carry out reproductive health research at the community level in the developing world to provide adequate information on patterns of prevalence. Such information can help determine the appropriate focus of concern of family planning programs with reproductive morbidity for different communities.

2. *Addressing reproductive morbidity conditions within family planning programs:* An expansion of family planning policy to include a concern with specific reproductive morbidity conditions must be accompanied by a realistic strategy for dealing with these conditions. The practice of screening for a limited number of conditions is currently part of the requirements of service in family planning programs. However, the extent of overlap that we found in the study community between contraceptive use and contraindicated morbidity conditions suggests that the practice of screening is not systematically applied. This situation was supported by field observations and certainly generalizes widely beyond the study villages.

One of the reasons for the current neglect of the required screening of clients in family planning programs is probably that the cost of proper screening for some disease conditions is too high and outside of the scope of program budgets. Nevertheless, another reason for this neglect is clearly that screening is not emphasized as a priority requirement, nor monitored as program policy. This stands sharply in contrast to the strong emphasis on recruitment of acceptors, sometimes encouraged through special quotas and incentives. In fact, the strong emphasis on recruitment of acceptors may even create pressure on program staff that leads to avoidance of the screening requirement.

The perception that cost is a barrier to the screening of those disease conditions contraindicated for contraceptive practice probably arises from the current focus on sexually transmitted diseases and on reproductive tract infections more generally. However, not all relevant disease conditions require costly diagnostic procedures. Measuring height and weight and reading blood pressure are easy, inexpensive procedures that can be undertaken by the provider of oral contraceptives, including the pharmacist, who needs to be involved in the screening process. An examination for genital prolapse is also a simple procedure to undertake before IUD insertion. On the other hand, if the cost of screening for the conditions of reproductive tract infections, anemia, and urinary tract infection that require laboratory examinations cannot be borne by a family planning program, it is necessary to refer the physical exam and the clinical judgment to a trained provider. A provisional diagnosis of any of these conditions would only postpone for a short time the desired method until proper diagnosis and treatment can be sought.

A woman with a contraindicated health condition must be encouraged to use the appropriate contraceptive. A family planning clinic must provide an alternative contraceptive that the woman accepts and can effectively use—either as a permanent substitute or as a temporary method until she is cured of her condition. Steps must be taken to ensure that she returns for the desired method. For such a process to work, a holistic approach to family planning policy is required that supports women and encourages them to seek the necessary health care and return to the service.

3. The reproductive health concern: The gravity of the reproductive health situation observed for women in the Giza study suggests the need to broaden the scope of our concern with reproductive health beyond morbidity conditions that are contraindicated for contraceptive methods. Family planning would thus become one part of a comprehensive set of services dealing with women's reproductive health throughout their life cycle.

The Giza study shows that despite the prevalence of gynecological disease and related conditions, two-thirds of women reporting symptoms have not sought health care, even though a health center is available in each village studied. This pattern suggests that a family planning visit should be used as an opportunity to give greater attention to healthy reproduction. Thus, information on how to prevent reproductive health conditions could and should become a component of the services provided by family planning programs. It is very relevant, for example, for a family planning program to emphasize the link between the number of deliveries and prolapse, and to present spacing and number of children as part of the factors affecting women's health. By offering information and education, the family planning program would contribute at very little cost to reducing the disease burden of women. This is only a first step in providing services that are more acceptable to women and to communities because they address reproductive health holistically, with family planning as part of a whole.

Another important implication of our research is that attention can no longer be limited to women in the reproductive age period. Our data have shown that the prevalence of most gynecological and related conditions tends to rise with age, so that women most in need of attention and advice are older women, some of them past reproductive age. The family planning program can act as a referral point for these women to other curative facilities. It would certainly help the credibility of the program to receive older women, who are powerful and influential in the community of women, in addition to the younger ones currently served.

Reorienting the perspective of family planning policy toward a concern with the wider reproductive health situation of women is a major shift. It necessitates working on a change of attitude that would permeate all the echelons of the family planning activity, from national policy makers to program managers to providers. What would certainly assist such a shift is the realization that a concern with individual well-being and healthy reproduction serves, sometimes at very little extra cost, to increase the number of effective users of contraceptives in a way that can never be achieved by a single-minded emphasis on targets. Research such as that described here can provide the hard evidence needed to convince the cautious or skeptical.

QUALITY OF CARE OF SERVICES

Another significant finding of the Giza study is that prevalence rates for some disease conditions among women who had consulted a physician for symptoms are similar to those among women who had not. This fact highlights for consideration the issue of the efficacy of services, in addition to the issue of their underutilization, and emphasizes that merely expanding family planning services is not enough. A primary concern must be the quality of care and effectiveness of services provided.

We have already dealt with some components of quality of care in terms of the technical management, provision of choice, and follow-up of the screening process. Here we focus on the client–provider interaction and its potential contribution to utilization and compliance. We believe that the limited interaction and exchange that takes place during clinic visits is one of the major reasons that consultation with a physician did not seem to affect disease prevalence in our study. To ensure the cooperation of women, who are not always aware of their own reproductive morbidity and health, providers must be willing to approach women holistically, encouraging them to talk, listening to them, and taking into account the socioeconomic conditions of their lives. Such a practice may be considered time-consuming when the load of clients is high, but the cost in time is well worth the benefit of sustainable use and satisfied users. Gender sensitization and changing attitudes of providers (male and female) are particularly necessary.

WOMEN'S PERCEPTIONS AND SOCIAL CONDITIONS

We consider next the factors affecting utilization of health services that are related to women themselves, particularly to women in disadvantaged communities such as those we have studied. The Giza study has revealed that women perceive some disease symptoms as normal consequences of their reproductive function, rather than as indications of health problems. The majority of women responded positively when asked about the occurrence of discharge, but only a small proportion considered the discharge as "different from their nature" (not normal), although many proceeded to report characteristics that could be considered suspicious in terms of color, odor, and other factors. Also, some women did not report feeling the symptoms of prolapse, reflecting a high tolerance for pain and discomfort. Thus the 'culture of silence' related to health problems, observed for women in many countries of the developing world (Dixon-Mueller and Wasserheit, 1991) was reflected clearly in our study community (Khattab, 1992).

These findings emphasize the need to understand women's perceptions of health in order to be able to reach them and attract them to use health services. It may be necessary, in fact, to consider women's perceptions of a larger associated group of concepts, including health and morbidity, treatment options, the body, sexuality, and even women's perceptions of the self (The Population Council, 1993). Such understanding, appropriately and respectfully utilized, will help providers to communicate better with women. It would also form an essential base for health education to raise the awareness of women of their reproductive health situation and the need to seek health care for disease conditions.

Social constraints on women's use of health services are certainly not to be neglected. In-depth case studies undertaken as part of the

Giza morbidity study (Khattab, 1992) have demonstrated the extent to which social and economic constraints prevent women from seeking health care. Such constraints are well illustrated by the case of one woman (Khattab, 1992), diagnosed to have had an incomplete hysterectomy, as she voiced one concern after another in response to the invitation of the study team to take her to a hospital in Cairo for follow-up of this condition:

> Sahar left the unit looking very preoccupied and upset. The researcher accompanied her back home and on the way she asked: "Will they mistreat me?" The researcher explained that she would be under the supervision of a very experienced senior professor who was a member of the research team and who also headed the Department of Gynecology and Obstetrics at the hospital. Sahar then said: "This is surely a serious operation which will cost a lot and my husband and I have no money." The researcher assured her that everything was free of charge, and the project would finance the cost of the medical care and all other expenses needed for the operation. Sahar showed renewed interest and said: "It seems unbelievable that I won't pay any money. Well, that's very good! But how will I get there? I don't know the hospital at all. Cairo is a big place and I'm afraid I might get lost." The researcher said she would pick her up from her house and drive her to hospital in the project car, and bring her back home, without any trouble. This made Sahar feel more comfortable, but after a short while, she asked "But the children, what shall I do with them? They don't know how to look after themselves. And my husband, who's going to look after him?" The researcher replied: "You'll be back after two or three days. Since your daughters live nearby, they can look after their father and their brothers; for your sake, they have to put up with your absence till you come back to them in good health."

The field team in charge of following up on women such as Sahar discovered that women need support in the community to leave their families for medical procedures and need support at the hospital for better communication with providers. These findings suggests that in order to be effective, reproductive health services operating in disadvantaged communities must provide special support to women in seeking and undertaking health care. We find that this role is best played by a counselor who can reach out to women, listen to them, give them information, encourage them to give their health priority in the face of all their family responsibilities, and show them where to go for care. The counselor would also work together with the physician to ensure follow-up and return to service when necessary. Such a role is an essential component of a transformed policy that understands the reproductive health needs and realities of women in disadvantaged communities of the developing world.

ACKNOWLEDGMENTS

The authors acknowledge the participation of Dr. Mawaheb El-Mouelhy, of the Cairo Family Planning Association, and Dr. Mohamed Fadel Amin, of the Department of Clinical Pathology at al-Azhar University, as part of the research team that implemented the reproductive morbidity study in the two villages of Giza. They wish to thank Mahinaz El-Helw and Olfia Kamal for their contribution to the data analysis and their comments on the manuscript. They also wish to thank Barbara Ibrahim and Carla Makhlouf Obermeyer for their comments. Permission for the project was given by the Ministry of Health and the Central Agency for Public Mobilization and Statistics in Egypt. Activities of the project are sponsored by grants from The Population Council, the Ford Foundation, the World Health Organization, UNICEF, and the Government of the Netherlands.

REFERENCES

Bang, R. A., A. T. Bang, M. Baitule, Y. Choudhary, S. Sarmukaddam, O. Tale. 1989. High prevalence of gynecological diseases in rural Indian women. *The Lancet.* 1/8,629:85–87.

Belsey, M. A. and E. Royston. 1987. *An overview of the health of women and children.* Technical background paper prepared for the International Conference on Better Health for Women and Children through Family Planning, Nairobi, October 5–9.

Berer, M. 1993. Population and family planning policies: Women-centered perspectives. *Reproductive Health Matters.* 1:4–12.

CAPMAS. 1986. *Egyptian population census 1986.* Cairo: Central Agency For Public Mobilization and Statistics.

Dixon-Mueller, R. 1993. *Population policy and women's rights.* Westport, Connecticut: Praeger.

Dixon-Mueller, R. and A. Germain. 1992. Stalking the elusive "unmet need" for family planning. *Studies in Family Planning.* 23/5:330–35.

Dixon-Mueller, R. and J. Wasserheit. 1991. *The culture of silence: Reproductive tract infections among women in the Third World.* New York: International Women's Health Coalition.

Elias, C., A. Leonard, J. Thompson. 1993. A puzzle of will: Responding to reproductive tract infections in the context of family planning programs.

Paper presented at the Population Council Operations Research and Technical Assistance End-of-Project Conference, Nairobi, October 1993.

Eschen, A. and M. Whittaker. 1993. Family planning: A base to build on for women's reproductive health services. In M. Koblinsky, J. Timyan, J. Gay, eds., *The health of women: A global perspective.* Boulder: Westview Press.

Hartmann, B. 1987. *Reproductive rights and wrongs: The global policies of population control and contraceptive choice.* New York: Harper and Row.

Jain, A. and J. Bruce. 1993. *Implications of reproductive health for objectives and efficacy of family planning programs.* New York: The Population Council, Programs Division. Working paper no. 8.

Kabeer, N. 1992. *From fertility reduction to reproductive choice: Gender perspectives on family planning.* Brighton: Institute of Development Studies, University of Sussex. Discussion paper no. 299.

Khattab, H. 1992. *The silent endurance: Social conditions of women's reproductive health in rural Egypt.* Amman: UNICEF; and Cairo: The Population Council.

Koblinsky, M., J. Timyan, J. Gay, eds. 1993. *The health of women: A global perspective.* Boulder: Westview Press.

Muir, D. G. and M. A. Belsey. 1980. Pelvic inflammatory disease and its consequences in the developing world. *American Journal of Obstetrics and Gynecology.* 138/7:913–28.

PAPCHILD. 1993. *Egypt maternal and child health survey 1991.* Cairo: Central Agency for Public Mobilization and Statistics; and League of Arab States.

Ravindran, T. K. S. 1993. Women and the politics of population and development in India. *Reproductive Health Matters.* 1.

The Population Council. 1990. *A program of research and technical consultation on family resources, child survival and reproductive health in the West Asia and North Africa region: Report of the first phase, 1988 to 1990.* Cairo: The Population Council.

———. 1993. Notes of the meeting on women's perceptions. Cairo: The Population Council. May 22–28.

United Nations. 1993. *Report of the expert group meeting on family planning, health and family well-being.* United Nations Economic and Social Council (E/CONF.84/PC/7).

Wasserheit, J., J. R. Harris, J. Chakraborty, B. A. Kay, K. Mason. 1989. Reproductive tract infections in a family planning population in rural Bangladesh. *Studies in Family Planning.* 20/2:69–80.

Wasserheit, J. and K. Holmes. 1992. Reproductive tract infections: Challenges for international health policy, programs and research. In A. Germain, K. Holmes, P. Piot, J. Wasserheit, eds., *Reproductive tract infections: Global impact and priorities for women's reproductive health.* New York: Plenum Press.

Younis, N., H. Khattab, H. Zurayk, M. El-Mouelhy, M. F. Amin, and A. M. Farag. 1993. A community study of gynecological and related morbidities in rural Egypt. *Studies in Family Planning.* 24,/3:175–86.

Zurayk, H., H. Khattab, N. Younis, M. El-Mouelhy, M. F. Amin. 1993a. Concepts and measures of reproductive morbidity. *Health Transition Review.* 3/1:17–40.

Zurayk, H., H. Khattab, N. Younis, O. Kamal, M. El-Helw. 1993b. *A comparison of women's reports and medical diagnosis of reproductive morbidity conditions in rural Egypt.* Paper presented at the International Union for the Scientific Study of Population (IUSSP) General Conference in Montreal, August 24–September 20.

NOTES

1 The report of the United Nations Expert Group Meeting on Family Planning, Health and Family Well-Being (written in preparation for the International Conference on Population and Development), for example, deals very superficially with health, failing to address at a minimum the need for better concern with the health contraindications and side effects of contraceptive methods.

2 It is also important to note that very little consultation is done other than with physicians.

3 Diabetes, which we did not cover in our study, is also a condition worth considering.

Notes on Contributors

Cem Behar is professor of economics and chair of the Economics Department, Boğaziçi University in Istanbul, Turkey.

Rahma Bourqia is professor of sociology at Mohammed V University in Rabat, Morocco.

Youssef Courbage is a senior researcher at the Institut National d'Etudes Démographiques in Paris.

Philippe Fargues is director of the Centre d'Etudes Démographiques, Economiques, et Juridiques in Cairo.

Mahmoud Fathalla is the former chair of the Department of Obstetrics–Gynecology and dean of the Medical School at Asyut University, Egypt, and is presently a professor there. He is a senior advisor to the Rockefeller Foundation.

Ezzeldin O. Hassan is the former department head of the Department of Obstetrics–Gynecology at Mansura University, and is currenly a professor there. He is the head of the Egyptian Fertility Care Society in Cairo.

Homa Hoodfar is assistant professor of anthropology at Concordia University in Montreal, Canada.

Barbara Ibrahim is senior representative for West Asia and North Africa at The Population Council in Cairo.

Saad Eddin Ibrahim is professor of sociology at the the American University in Cairo, and director of the Ibn Khaldoun Center for Development Studies in Cairo.

Karima Khalil is a physician and consultant to The Population Council.

Hind Khattab is the director of social research at Delta Consultants in Egypt.

Cynthia Lloyd is senior associate and deputy director of the The Population Council in New York.

Carolyn Makinson is program officer, the Andrew Mellon Foundation.

Cynthia Myntti is a senior fellow at The Humphrey Institute in Minnesota.

Laila Nawar is host country advisor to The Population Council, Cairo.

Carla Makhlouf Obermeyer is associate professor of anthropology and population, Harvard University, and associate, The Population Council, Cairo.

Nabil Younis is professor of obstetrics–gynecology at al-Azhar University, Egypt.

Huda Zurayk is senior associate, The Population Council, Cairo, and professor of epidemiology and biostatistics, American University of